Sports of Our Times

Also by Dave Anderson

Upset: The Unexpected in the World of Sports
Countdown to Super Bowl
Sugar Ray (with Ray Robinson)
The Return of the Champion: Pancho Gonzales' Golden Year 1964
Always on the Run (with Larry Csonka and Jim Kiick)
Frank—The First Year (with Frank Robinson)
The Yankees (with Murray Chass, Robert Creamer
   and Harold Rosenthal)

Sports of Our Times

DAVE ANDERSON

Random House · New York

Grateful acknowledgment is made to the following for permission to reprint previously pub-
lished material:

The Hearst Corporation: Column entitled "By Sam Huff," *New York Journal American*,
April 11, 1964. © 1964 The Hearst Corporation. Reprinted from the original article by
permission of Sam Huff and the Hearst Corporation.

The New York Times: Articles by Dave Anderson. © 1967, 1970, 1971, 1972, 1973, 1974,
1975, 1976, 1977, 1978 by the New York Times Company. Reprinted by permission.

Library of Congress Cataloging in Publication Date

SPORTS OF OUR TIMES
   Dave Anderson.
   A selection of the author's sports columns.
   1. Sports—Addresses, essays, lectures.
I. Title.
GV707.A48   796   78-57097
ISBN 0-394-50122-5

Manufactured in the United States of America

9 8 7 6 5 4 3 2

First Edition

For Red Smith
and
Jimmy Cannon

Contents

Introduction

I have a job that many people would like to have. I go to the big sports events. I'm around the big sports personalities. Quite naturally, I'm often asked which sport is my favorite.

"The one," I like to say, "that provides the subject for my next column."

As soon as I finish one column, I'm wondering what I'm going to write about in the next column. I can't call the sports desk at *The New York Times* and say, "I couldn't think of anything to write, I'm taking the day off." I've got to produce a column. Four times a week. Within those four columns, I like to take readers where they can't go, or tell them something they don't know. That means I'm usually juggling six or eight ideas each week, hoping to catch the four with, I hope, the most appeal to readers for whatever reason—timeliness, controversy, insight, humor, pathos.

My four ideas also must not duplicate those of Red Smith, my colleague and the most admired sportswriter of our time. Morrie Siegel of the Washington *Star* once was being heckled good-naturedly by some other sportswriters as he and Red left a press box. Putting an arm around Red, he said, "Be careful, between us we've won one Pulitzer Prize."

Only once did Red and I have a mix-up over a column subject. Looking ahead to a saver for a Tuesday column if nothing else developed, I once asked Walter Fletcher, then the dog writer at the

Times, to arrange a Monday working-press ticket for me to the Westminster Dog Show at Madison Square Garden.

Unknown to me, Red later phoned Walter and asked for a Tuesday ticket. But when Walter told him that I was planning to go to the dog show Monday for a Tuesday column, Red backed off. Two consecutive dog-show columns, he knew, would be overkill. But on Sunday morning I read where Darryl Sittler of the Toronto Maple Leafs had set a National Hockey League record with 10 points in a Saturday-night game—six goals, four assists. To me, Sittler's feat was a better subject for Tuesday than the dog show.

Tuesday morning Red was having breakfast with a friend who happened to ask him what many people ask us, "How do you know what the other guy is writing about?"

"No problem," Red said, opening the *Times* to the sports section. "We check with each other every so often. Now today, I happen to know that Dave is writing about the dog show." He had folded the paper and was about to show my column to his friend when he noticed that I had written about a hockey player instead.

"The son of a bitch," Red said, true to the dog show.

Other than that, we've never had a problem. If a newsbreak creates a column subject, it's the property of whoever is writing next or whoever is more qualified to write about it. Horse racing, for example, is one of Red's favorite subjects. But it's still strange for me to be sharing the column with Red Smith; growing up, Red Smith and Jimmy Cannon were my patron saints. Some people like to put down sports as not "important." Compared with the larger issues of life, it's not. But if Red Smith and Jimmy Cannon can devote their lives to writing about sports, it's important enough for me. I've worked and traveled with Red for almost a decade; I worked and traveled with Jimmy for more than a decade before his 1971 stroke that shattered this fussy bachelor who was married to his column. He never really recovered and I visited him often. In his East Side apartment shortly before his death in 1973, he turned to me. "I envy you your wife," he said softly.

He was fond of my wife, Maureen, and perhaps too late he realized what a good wife means to any man. I'm fortunate to have a good wife and good children who understand that their husband and father often has to be away from home to do his job properly. I didn't go to the Billie Jean King–Bobby Riggs tennis match in Houston in

1973, but we were in the family room watching it on television—Maureen, Stephen, Mark, Mary Jo and Jean-Marie—when Mary Jo, then fifteen, looked up at me. "Daddy," she said, "you should be there."

It makes traveling easier when your family realizes that. And sometimes Maureen or one of the kids will suggest a subject for my next column. No greater love.

Sports of Our Times

1 · Baseball

Of all our sports in America, baseball is the roots game, the first sport I was aware of. In other areas of the world, soccer is the roots game, the sport virtually all the kids play. But most Americans grow up with baseball. More than any other sport, baseball is the reason I write sports. Living in Brooklyn when the Dodgers were there, I didn't want to be a sportswriter as much as I wanted to be a *baseball* writer who traveled with the team, who went to spring training. And strangely, I wasn't that devoted a Dodger fan. I preferred the St. Louis Cardinals, which occasionally jeopardized my health in street-corner debates. But instead of following any one team, I considered myself a baseball fan. I took the subway up to the Polo Grounds and Yankee Stadium occasionally, an expedition resisted by some Brooklyn residents who didn't recognize any horizon beyond Ebbets Field, where I sat in the center-field bleachers.

In those years before jets and satellites, horizons were closer. And sports were simpler.

Television gorges us with sports now. But before TV there were only four sports of consequence—baseball, boxing, college football and horse racing. Pro football was struggling. Pro basketball had just escaped from dance halls. Hockey was still considered a Canadian game. Except for the Indianapolis 500, auto racing didn't mean much. Olympic sports, such as track-and-field and swimming, weren't taken too seriously except in Olympic years. And golf and tennis were country-club sports.

But there were no country clubs in my neighborhood; no tenements either.

I grew up in Bay Ridge, out where the Verrazano Bridge now stretches from Brooklyn to Staten Island across the mouth of New York Bay, a quiet area of middle-class two-family homes and six-story red-brick apartment houses on leafy streets. My father was an advertising salesman for the old New York *Sun;* my mother an insurance broker. Between them, they brought home half a dozen of the eight New York newspapers that flourished then. I spread them out, one by one, on the living-room floor and read them. I played sports, not well but often—baseball, basketball, football, roller-hockey—but mostly I *read* sports. As a sportswriter now, I'm occasionally asked if I'm a frustrated athlete. Those people don't understand that I never wanted to play baseball like Stan Musial and Joe DiMaggio; I wanted to *write* baseball like Red Smith in the *Herald-Tribune* and Jimmy Cannon in the *Post*—the two patron saints of modern sportswriting. My parents didn't bring home the *Post,* but I did.

"Why?" my mother once asked me.

"To read Jimmy Cannon," I said.

I was going to Xavier High School in Manhattan then, a forty-minute subway ride on the old Sea Beach Express; my senior year I covered the basketball team (coached by Frank McGuire, who later went to St. John's, North Carolina, South Carolina and the Basketball Hall of Fame) for the school paper and worked on Saturdays as a copy boy in the *Sun* sports department. That $5 payday made me relatively wealthy. I read all the sports columnists of that era—Smith and Cannon, Arthur Daley in the *Times,* Frank Graham in the *Journal-American,* Bill Heinz and Grantland Rice in the *Sun,* Dan Parker in the *Daily Mirror,* Joe Williams in the *World-Tele-gram,* Tommy Holmes in the Brooklyn *Eagle*—studied them, really. And when I went off to Holy Cross in Worcester, Mass., for four years, I thought I might have a job waiting for me at the *Sun* after my graduation. But in the winter of my junior year, the *Sun* folded.

As it turned out, I would work for several other now defunct newspapers. But having newspapers collapse was somewhat hereditary; somewhat fortunate too.

I had been born in Troy, N.Y., where my grandfather was the publisher of the *Troy Times* and my father the advertising director. But in 1936, in the midst of the Depression, that newspaper went out of business. We moved to Brooklyn the next year when I was eight, leaving our little yellow cottage in the Sycaway section of Troy and taking a big noisy New York Central train down along the Hudson River to the big city. Every so often I wonder what I would be doing now if we had not moved. For that matter, I wonder what I would be doing now if Lou Niss hadn't hired me. Back when I got out of Holy Cross in 1951, I had a degree in English lit. and a scrapbook of my columns and stories as the sports editor of the *Tomahawk,* the college weekly. But not many people were impressed.

"Sorry, kid," sports editors kept telling me. "We're not hiring anybody now."

Max Kase of the *Journal-American* told me that, and Joe Val of the *World-Telegram and Sun,* and Bob Cooke of the *Herald-Tribune.* But then I walked into the old Brooklyn *Eagle* office, which was literally a block from the ramp to the Brooklyn Bridge, and Lou Niss, then the sports editor and now the New York Mets' traveling secretary, looked through the scrapbook.

"We've got an opening," he said. "But we've got a lot of applicants. Give me a call Monday."

The opening had developed because the *Eagle* was no longer using a Western Union operator with a Morse-code key to take its horse-racing charts. It had converted to a teleprinter, creating an opening for someone to edit the racing charts. And when I phoned Lou on Monday, he told me I had the job.

"See that batch of pictures over there," he said, my first day. "File them."

There must have been three thousand photos strewn in wire baskets. I don't think I ever finished that job. Too many interruptions to do other things, like going for coffee or taking high school games on the phone. Or hoping the Dodgers would hold off the Giants and win the 1951 National League pennant. Around the time that I started filing all those photos, the Dodgers had a 13 1/2-game lead. But that's when the Giants started a 16-game winning streak. And then I realized what it was like to root as a newspaperman roots— not for a team to win but for a good story to develop.

To many people, the Giants overtaking the Dodgers was the better story. But on the Brooklyn *Eagle,* the Dodgers were *always* the better story.

Late on the afternoon of October 3 that year I was in the composing room, where the words "Dodgers Win" were already set in big black type in the front-page form that would be stereotyped and put on the presses as soon as the decisive third game of the National League pennant playoff ended. The Dodgers were leading the Giants, 4–1, going into the bottom of the ninth inning at the Polo Grounds, and just about everybody at the *Eagle* was grinning and laughing and adding up how much they had won in friendly bets. But the Giants put together a few hits and then Bobby Thomson hit a home run off Ralph Branca for a 5–4 victory and the pennant.

All of Brooklyn was in shock; all of the Brooklyn *Eagle* too. But our last edition had a new headline and a new story that nobody in Brooklyn wanted to read; and yet nobody could resist reading it.

When the 1952 season began, Lou Niss let me write some baseball. I covered many of the Giants' and Yankees' home games. But not all. And not too well. My first assignment was a Yankee double header. In the office the next day I was basking in the glow of my by-line when Lou Niss called me over to his desk.

"You forgot something," he said.

"What's that," I wanted to know.

"The scores," he said. "You forgot the scores of the two games. You say the Yankees won both games but you don't have the scores. Always make sure the scores are in there."

What a dumb mistake. Another sports editor might have sent me back to filing pictures again.

Ever since, I've checked every piece I've written to make sure the score is in there. All the rest of my Yankee and Giant stories that year might not have been very well written, but they had the score in them. I was handling the same Giants-Yankees assignment early in the 1953 season when Lou called me aside one morning.

"Harold Burr broke his hip in a fall in Cincinnati," he told me. "You're covering the Dodgers until he gets well."

Harold Burr was a wonderful old man, a baseball writer for thirty years on several newspapers, a bachelor who sat around the offseason spinning stories. His favorite was the time he was riding with Arch

Murray of the *Post* on a bus taking the Dodgers from Vero Beach to Miami during spring training.

"The sunset was spectacular," Harold said, "and I asked Arch if he had ever seen anything more beautiful and Arch said he had. I asked him what could possibly be more beautiful than that sunset and Arch said, 'Reiser tripling off the exit gate at Ebbets Field.' "

Once the Dodgers' most exciting player, Pete Reiser was a switch-hitting center-fielder who liked to steal home. But he kept smashing into outfield walls. Dizzy spells wrecked his career. By the time I started covering the Dodgers, he had been succeeded by "the boys of summer," as they have been known ever since Roger Kahn's thoughtful book about them—Pee Wee Reese, Duke Snider, Gil Hodges, Roy Campanella, Carl Furillo, Billy Cox, Jim Gilliam, Carl Erskine, Preacher Roe and Don Newcombe and, especially, Jackie Robinson. Not long ago somebody asked me to name the best baseball player I had ever seen.

"Jackie Robinson," I said.

In his time, Jackie Robinson was not the best hitter or the best power hitter or the best base stealer or the best second baseman or the best third baseman. But he was the best *baseball player*, surely the best clutch hitter, the best clutch base runner and the best clutch competitor. To me he will always symbolize the spirit of those Dodger teams. I once discovered what it was like to be stung by that spirit. After a big loss to the Giants, he was still angry about an umpire's call. His voice kept rising, higher and louder. Across the clubhouse, I was talking to Roy Campanella when the catcher said softly, "Oh, Robinson, why don't you shut up?" The next day that quote appeared in my story. That night the Dodgers were leaving on a road trip. On the railroad platform at Penn Station, somebody warned me that Robinson was looking for me.

"What for?" I asked.

"That quote from Campanella," I was told.

"I thought that was funny."

"Jack doesn't think it was."

Moments later I could hear Jack's voice, high and loud from about two pullman cars away. "Where's that Dave Anderson," the voice kept roaring, louder and louder as it got closer and closer. "I'm going to kick his ass." By this time I was sitting in my roomette with the door open. No use hiding. And soon he was staring down at me, yelling about Campy's quote.

"You made me look bad in front of my teammates," he roared. "I'm going to kick your ass."

"Take it easy, Jack," I said. "Campy said it with a smile, I wrote it that way and the readers will take it that way."

"No, they won't," he said.

"Yes, they will," I said.

He grumbled some more, then stalked off.

He never brought it up again. But looking back, I've always been grateful for the memory of that confrontation. For once I had seen Jackie Robinson the way his opponents often had—in full flame. Traveling with those Dodgers was a special experience. As it turned out, I would be the last baseball writer to cover the Brooklyn Dodgers for the Brooklyn *Eagle*.

When the *Eagle* folded in 1955 and I moved to the *Journal-American,* my life as a traveling baseball writer ended, except for a few road trips in 1967 after the *Times* hired me.

But by the time the *Eagle* closed I wasn't that disappointed at leaving baseball. Maureen and I had been married in 1953 and Stephen had been born. Traveling had lost some of its appeal. By the very nature of spring training, the regular-season road trips and the World Series, a baseball writer is away more than half the time for eight months. To be where the action is, I travel about fifty thousand miles a year now, but it's not the same as the grind of baseball travel. And having been a baseball writer, I wanted to cover other sports, which I did at the *Journal-American*—pro football, boxing, hockey and tennis. I had discovered that because many baseball writers, then more than now, seldom covered other sports, they often developed tunnel vision. And that's bad, as a sportswriter and as a person.

To be a good sports columnist, I believe it's important to have covered as many sports as possible as a beat reporter—someone assigned to a particular team or a particular scene. Being a beat reporter is the best way to develop an understanding of a sport, to develop an appreciation of its lore. It's also the only way to develop contacts in each sport—people you can trust to tell the truth, people who know what's really going on. Contacts don't develop instantly. It takes time, sometimes years, to nurture them. The contact must be able to trust you too.

Since a sports columnist has to write on a variety of sports, he must have contacts in as many sports as possible. The sports columnist cannot have been, or *should* not have been, a one-sport sportswriter.

Suddenly, in 1971, I was a sports columnist. Bob Lipsyte, a fine writer, had shared the "Sports of the Times" column with Arthur Daley, but Bob resigned. Abe Rosenthal, then the managing editor, and Jim Roach, the sports editor, selected me to replace him. At the same time they hired Red Smith; the kid who grew up reading Red Smith and Arthur Daley on the subway now was checking with them to make sure there was no duplication of column ideas.

I was around baseball again and enjoying it. Especially during the memorable fifth game of the 1975 World Series between the Cincinnati Reds and the Boston Red Sox—a game that defined the beauty of baseball:

BOSTON—At center stage in the Fenway Theater tonight for the start of the seventh World Series game were two contrasting left-handed actors, Bill Lee and Don Gullett, each hoping to perpetuate a script that not even Abner Doubleday, much less William Shakespeare or Neil Simon, would have submitted. Bill Lee, who outraged many of his Boston Red Sox followers by speaking out in favor of school busing, occasionally has outraged Darrell Johnson, his narrow-eyed manager.

"He's been falling out of trees all year," Lee said the other day, "but he keeps landing on his feet."

Bill Lee was complaining about Johnson's decision to bypass Bill Lee for Luis Tiant in the sixth game after it had been delayed by rain. Don Gullett, the country kid from Kentucky, would never talk like that about Sparky Anderson, the Cincinnati Reds' mentor. Don Gullett is quiet and polite. As a high school football player, he once scored 72 points in a game—11 touchdowns and 6 extra points. When his teammates needle him about having missed the 5 other extra points, Don Gullett shrugs shyly and smiles. Don Gullett doesn't smile when he throws his fast ball, just as Bill Lee doesn't outrage his manager when he has his best stuff. But tonight each went to the mound with the burden not only of winning the World Series, but also of following the histrionics of the sixth game.

In the hours before the decisive game, the more excitable critics were calling the sixth game "the greatest" in baseball history. The more restrained observers were describing it as "one of the best," which indeed it was as the Red Sox won, 7–6, on Carlton Fisk's home run off the left-field pole in the twelth inning.

But the true significance of the sixth game involves the beauty of baseball when a game means something. Baseball is often put down as slow and boring, out of step with the violence of our times that the National Football League thrives on. And on a Tuesday night in June, with virtually nothing at stake and with another game tomorrow night in a 162-game schedule that can become dreary, baseball is slow and boring to many people. The pitcher fingers his cap. The batter fouls off several pitches. The infielders and outfielders stand around like so many statues. But when a baseball game means something, as it does in a World Series or the league playoffs or in a pennant race, baseball is the best game. The same elements that make it slow and boring on a Tuesday night in June make it thrilling on a Tuesday night in October, because those same elements build the tension. When the sixth game had ended, even many of the Reds realized that the game had been the thing, not the outcome.

"What a game!" Pete Rose told Sparky Anderson. "Now the Super Bowl people got it on their back to match this."

Pete Rose meant that the N.F.L. had a monkey on its back now, which isn't quite fair. If the Super Bowl were conducted in a four-of-seven-game series, surely some spectacular games would hypnotize the nation, as the sixth game of the World Series did. But the appeals of baseball and football are different. Football depends on the brutal assault of twenty-two players. Baseball depends on solitary artistry. Seldom has that solitary artistry been more obvious than in the sixth game, when so many moments deserved to be etched in the minds of millions.

Fred Lynn hitting a towering three-run homer beyond the Red Sox bullpen for a 3–0 lead in the first inning.

Luis Tiant whirling, jerking and tantalizing the Reds' batters with his variety of pitches in the early innings.

Ken Griffey lining a triple off the center-field wall in the fifth and Lynn, unable to make a leaping catch, falling grotesquely to the ground and remaining there for several minutes in the hush of thirty-five thousand concerned spectators.

George Foster lofting a two-run double off the left-center wall to put the Reds ahead, 5–3, in the seventh.

Cesar Geronimo pulling a home run inside the right-field foul pole to put the Reds ahead, 6–3, in the eighth.

Bernie Carbo drilling a three-run homer into the center-field bleachers to tie the score, 6–6, in the eighth after Rawly Eastwick, the Reds' sixth pitcher, had been within one strike of holding a 6–3 lead.

Foster throwing out Denny Doyle at the plate, with Johnny Bench making a swipe tag the way first basemen do, after the Red Sox had loaded the bases with none out in the ninth.

Fisk throwing out Rose at second base on Griffey's bunt in the eleventh, then Dwight Evans making a desperate, running one-handed catch of Joe Morgan's drive near the low right-field wall and throwing wide to Carl Yastrzemski at first, who tossed the ball to Rick Burleson, the alert shortstop covering the bag, for a double play.

And then Fisk, after waving his arms in a plea for the ball to stay fair, completing his home run through a swarm of idolaters.

In each case the solitary artistry was not obscured in a trample of bodies, which occurs in football, or in collisions near the backboards, which occur in basketball, or in a scramble near the goal, which occurs in hockey. The solitary artistry of baseball is there to be seen, not obscured. Throughout the history of baseball, there have been too many games to label the sixth game of the World Series the greatest. Value depends on allegiance. To those loyalists of the New York Giants at the Polo Grounds that day, Bobby Thomson's home run probably completed the greatest game. To those who suffered until the Brooklyn Dodgers finally won a World Series, perhaps Johnny Podres pitched the greatest game. To those who enjoyed the dominance of the New York Yankees, then perhaps Don Larsen's perfect game was the greatest game. To those in Pittsburgh, perhaps Bill Mazeroski's home run that won the 1960 World Series decided the greatest game. Everybody has his own memory of what to him was the greatest game.

But the sixth game was a reminder that baseball, when it means something, is the greatest game.

(October 23, 1975)

If any one player projected the beauty of baseball, Willie Mays did. With him, baseball always seemed to be fun. But eventually it became work. And near the end of the 1973 season he didn't want to work anymore:

For two decades, Willie Mays played baseball as if he were twenty-two years old. Then suddenly he was forty-two and his body wouldn't let him do what his mind wanted to do, which was to play baseball forever. With three sore ribs that won't let him swing a bat, with a sore arm that won't let him make the long throw from center field, Willie Mays has surrendered to his body. He announced yesterday that he wouldn't play baseball next season. He stood behind a long table in the Diamond Club at Shea Stadium with the New York Mets' hierarchy around him, a significant setting. His absence from New York, when the Giants moved to San Francisco in 1958, contributed to the creation of the Mets' franchise. But that didn't make his surrender any easier. For him, baseball has been a refuge from the real world. In his mind, he'd still like to play forever. Perhaps subconsciously, a few phrases betrayed that feeling.

"I'm trying to retire," he said at one point. "I'm here," he also said, "to renounce my retirement."

But now the formalities were over. The cameras and the tape recorders had been turned off. In his green-checked beige sport jacket he was sitting at a table near a long low window. Through the glass, center field shone in the sun.

"My best play," he reflected, "was the Billy Cox play."

As a rookie in 1951 at the Polo Grounds, he had run to his left, caught a liner hit by Carl Furillo of the Brooklyn Dodgers, spun completely around and thrown to the plate, where Wes Westrum tagged Cox.

"The throw was on the fly," he said, his eyes flashing.

"After the game," somebody recalled, "Charlie Dressen said, 'I'd like to see him do it again.' "

"What about the catch on Bobby Morgan at Ebbets Field?"

"He hit it over shortstop on a line and when I dove for it, my left arm hit me under the chest. I knocked myself out. The first guy I saw when I woke up was Jackie Robinson looking in my glove to see if the ball was there."

"Was the Vic Wertz catch your best?"

"I never thought about them that way. If you start thinking about the catches you make, you don't make them."

"Was any particular hitter difficult for you to play?"

"Not if I had a pitcher who worked with me, who let me know what he was throwing. That was all I asked. The best for that were Juan Marichal and Gaylord Perry."

"Did you know when Perry was throwing a spitball?"

"I was too far away," he said, his face straight.

"Who were the toughest pitchers for you to hit?"

"When I broke in, Robin Roberts and Don Newcombe," he said. "Newk threw harder, but Roberts had the best control. Later on, anybody who threw hard was tough."

"Any regrets?"

"When they talked about putting a bowl in San Francisco to keep the wind out, I thought I'd have a chance to beat Babe Ruth's record," said the man with 660 home runs. "But it didn't work out and I lost about seventy-five homers when I was in service. That's the only thing I wanted to do that I didn't do. But all the records, I'm close to 'em."

"Which of the Giant teams was the best?"

"I don't want to rate them, but the most memorable year was in '71 when we won the division in the last game."

"Why is '71 more memorable than '51?"

"Because in '51, I'd just come in, I didn't know what was going on, when Bobby Thomson hit the home run, I was the last man to get to the plate to greet him. I didn't even realize we had won the pennant."

"You're often described as the most exciting player in baseball history, but who was the most exciting player you ever saw?"

"That's hard. I like complete ballplayers. Joe DiMaggio was a complete ballplayer. Right now Bobby Bonds and Cesar Cedeno are complete ballplayers. They can throw, run, field, hit and hit with power. As a kid DiMaggio was my man. On the radio in Birmingham, all I heard was DiMaggio and Williams, the Yankees and the Red Sox, the rivalry. DiMaggio was smooth. Ted was an authority on hitting, but DiMaggio was smooth, he could do everything."

As a teenager with the Birmingham Black Barons, his contract gave the Boston Red Sox the first negotiation rights.

"But they didn't pick me up. Then our shortstop, Artie Wilson, was supposed to take me to Oakland of the Pacific Coast League, where Charlie Dressen was managing, but that didn't work out. Jackie Robinson knew about me, too."

But a Dodger scout, Wid Matthews, wasn't impressed.

"I was told the Dodgers didn't want me because I couldn't hit the curve ball. I was fifteen years old."

Now he's forty-two and he can't hit the fast ball.

"But if the Mets get in the World Series, I'm playing," Willie Mays said, trying to postpone his surrender.

(September 21, 1973)

The Mets made the World Series that year, which Willie Mays remembered mostly for losing a line drive in the low glare of the sun at Oakland Coliseum while the Mets were losing to the A's in seven games. That was the A's second of three consecutive championships. When the Cincinnati Reds won the World Series in both 1975 and 1976, they were touted by some baseball people as one of the most dominant teams in baseball history.

But to me, the Reds had not accomplished what the A's had. The

A's also had better pitching in Catfish Hunter, Vida Blue, Ken Holtzman and Rollie Fingers.

The A's also had more controversy. Perhaps that's why their reign was relatively unappreciated, even after they won the 1974 World Series:

In winning a third consecutive championship, the Oakland A's accomplished in the World Series what the Miami Dolphins hope to accomplish in the Super Bowl game.

"We're a lot alike," Reggie Jackson was saying even before the World Series began. "Catfish Hunter is like Bob Griese, steady and reliable. Joe Rudi is like Larry Csonka or Larry Little, and me, I'm like Paul Warfield. Either three catches and three touchdowns, or no catches and nothing. But just like the Dolphins are one of the great teams in football history, we're one of the best teams to come along in baseball since the great Yankee teams—the Babe Ruth teams and the Joe DiMaggio teams."

Old-timers probably will snort at that appraisal, especially New York old-timers. They wouldn't if the A's were a New York team.

Anyone who doesn't appreciate the A's has been too busy observing their appearance and their antics instead of noticing how they play baseball. It's easy to be distracted by their mustaches and beards, by their green-and-gold uniforms, by their turmoil and tantrums, by their owner and egomaniac, Charles O. Finley, but the A's are a superbly skilled baseball team. Reggie Jackson, talkative and challenging, is their symbol but Joe Rudi, quiet and contemplative, is really their essence.

Joe Rudi proved his stature in two World Series moments that were the antithesis of each other—a sacrifice bunt that generated a four-run rally for a 5–2 victory in the fourth game and his home run that won the final game, 3–2.

With one run in, Sal Bando on second and Jackson on first, Joe Rudi dutifully executed a perfect bunt to move the runners along. After an intentional walk to Claudell Washington, they both scored on Jim Holt's pinch single. To some players of Joe Rudi's accomplishments in that situation, the bunt sign would have been an insult. Some players might have deliberately fouled off two bunts in order to swing away. But not Joe Rudi.

"If the bunt sign's on," he said later, "you bunt."

"But some guys don't accept that," he was reminded.

"They're not on a winning ball club either," he said.

The next night, Joe Rudi noticed that Mike Marshall stopped warming up in order to persuade Bill Buckner, the left-fielder of the Los Angeles Dodgers, to ignore a whisky bottle that had been thrown onto the grass near him. And when Marshall returned to the mound, he declined to take any more warm-up pitches.

"When he was ready to pitch," Joe Rudi said later, "I thought he'd try to sneak a fast ball by me on the inside."

That fast ball turned into Joe Rudi's home run. It was another of many mistakes by the Dodgers, who pride themselves on being products of an organization that flourishes on fundamentals. Al Campanis, the Dodgers' general manager, once authored a book titled *The Dodgers' Way to Play Baseball* that has become the team's textbook. But in the World Series, the Dodgers forgot the commandments. In each A's victory, a small Dodger mistake emerged as a large factor.

Steve Yeager, the twenty-five-year-old catcher, let a change-up get by him as Ken Holtzman moved to third, then scored on a squeeze bunt.

Joe Ferguson, the outfielder-catcher, bobbled Jackson's topped ball in front of the plate to set up a two-run inning. "He tried to make that play with one hand," a learned baseball executive said later. "You make it with two hands."

Andy Messersmith's wild pick-off throw to first base contributed to a four-run inning. Yeager made a slow tag at the plate as Jackson scored.

Dave Lopes, with a slow pivot, sabotaged a possible double play that would have averted the A's first-inning run. Buckner was thrown out at third base when he should have stopped at second, with the Dodgers only a run behind and none out.

The A's, meanwhile, were making the double play, making the perfect throw, making the perfect tag, making the perfect slide. The A's, mature and certain, simply showed the Dodgers, young and uncertain, the way to play baseball.

"We were at our best," said Don Sutton, the Dodgers' right-hander, "when we played the Pirates in the playoffs."

The Dodgers were at their best then, because the Pirates didn't have the pitching to stop them, as the A's did. Another factor was that Alvin Dark, the A's pious manager, acted decisively in employing Rollie Fingers, his bullpen ace. Alston, by comparison, waited too long to use Mike Marshall when the fourth game might have been preserved. But when the World Series ended, Dark didn't take any credit for his strategy that Charles O. Finley often has to approve.

"Glory to God," said the A's manager. "I've leaned on Him all through this season and I'll continue to do so."

Charles O. Finley probably considered that to be the nicest thing that Alvin Dark has ever said about the A's owner.

(October 20, 1974)

As it turned out, Charles O. Finley destroyed the A's himself. His contract squabbles alienated the players, who either departed as free agents or were traded out of spite. The balance of power in the American League shifted to the Yankees, who were in the playoffs against the Kansas City Royals when I accidentally bumped into what turned out to be one of my favorite columns. Catfish Hunter had stopped the Royals, 4–1, with a five-hitter in the opening game and I stopped for a drink in the Royals Stadium club. After my first swallow of a vodka and tonic, Bob Fishel, once the Yankees' public relations director and now the assistant to American League president Lee MacPhail, nudged me.

"C'mon with me," Bob said. "Satchel Paige is sitting over here with his wife."

For the next hour ol' Satch, whose age is baseball's best mystery, entertained us:

"Best pitchers I ever saw," Satchel Paige was saying, "was Slim Jones, Bob Feller, Dizzy Dean—people forget how hard Dizzy could throw."

"What about Catfish Hunter?"

"Tops. Right with anybody who ever pitched. He can't throw hard but what would you do with him, nothin'."

"How about Mark Fidrych, the rookie who talks to the ball?"

"He looks good but the ball can't hear him. The ball don't go where he tell it. Talkin' to the ball don't make him a pitcher unless he's been to Algiers and got somethin'." Over the weekend, Leroy Robert (Satchel) Paige was talking baseball in Kansas City, where he lives. Spry and sharp, his hair still more black than gray, he was sitting with his wife, Lahoma, in the dining room at Royals Stadium, and as he talked, his Hall of Fame ring flashed on his right pinkie. According to the *Baseball Encyclopedia,* he was born on July 7, 1906, at least twenty years too soon. If that birthday is accurate, he was forty-two when he followed Jackie Robinson into the major leagues after having dazzled the black leagues for two decades. If he were pitching now, he might be baseball's most expensive performer. "But the Hall of Fame is all I got to depend on," he was saying now. "You never miss nothin' you never had. I never had no money."

"What did you think," he was asked, "when you read about Catfish's big contract?"

"I wouldn't know how to count that. Banks didn't have that much when I was young, much less one man makin' that much. I was makin' two hundred and fifty dollars with the Chattanooga Black Lookouts in 1926 and I thought that was a lot. That's two hundred and fifty a month."

"How old were you then?"

"Oh, that's the onliest catch," he said with a smile. "You can say sixteen or seventeen nobody gonna believe you. I don't care what you say."

"Who's older," a man joked, "you or Luis Tiant?"

"I pitched with Tiant's father in Cuba, but you don't know how old Tiant's father is."

"When did you start collecting Social Security?"

"Ever since 1971," Satchel Paige said seriously.

"If you started collecting at sixty-five, you're seventy now."

"I ain't sayin' nothin'. Whatever you write is all right."

"You've never been misquoted?"

"I ain't never been misquoted," he said with a smile, his eyes twinkling behind dark horn-rimmed glasses.

"Anybody ever dispute what you say?"

"Lot of people, but they can't pinpoint me. My mother told me, 'If you tell a lie, always rehearse it. If it don't sound good to you, it won't sound good to anybody else.' No, I didn't rehearse this, but my birth certificate was in our Bible. In those days you put everything like that in the Bible. What happened was that my grandfather was reading the Bible under a chinaberry tree."

"Under a what?"

"Chinaberry tree. You ain't never heard of a chinaberry tree? I guess they're only in Alabama."

"If you were called into court and had to take an oath on your age, what would you tell the judge?"

"Yessir, I'd tell him how the goat ate it."

"How the goat ate what?"

"The goat ate the Bible with my birth certificate in it. My grandfather got up from the chair to talk to the lady next door and he forgot about the Bible and the goat ate the Bible with the birth certificate in it."

"You never got it back?"

"They couldn't follow that goat around all the time. But that goat lived to be twenty-seven. That goat's name was Bill Summers."

"When did the goat eat the Bible?"

"Oh, '25 or '26. I was ten or twelve."

"But you said before you were sixteen or seventeen in '26."

"I said I did which?" he asked.

"Remember when the St. Louis Browns had five different ages for you in their press guide?"

"It's still like that now. I got 'plus' on a few cards. Like on my driver's license, I'm seventy-plus. I got a ticket the other day. The cop asked me, 'How old are you?' and I laughed. He said, 'You one of those smart guys?' I thought the cop was kidding me because my name's on the license. I told him, 'I been around a long time.' He said, 'You ain't been around long enough to know you don't get smart with the police.' I got the ticket."

"Were you speeding?"

"No, but I was fixin' to," Satchel Paige said.

"How did the cop know that?"

"My tires were spinnin'. I was gettin' off fast."

"Do you take Geritol?"

"No, I don't take nothin'."

"No vitamins either?"

"Not yet," he replied.

"When did you get old?"

"I'm tryin' to think."

"Did you tell your wife how old you were when you got married in 1947?"

"Yeah, but she forgot."

"Will anyone ever know?"

"Never. I want to be the onliest man in the United States that nobody knows nothin' about. I say I saw Jack Johnson fight in 1912 and people believe me because I can say it so straight."

"Did you see Abner Doubleday?"

"I could talk about him, too."

"Who is the most important person you ever met?"

"I met Presidents and King George VIII."

"King George VI was the last King George."

"That was that," Satchel Paige said. "Maybe it was a queen I met. You gotta give me a little time to think about that, like my birth certificate."

(October 12, 1976)

The Yankees won that playoff on Chris Chambliss's ninth-inning home run in the decisive fifth game, then lost the World Series to the Reds in a four-game sweep. But they soon signed Reggie Jackson, a $3 million decision that added another ego to the Yankees' already sensitive situation. In addition to the continual conflict between George Steinbrenner, the Yankees' principal owner, and manager Billy Martin, a conflict soon flared between Jackson and Thurman Munson, the Yankees' catcher and captain.

"I'm the straw that stirs the drink," Jackson was quoted as saying in *Sport* magazine early that season. "It all comes back to me; maybe I should say me and Munson but really he doesn't enter into it."

Munson, naturally, was outraged. Then the Jackson-Martin feud was there on a Saturday-afternoon televised game for the nation to see. Martin benched Jackson in mid-inning for allegedly loafing on a looper that became a double. They almost had a fight in the dugout. Not long after that, Reggie suggested we have a drink after a game.

"I need somebody to talk to," he said.

We went out for a drink again a few weeks later. At the time both conversations were off the record. But when I got home, I made notes on what Reggie had talked about. I've learned that, sooner or later, what is said off the record often becomes on the record. And if that happened in this situation, I wanted the quotes to be accurate. The night he emerged as the World Series hero, I asked him if, in order to put his accomplishment in perspective, I now could write what he told me when he was discouraged. He agreed:

Nearly three hours after his three home runs had won the World Series for the Yankees and redemption for himself, Reggie Jackson, like almost everyone else, appeared in awe of what he had accomplished. "There's a part of me I don't know," he was saying softly at his locker. "There's the ballplayer in me who responds to all that pressure. I'm not sure I hit three home runs but the ballplayer in me did."

And above all his complex parts, Reggie Jackson is a ballplayer. When he took nearly $3 million from the Yankees, most people scoffed that he wasn't worth it. He even agreed he wasn't worth it. But he's worth it now. No matter what he does from now on is a bonus. What he did Tuesday night put Reggie Jackson up there with Muhammad Ali winning back the heavyweight title in Zaire, up there with Joe Namath and the Jets winning Super Bowl III, up there with Tom Seaver and the Mets winning the 1969 World Series, but to appreciate how the "part of me I don't know" put Reggie Jackson up there, it is necessary to remember how another part, his sensitive ego, put Reggie Jackson down so that he might ascend.

"I got to get dressed," he was saying now. "I told some people I'd meet them at Seventy-sixth and Third."

In that same East Side area, at a sidewalk table at Arthur's Court in July, he was sipping white wine and saying, "I'm still the straw that stirs the drink. Not Munson, not nobody else on this club."

All the other Yankees had dressed and departed Tuesday night except for Thurman Munson, who was on his way out now.

"Hey, coon," called the catcher, grinning. "Nice goin', coon."

Reggie Jackson laughed and hurried over and hugged the captain.

"I'm goin' down to that party here in the ballpark," Thurman Munson said, grinning again. "Just white people but they'll let you in. Come on down."

"I'll be there," Reggie Jackson said. "Wait for me."

"I got to make myself go to the ballpark," he said in July. "I don't want to go."

"You'll change your mind," somebody told him.

"I don't want to change. I've closed my mind. Remember the thing in Boston," he said, referring to his dugout confrontation with Billy Martin in Fenway Park, "the next day we had a meeting in Gabe Paul's suite and Billy challenged me. He stood over me and said, 'I'll make you fight me, boy.' But there was no way I was going to fight him. I'm two hundred and fifteen pounds, he's almost fifty years old. I win the fight, but I lose."

In the manager's office half an hour earlier, Reggie Jackson and Billy Martin had finished a TV interview together when the slugger overheard the manager talking about punching somebody.

"Anybody fights you, Skip," Reggie Jackson said, "he's got to fight both of us."

"And anybody who fights you," Billy Martin said, "got to fight the both of us."

"We can't win this way," he said in July. "The Red Sox can hammer. We got nobody who can hammer except me. I should be batting third or clean-up, not sixth. I always hit third or clean-up."

"How far did that last homer go?" the clean-up hitter asked.

"I figured it to be about four hundred and fifty feet," a sportswriter said.

"Make it four hundred and seventy-five, it sounds better," the clean-up hitter said, laughing. "I hit that one off a knuckler, the first two off fast balls. The general consensus on how to pitch to me is hard and in.

On the first one. I knew [Burt] Hooton would pitch me there, but I had an inkling I'd hit one. As soon as they brought in [Elia] Sosa, I got on the phone to Stick [Gene Michael, the Yankee scout] upstairs and asked him about Sosa, because Sosa popped me up with a fast ball in spring training. Stick told me he throws hard stuff—fast ball, slider, good curve. I hit another fast ball. I hit the second one even better than I hit the third, the one off [Charley] Hough's knuckler. Brooks Robinson taught me how to hit a knuckler. Just time the ball."

"Hough said that knuckler didn't move much," somebody said.

"It didn't," Reggie Jackson said, "until I got hold of it."

"I should've signed with the Padres," he said in July. "I'd be happy there. Or with the Dodgers."

"Did you hear," Reggie Jackson was told, "what Steve Garvey said—that after your third homer, he applauded in his glove?"

"What a great player Steve Garvey is, what a great man," Reggie Jackson said. "He's the best all-around human being in baseball. My one regret about not playing with the Dodgers is not being around Steve Garvey, but I got a security blanket here, Fran Healy [the Yankees' bullpen catcher]. Before the game he told me I was swinging the bat good."

"I don't need baseball," he said in July, "I'm a businessman. That means as much to me as baseball. I don't need cheers."

"When you hit the third one," a visitor was saying now, "George Steinbrenner had tears in his eyes."

"Get my bat, Nick, please," Reggie Jackson told a clubhouse man. "I started using this bat Saturday after I broke one in Friday's game. Look at the wide grain. The older the tree, the wider the grain, the harder the wood. I think I'll give this bat to George, he'll appreciate it."

"George," somebody said, "ought to put a marker out there halfway up the bleachers where that third homer landed."

"That'd be something, Babe Ruth, Lou Gehrig, Joe DiMaggio, Mickey Mantle and Reggie Jackson. Somehow I don't fit."

"You know what Bobby Vinton sings, 'Color Me Gone,' that's me," he said in July. "Color me gone. I want to hit .300, thirty homers, fifty doubles, drive in ninety runs, be the most valuable player in the World Series, get to win the World Series, and then go. Color me gone."

Thurman Munson reappeared. "Hey, nigger, you're too slow, that party's over but I'll see you next year," the captain said, sticking out his hand. "I'll see you next year wherever I might be."

"You'll be back," Reggie Jackson said.

"Not me," said Thurman Munson, who has talked of demanding to be traded to the Cleveland Indians. "But you know who stuck up for you, nigger, you know who stuck up for you when you needed it."

"I know," Reggie Jackson said. "But you'll be here next year. We'll all be here."

(October 20, 1977)

Just as Reggie predicted, they were all there the next year, at least at the start. But by late June the Yankees had dropped eight and a half games behind the Red Sox in the A.L. East and Billy Martin was facing a firing squad, the front office. Even worse, he looked as if he knew he was about to be executed. His face was haggard, his body and patience thin. I was alone with him in his Yankee Stadium office when he closed the door.

"I want to tell you something," he said, "but it's got to be off the record. I'm not well. I've got a spot on my liver."

I agreed to keep his secret, especially since he mentioned I was only the second person who knew about his liver problem; as I remember, his pal Mickey Mantle was the other who knew. But at the All-Star Game in San Diego two weeks later I heard other people talking about Billy's liver ailment. Two days later I stopped at Anaheim Stadium to visit Jim Fregosi, the California Angels' manager.

"Did you know," Jim asked, "that Billy has a spot on his liver?"

I knew—but when Billy asked me to keep his ailment a secret, I expected him to keep it a secret too. Instead, it had become common knowledge among baseball people. That same day George Steinbrenner had granted Billy the opportunity to resign for "health" reasons, ostensibly a nagging virus. I decided to write the truth about Billy's health. I was in Los Angeles at the time and tried to phone him. I wanted to let him know that I no longer considered his liver ailment to be off the record. But the Yankee Stadium switchboard operator would not put me through to his office in the clubhouse. I talked to Mickey Morabito, the Yankees' publicity director, and asked him to give Billy my phone number. Billy never called:

Up to now the primary plot of the Yankees' soap opera has involved the continuous conflict of egos between George Steinbrenner and Billy Martin, but suddenly a medical crisis has surfaced. The volatile owner has offered the volatile manager an opportunity to resign for "health reasons." George Steinbrenner identified a nagging "virus" that Billy Martin has been unable to shake all season. But his ailment might be much more serious. Billy Martin has told friends, "I have a spot on my liver," and has been advised by physicians to stop drinking. True to his stubbornness that he can't live with or without, Billy Martin has spurned that medical advice as well as George Steinbrenner's offer.

"I'm not a quitter," Billy Martin has said. "I want to try to win this thing. I owe it to the Yankee fans."

But more important, Billy Martin owes it to himself to undergo extensive tests. He should not risk collapsing and needing to be rushed to a hospital, as Mickey Mantle was recently with bleeding ulcers. And the Yankee hierarchy should overrule his stubbornness. If a player is hurting, the Yankees surround him with doctors. But with the manager ill, the demand for medical attention has not had the same urgency. Hell, the manager does not pitch or swing a bat or run the bases.

Scrawny even when the picture of health, Billy Martin is the picture of tension now. His narrow face appears to be clenched. His smile is tight and sad.

The problem apparently is in Billy Martin's liver. But it's also in his head. Billy Martin won't surrender to the tension that keeps tightening its grip on him. The tension was brutal even when the Yankees won the World Series last year. It's worse now that they're virtually out of the American League East race halfway through this season. But in Billy Martin's mind, the Yankees can still win. So he tries to relax with a drink after a game. But that only aggravates his liver ailment.

"I still got my key," Billy Martin was saying three weeks ago when George Steinbrenner announced that the manager was safe for the remainder of this season. "I still got my key."

Billy Martin meant the key to his private liquor cabinet behind the bar in the Yankee Stadium press room where he often drinks after a game. When the bartender, Lou Napoli, goes home, Billy Martin uses the key to keep his glass full. To him, the key to that liquor cabinet is as much a status symbol as the key to the executive washroom is to a corporate vice president.

"As long as I got my key," Billy Martin said with a laugh that night, "I'm all right."

But physically, Billy Martin is not all right. And he knows it. But he also knows that if he goes into a hospital for tests now, he'll never manage the Yankees again during George Steinbrenner's regime. He knows that George Steinbrenner is searching for a reason to replace him. And there's no better reason than a medical reason. That gets George Steinbrenner off the hook with the Yankee fans who keep giving Billy Martin standing ovations.

The liver ailment also was a factor in George Steinbrenner's sudden support of Billy Martin three weeks ago.

That crisis developed when the Yankee front office decided to transfer Billy Martin's pitching coach and pal, Art Fowler, to the role of minor league instructor. Billy Martin was furious. In retaliation, he threatened to go to a hospital for liver tests. He also threatened to call a news conference and blast George Steinbrenner so severely that the Yankees' principal owner would virtually be forced to dismiss him. Either way, the Yankees would have had to honor Billy Martin's contract through next season.

That contract, at a salary of more than $100,000 annually, is more important than ever to Billy Martin now, especially with a liver ailment that might prevent him from managing elsewhere in the future.

George Steinbrenner talks of Billy Martin becoming a Yankee "consultant," but a consultant often is not consulted. Just ask Red Holzman, the Knicks' former coach. Billy Martin yearns to be in a front office someday, but he is a manager, not an executive. If he thinks he has problems with George Steinbrenner looking over his shoulder now, imagine the problems of another manager with Billy Martin looking over his shoulder. Leo Durocher was never the type to be in the front office. Billy Martin is not the type either. He belongs in the dugout.

Ironically, because of their continuous conflicts, Billy Martin and George Steinbrenner taped a Miller Lite beer television commercial Friday, the perfect pair for that argumentative series. They probably had a script, but they didn't need one.

Already there is speculation that after the season, or perhaps after the Yankees have been eliminated, Billy Martin will accept George Steinbrenner's offer to retire. That way Billy Martin will still have his pride. But maybe not his health.

(July 16, 1978)

When the column appeared, Billy denied he had a liver ailment. That didn't surprise me. Denials often occur even when the denial is a lie. What annoys me is that people who know their denial is a lie never seem to think of it as a lie. But that's a subject for an ethics professor.

Billy's denial was quickly eclipsed by another controversy. In the tenth inning of a game, Reggie Jackson kept trying to bunt, instead of obeying Billy Martin's orders to swing away. Reggie was suspended for five days.

The day Reggie returned, Billy uttered his famous description of Reggie and George Steinbrenner—"They deserve each other; one's a born liar, the other's convicted" (words he also denied for several days before apologizing to Steinbrenner). The next day Billy suddenly resigned. Of all his explanations that day, the most significant to me was, "I owe it to my health . . . to resign," almost the exact phrase I had used. Incredibly, he was rehired by Steinbrenner five days later, effective with the 1980 season if his health permits. A brilliant public relations move by Steinbrenner to placate Yankee fans. When the rehiring was announced, at the Old-Timer's Day introductions, Martin received a seven-minute standing ovation. Appearing on the ABC television network, Billy acknowledged having a "slight spot" on his liver.

But say this for Billy Martin—even when the Yankees were fourteen games behind the Red Sox, he insisted they could still win. And they did—with Bob Lemon as their manager.

Around that same time Pete Rose had his hitting streak stopped at 44 games; close to and yet so far from Joe DiMaggio's monument of 56 games. But for the last two weeks of his streak the Cincinnati Reds' third baseman created the same suspense that DiMaggio had in 1941, the suspense of "Did he get a hit today?"—the suspense that only a consecutive-game hitting streak generates. In nearly forty years they have been the only baseball players to have embedded themselves in the nation's memory that way. His 44-game hitting streak further enhanced the stature of Pete Rose who three months earlier got his 3,000th hit:

He works now at Riverfront Stadium, which is perched above the traffic rumbling along the interstate between the downtown Cincinnati office buildings and the Ohio River bridges. But about two miles away, in an old neighborhood of old warehouses, Pete Rose was returning to his baseball roots. He was driving down old streets toward where Crosley Field once was. Growing up in Cincinnati, he often saw the Reds play in Crosley Field and he played there himself for half his career. "Here's where it was," he announced now to the visitor he was taking on a guided tour. "What a great little ballpark it was." But there was no evidence that a ballpark had been there. No ruins, no commemorative stone. Merely a vast empty lot with small rocks and other debris all over it.

"You'd never know," the visitor said to Pete Rose, "that you got a lot of hits here."

"With the bad hops off them rocks," he said, laughing. "Think of the hits I'd get now."

Hits—perhaps no other major league baseball player has been so obsessed by hits as Pete Rose, the Cincinnati Reds' third baseman who now has 3,002 of them. Recently turned thirty-seven years old, he has the time and the tenacity to accumulate more hits than Stan Musial, who had 3,630, or Henry Aaron, who had 3,771; he might even approach Ty Cobb's record of 4,191 hits.

"That's why I don't smoke or drink," he says. "To me, to play three years extra is worth maybe five-hundred hits."

He has won three National League batting titles and invariably he is among the league's top-ten hitters.

"I love to get my hits," he once said. "I don't want to be one of those guys who has to wait for the Sunday papers to find out what his batting average is. I want to be able to see it every day."

When he doesn't get at least 200 hits in a season, Pete Rose is disappointed. If he collects that many again this season, he will have done it 10 times, breaking the record he now shares with Ty Cobb.

"I'm proud to see I only needed fifteen years to do it nine times," Pete Rose says. "Ty Cobb needed twenty-three years."

Ted Kluszewski, the Reds' coach who was their slugging first baseman when Pete Rose was a kid going to Crosley Field, has warned that Pete Rose is "an original, you won't see another one like him in a thousand years." But old-timers can't resist comparing Pete Rose with Ty Cobb, with Pepper Martin, with Enos Slaughter—three players whose best was matched only by their zest. Of the three, only Ty Cobb had more hits than Pete Rose has.

"But with all the good relief pitchers there are now, Ty Cobb would hit maybe .315 and that's all," Pete Rose has said. "I'm not trying to belittle him. It's just that the game has changed."

In his 16th season with the Reds, Pete Rose has not changed. When he is awarded a base on balls, he still runs to first base. Between innings, he runs to and from his position at third base. And he still slides head first.

"I have so much fun playing baseball," he often explains, "that's why I play the way I do."

Maybe that's why Pete Rose has never been booed in Cincinnati; in other towns he has been hooted, notably Los Angeles when the Reds were battling the Dodgers for the National League West title and New York after his fistfight with Bud Harrelson of the Mets following a hard slide in the 1973 playoffs. But another reason for his popularity in Cincinnati is that he was born and raised there. He also has remained there.

"I don't know why," he has said, "anybody would want to live anywhere else."

To emerge as a Hall of Famer in your hometown—as Pete Rose surely will—is a rarity in baseball. Honus Wagner, a native of suburban Carnegie, Pa., was the Pittsburgh Pirates' legendary shortstop. Lou Gehrig and Whitey Ford were New Yorkers who made it big with the Yankees, but because of New York's distinctive borough borders perhaps they deserve an asterisk. Lou Gehrig grew up in Manhattan and Whitey Ford in Queens; neither grew up in the Bronx where the Yankees play. Another asterisk should be attached to Frank Frisch, who came out of the Bronx to be the New York Giants' second baseman at the old Polo Grounds. Sandy Koufax joined the Dodgers from the Brooklyn sandlots but he did not emerge as a Hall of Fame pitcher until the club had moved to Los Angeles—too late to be classified as a hometown product. But there is no question about Pete Rose's identification with Cincinnati then or now.

"The thing that impressed me most about Johnny Bench," he has said, "is that he moved to Cincinnati year-round."

Down near the Ohio River there is a plaque identifying Pete Rose Park where he played baseball as a youngster.

"I could have played other places," he says with a smile, "but the kids in that park were more aggressive."

When he finished his sandlot games, Pete Rose would go to Crosley Field with his father to see the Reds play. His father would buy a ticket but, perhaps to instill the hustler's attitude in his son, he would make little Pete bum a ticket to get in. Once inside, little Pete did not stuff himself with hot dogs and peanuts.

"My dad believed in going to the ballpark to see the game, not to eat," Pete Rose remembers. "We ate at home."

But they always got to Crosley Field early enough to see the infield drill. Pete Rose was a second baseman then.

"I liked to watch Roy McMillan and Johnny Temple turn the double play," he says. "Johnny Temple was my favorite."

And now Pete Rose is Cincinnati's favorite, if not baseball's favorite, one of the new millionaire athletes that fans do not resent, probably because he's always hustling, always earning every penny of his estimated $350,000 salary. And when they see him driving his burgundy Rolls-Royce, people invariably smile instead of smirk.

"Yeah," says Pete Rose, "that Rolls-Royce is a lot of hits."

(May 7, 1978)

• • •

When the Red's front office did not agree that Pete Rose should be their highest-paid player in 1979, he hustled off to the Phillies for a $3.2 million four-year offer that made him *baseball's* highest-paid player. That offer, of course, had been enhanced by his 44-game hitting streak.

With his obsession for hits, Pete Rose deserved to put together a memorable hitting streak. I've always been fascinated by hitting streaks. I've even had my life influenced by one. I did a magazine piece in 1961 for *Sports Illustrated* on DiMaggio's streak, and the week the article appeared, I had a drink with an attorney who was offering me a job as an investigator for a House subcommittee. The money would be better than I was making at the *Journal-American* and working in Washington during John F. Kennedy's administration was appealing. We were having a drink in the old Forest Hills Inn when a friend of the attorney stopped by our table.

"I know you," his friend said after we were introduced. "You're the guy who wrote the piece about DiMaggio's hitting streak. I couldn't stop reading it. I kept reading it even while I was shaving tonight."

I thanked him and he left. I turned back to the attorney, who was shaking his head and saying, "Well, that's the end of the Washington job. I thought I had you but I can't offer you anything to match that."

I stayed a sportswriter.

2 · Aaron

Back when I was covering the Dodgers for the Brooklyn *Eagle,* I was in the office one day in 1954 after my first trip to spring training. The noisiest baseball fan there was a cityside rewrite man, Clarence Greenbaum, a delightful cynic who often wandered over to the sports department. Seeing me, he sneered and said, "Well, kid, what did you see in spring training that you never saw before?"

"Henry Aaron," I said.

"Who?" asked Clarence.

"Henry Aaron," I said.

That was the year Henry Aaron joined the Milwaukee Braves as a rookie. He was Henry Aaron then, not Hank, and that's probably why he's always been Henry to me. Not that I was a talent scout. I had simply been listening to the Dodgers talk about him. That year the Dodgers had traveled north with the Braves by train, stopping for exhibition games in Mobile, Birmingham, Nashville and Chattanooga, and the more the Dodgers saw of Henry Aaron, the more they talked about him. They knew this skinny twenty-year-old kid was a hitter. Not a home-run hitter. None of the Dodgers, or anybody else for that matter, believed then that he would hit 755 home runs. But if they had been told that his batting average for twenty-three major league seasons would be .305, none would have been surprised.

But season by season, Henry's home runs began to add up—400,

500, 600—and when he hit his 700th, the countdown began to Babe Ruth's record of 714.

Entering the last week of the 1973 season, Henry had 712 home runs. He had to be covered now. He might hit two in one game to tie the record, or even three in one game to break it. Babe Ruth, remember, had hit his last three homers in one game on May 25, 1935, for the old Boston Braves at Forbes Field in Pittsburgh. The next week Babe retired.

The Braves, who had moved from Milwaukee to Atlanta after the 1965 season, were playing in Atlanta that last week in 1973 against the Los Angeles Dodgers and the Houston Astros.

About fifteen other out-of-town sportswriters also arrived for the final countdown. That invasion would have bothered some athletes but Henry took it in stride. Before the night games, he would get to Atlanta Stadium about four o'clock and go into the trainer's room for a rubdown and a cigarette. Then he would sit at his locker with us for about an hour in what was more a casual conversation than an interview. By making it easy for us, he also made it easy for himself.

But somehow the city of Atlanta didn't seem aware of the drama that week:

ATLANTA—Maybe the people here are too close to it to appreciate the significance. Maybe they just don't understand. Or maybe they don't want to understand. Whatever the reason, the panorama of Atlanta Stadium is dominated by empty blue seats as Henry Aaron approaches Babe Ruth's record of 714 home runs. In a modern ballpark with 52,870 seats, there were 47,299 empty seats last night, 42,659 empty seats the night before. Of those who came, the majority were white. One reason is that the Atlanta Braves' ticket prices are too high for many blacks. When the Braves end their season against the Houston Astros on Saturday night and Sunday afternoon, bigger crowds are anticipated. But until more people appear, Atlanta is the disgrace of baseball. It prides itself as a historical city, but it's ignoring history. Atlanta doesn't deserve Henry Aaron's drama. He'd be better off on a barnstorming tour.

"One day, too late," says a member of the Braves' organization, "the people here are going to realize what they had."

What they have is not only a great baseball player but a great person. To judge somebody properly, observe him under stress. Henry Aaron is under stress now. But he remains quiet, almost gentle. He remains pleasant and polite, so polite that he pretends the small crowds don't bother him.

"I've got a job to do," he says. "It doesn't make any difference to me if there are seven hundred and fifty people watching or seventy-five thousand."

He was sitting by his open locker in the Braves' clubhouse. In his free time, he maintains his privacy. But at the ballpark, he is a man of history. Cameras follow him. When he sits at his locker in the hours before a game, a group of about fifteen newsmen from all over the country surround him. They're here to cover him, nothing else. When he comes to bat, it's as if they were covering a time bomb. On every pitch, the time bomb ticks. After a game, he appears in a special interview room adjacent to the clubhouse.

"Are you enjoying this?" he was asked the other night.

"I refuse," he said with a big grin, "to answer that."

It's not easy for him to enjoy it. Not after having answered many of the same questions for months. But he tolerates them patiently. Throughout his career he has performed the same way—stoically, without flair, without emotion. He seldom creates headlines with anything except his home runs.

"Things do bother me," he was saying now at his locker, "but I react differently than other people. Some guys go 0 for 4 and throw their helmets or kick things, but I think, Why did I pop up? Why did I strike out? This is how I try to teach my kids—to sit down and figure it out."

He has four children—Gaele, a junior at Fisk University in Nashville, Henry Jr., Larry and Dorinda.

"I always feel there's room for improvement," he continued. "Like if I hit two homers and a double, I wonder why I wasn't able to hit three homers. In a way I'm never satisfied, but I also believe that in playing baseball or any sport, you can't be as good as the other guy every day."

His attribute is consistency. Thickly muscled through the chest and shoulders, his body has supported that consistency. So has his mental outlook.

"The reason I'm not showing much emotion in all this," he said, "is that I've been doing it through the years. I don't recall having a bad year. I think my best year was 1959 for hitting the ball. I hit .355, but for a long time I was well over .400, then I sprained my ankle running after a fly ball in the old Philadelphia ballpark. I stepped on a bottle.

"I didn't begin to think of myself as a home-run hitter until I was around a few years. When I was a rookie in 1954, we had Eddie Mathews and Joe Adcock and I considered myself a guy who got on base. But when I got older and stronger, I also got more selective with the pitches I hit, and that turned me into a home-run hitter. Then it was my responsibility."

Henry Aaron rubbed the big yellow callus at the base of his left palm.

"I realized that home-run hitters drive Mercedes or Cadillacs," he said, smiling.

"What kind of a car do you drive yourself?" one of the newsmen asked him.

"I have a Caprice," he said, referring to a Chevrolet model. "It gets me around."

In the laughter, Henry Aaron smiled and stood up. He put on his uniform shirt with the big 44 on it and adjusted his red, white and blue cap.

"Let me go hit," he said.

In his unhurried manner, he walked through the long concrete tunnel to the field surrounded by the empty seats.

(September 27, 1973)

Suddenly, on Saturday night, he hit his 713th before 35,034 empty seats. But now that he needed only one to tie the record, the imminence of history filled 40,517 seats for the Sunday game. He got three singles that day to lift his batting average to .301, not bad at age forty, but his last time up, he popped out. When he trotted out to left field in his casual stride, the ovation began with the people in the left-field stands. Slowly, it circled Atlanta Stadium with virtually everyone on their feet. He was smiling now and waving every so often. After about three minutes, the game was resumed with the ovation still ringing.

"That ovation was tremendous," he was saying now. "That ovation was really great."

That ovation and that big crowd apparently got the Braves' front office thinking. The next February, their board chairman, Bill Bartholomay, issued a statement that scandalized baseball:

In brazen defiance of baseball's integrity, the Atlanta Braves have decreed that they will not fulfill their 162-game commitment to the National League schedule this year. Instead, the Braves will play 159 games. The other three, their opening series in Cincinnati, have emerged as exhibitions now that Henry Aaron won't be in the starting lineup.

Over the weekend, Bill Bartholomay, the Braves' chairman of the board, announced that Aaron, whose next home run will equal Babe Ruth's record, "will be available as a pinch hitter for the road games in Cincinnati and for part-time play if required by Eddie Mathews," the team's manager. It sounded as if the Braves were talking about three games in Florida during spring training instead of what are advertised as championship games. After the opening series in Cincinnati, the Braves return to Atlanta for an eleven-game home stand, beginning with a Monday-night game against the Los Angeles Dodgers that will be nationally televised. Bartholomay obviously is more concerned with preserving Aaron's historic 714th and 715th home runs as a box-office attraction and an Atlanta spectacular than he is with winning the three games in the Cincinnati series. If he could manipulate it completely, Bartholomay probably would prefer that Henry's next two homers occur in the final game of the season.

So brazen was the Braves' decision it even awoke that guardian of baseball's integrity, Commissioner Bowie Kuhn, who had been asleep on sentry duty.

Three weeks ago Aaron disclosed, "I would like the seven hundred fourteenth and seven hundred fifteenth home runs to be in Atlanta. I've talked it over with Bill Bartholomay and I think I'll play the second game in Cincinnati and sit out the other two." The Braves open there on Thursday, April 4, then play there Saturday and Sunday afternoons. "They don't need me in Cincinnati to sell out their opener. But they might need me to sell tickets for Saturday's game." Aaron's concern, and presumably Bartholomay's, for the Saturday game was subtle. It's expected to be the National Broadcasting Company's opening TV game of the week—the perfect tease for the long home stand. Those comments by Aaron didn't stir the commissioner, but at least Bartholomay roused him.

"I have discussed with Bill Bartholomay on the telephone the Braves' statement of last Saturday," the commissioner announced yesterday in a prepared statement. "He has assured me that the Braves will do their very best to win the opening three games in Cincinnati."

Unless the Braves' executive assured Kuhn that Aaron, if healthy, will be in the starting lineup, the Atlanta franchise won't be doing its "very best" to win. Aaron is forty years old but he is not an ornament of the team, he is its soul. He is a clean-up hitter whom pitchers fear. He is not dragging into his final season. He is coming off a remarkable year in which he hit 40 homers, batted .301 and drove in 96 runs. When his name isn't on the lineup card, the Braves are not using their "very best" team.

When a few pitchers mentioned last season that they might groove a pitch for Aaron when his home-run record is imminent, Kuhn branded it "detrimental" to baseball and scolded them. The current Aaron situation is, to borrow the commissioner's vocabulary, equally detrimental.

It's detrimental to the Los Angeles Dodgers, the Houston Astros and the San Francisco Giants, who hope to challenge the Reds in the National League West this year. If the Braves choose to preserve Aaron against the Reds in the final week of a pennant race instead of in the first week, the other contenders will squawk, and justly so. One of baseball's tenets is that a victory or a defeat in the first week counts the same in the standings as it does in the final week. And the Reds are chuckling. "If he never hits another home run against us," said Bob Howsam, the Reds' president, "it will be soon enough for me." In his career Aaron has hit more homers against the Reds than against any other team. And in four seasons at Riverfront Stadium, he has hit ten.

It's detrimental to Eddie Mathews, who isn't that secure as the Braves' manager.

It's detrimental to the Braves' pitchers who want Aaron swinging a bat for them.

It's detrimental to those in Cincinnati who purchase tickets for the first three games. They're entitled to see the Braves at their "very best" with Aaron, or else they're entitled to a cut-rate price. Exhibition games are never as expensive as championship games.

(February 19, 1974)

The day of the opener, Henry Aaron was in the lineup. With his first swing in the first inning against Jack Billingham, he hit a line drive over the left-field fence in Riverfront Stadium for his 714th home run. On our way to Saturday's game, Joe Durso of the *Times* and I were about to take a cab when Joe recognized a man on the sidewalk.

"Fabulous Howard," Joe said.

"Where's Aaron?" the man said. "I'm here to drive him to the ballpark. Where is he?"

As if on cue, Henry appeared:

CINCINNATI—On the sidewalk next to the shiny black Cadillac limousine the red carpet had been unrolled. On it in gold were the words "Fantastic Aaron," and when Henry appeared outside the Netherland Hilton Hotel shortly before noon today he was approached by a seventy-two-year-old man with a mustache who calls himself "Fabulous Howard." His full name is Howard Risner and he is America's most celebrated chauffeur, at least in his opinion. On his card is the phrase, "Have Cadillac, Will Travel" and he had driven over from Chicago to transport Henry Aaron to Riverfront Stadium in anticipation of the forty-year-old slugger's 715th home run.

"I'm taking you to the ballpark," Fabulous Howard was saying now. "Let's go. You're my guest."

Somewhat confused, Henry stared at him. In his travels, he had never met Fabulous Howard before.

"I'm all right," Risner said. "I drove Joe Pepitone to the ballpark when he was with the Cubs."

Aaron laughed. He and Pepitone had been teammates on the Atlanta Braves briefly. Risner might have mentioned other passengers, such as Bob Hope, Elizabeth Taylor and Richard Burton, Frank Sinatra, Marlon Brando, or even Bowie Kuhn, but he had chosen the psychologically magic name "Joe Pepitone." Said Aaron, chuckling, "All right, let's go to the ballpark."

He crossed the red carpet and slid into the front seat, then waited while Fabulous Howard rolled up the red carpet and put it in the trunk while bagpipe music blared in the back seat. When he got behind the wheel, Fabulous Howard honked his horn, which is not your ordinary horn. Fabulous Howard's horn is musical.

"What's that?" Aaron asked, surprised by the melody.

" 'The Bridge on the River Kwai,' " Fabulous Howard said.

He also has a loudspeaker, which he was talking into.

"Feast your eyes on royalty," he was saying as people on the sidewalks turned and stared. "The King is in this car, the King of Baseball."

Aaron laughed again in his enjoyment.

"I drove Babe Ruth, too," Risner said.

"In this car?" Aaron asked. Seriously.

"No," said Risner. "In a little jitney I had when I was in St. Louis years ago. I drove him in Chicago later on, in an open purple Marmon touring car with white spoke wheels. And now I'm driving Henry Aaron to the ballpark. I'll be in Atlanta, too."

As he approached Riverfront Stadium he turned on a siren. But a ballpark policeman stopped the limousine.

"I've got the King here," Fabulous Howard said. "I'm driving the King right into the Braves' locker room."

Not quite. He parked outside it. But when Aaron went to open his door, Fabulous Howard told him, "Not yet—wait until I come around." He hurriedly opened the trunk, took out the red carpet and unrolled it. Still laughing, Henry Aaron thanked him and strolled into the clubhouse, where the Braves' manager, Eddie Mathews, was announcing that "the King of Baseball" would not be in the starting lineup today or tomorrow.

"Eddie told me about it last night," Aaron said. "He made the decision. He's the manager, I can't put my name in the lineup."

Outside, in the Braves' dugout near a lineup card that listed Aaron under "extra men," Matthews was being cross-examined.

"On opening day," somebody asked, "you explained that Bill Bartholomay and Eddie Robinson had asked you, 'If the home run were not involved, would Henry be playing?' and you answered, 'Yes.' Doesn't the same question still apply?"

"The home run is involved," Mathews said. "That home run Thursday changed everything."

Don't blame Mathews, who simply was doing what he knows Bartholomay, the Braves' chairman, and Robinson, the general manager, preferred—preserving the possibility of the record 715th home run for the Atlanta audience, beginning Monday night. The decision, in defiance of Commissioner Kuhn's expectation that Aaron would play two of three games here, proved that the Braves were more interested in their receipts than in their record. They lost again today, 7–5, with Mathews using four other pinch hitters while Aaron sat in the dugout.

The decision also was a tribute to Aaron's integrity. When he's permitted to swing, as he was Thursday, he swings for home runs.

But tonight the commissioner wisely and firmly ordered Mathews to start Henry Aaron tomorrow and the Braves' manager agreed, reluctantly. Bartholomay and Robinson concurred, reluctantly. They still don't seem to understand that the commissioner simply wants them to use a player who might help them win a game with a home run. They would have preferred not to use Henry Aaron for that very reason—he just might hit a home run. Think about that.

(April 7, 1974)

Henry Aaron did not hit a home run Sunday, which meant he now returned to Atlanta for an eleven-game home stand. The next morning I was awakened in Atlanta by the sound of a musical horn blaring the tune from *The Bridge on the River Kwai*. Fabulous Howard had arrived after an all-night drive. And that night Al Downing threw a fast ball, Henry Aaron swung and I heard another sound—the sound of 715.

ATLANTA—In the decades to come, the memory of the scene might blur. But the memory of the sound will remain with everyone who was here. Not the sound of the cheers, or the sound of Henry Aaron saying, "I'm thankful to God it's all over," but the sound of Henry Aaron's bat when it hit the baseball tonight. The sound that's baseball's version of a thunderclap, the sound of a home run, in his case the sound of the 715th home run. The sound momentarily was the only sound in the expectant silence of 53,775 customers at Atlanta Stadium and then, as the sound faded, the ball soared high and deep toward the left-center-field fence. And over it. On the infield base paths, Henry Aaron was trotting now, trotting past Babe Ruth into history in his twenty-first season. On his first swing in tonight's game, the forty-year-old outfielder of the Atlanta Braves had hit another home run, just as he had hit his record-tying home run on his first swing at Cincinnati in last Thursday's season opener. At home plate, surrounded by an ovation that came down around him as if it were a waterfall of appreciation, he was met by his teammates who attempted to lift him onto their shoulders. But he slipped off into the arms of his father, Herbert Sr., and his mother, Estella, who had hurried out of the special box for the Aaron family near the Braves' dugout.

"I never knew," Aaron would say later, "that my mother could hug so tight."

Moments later he was accepting a diamond wristwatch from the commissioner of baseball, Bowie Kuhn, but not from Kuhn himself. Rather than expose himself to the boos of the Atlanta populace, Kuhn had dispatched an ambassador, Monte Irvin, to the scene of the pre-game festivities in the event the 715th home run occurred. When it did, Irvin presented the watch, and when he was introduced as being from the commissioner's office, the boos roared. In his jubilation, Henry Aaron smiled.

"I was smiling from the boos," he would say later. That's all he would say because that's the way Henry Aaron is. Henry Aaron doesn't gloat. Quietly, he has resented Kuhn's attitude toward him, whether real or imagined. It began when Kuhn ignored his 700th home run last season, and it simmered when Kuhn ordered Eddie Mathews to use him in the starting lineup in Cincinnati yesterday after the Braves' manager had planned to preserve him for the Atlanta audience. Kuhn was correct in that ultimatum, because the Braves were defying the integrity of baseball.

But the commissioner was wrong tonight in not being here. He had stood up gallantly, but suddenly he had sat down again. Henry Aaron should have ordered the commissioner to be here.

"I thought the lineup card was taken out of Eddie Matthew's hand," the man with 715 home runs said. "I believe I should've been given the privilege of deciding for myself."

It's unfortunate that controversy somewhat clouded Henry Aaron's moment. It's also untypical. Of all our superstars, Henry Aaron has been perhaps the most uncontroversial. But time will blow those clouds away. Soon only his home runs will be important, not where he hit them, not where the commissioner was. His eventual total of home runs will be his monument, although they represent only a portion of his stature as a hitter.

With a normally productive season, in what he insists will be his last, Henry Aaron probably will hold six major league career records for home runs, runs batted in, total bases, extra base hits, games and times at bat. Ty Cobb will retain the records for hits, runs, batting average and stolen bases. Babe Ruth will hold the records for slugging average and walks. Through the years, Cobb and the Babe were the ultimate in hitting, but now they must move over.

"With a good year," Henry Aaron has said, "I'll hold six records, Cobb will hold four and Ruth two."

Perhaps that will convince the skeptics who minimize his accomplishments as a hitter. Some of the skeptics are traditionalists, some are racists. Statistically, their argument is that Henry Aaron needed 2,896 more times at bat than Babe Ruth in order to break the home-run record. Those skeptics ignore Henry Aaron's durability and consistency, attributes as important as Babe Ruth's charisma. And when his 715th home run soared over the fence tonight, Henry Aaron never lost his dignity, his essence as a person.

"You don't know what a weight it was off my shoulders," he said later, "a tremendous weight."

Now the weight will be transferred to the hitter who someday challenges Henry Aaron, if that hitter appears.

(April 9, 1974)

Few have carried such a "tremendous weight" as easily. Just the burden of breaking baseball's most famous record, held by baseball's most famous player, would have been enough to shatter the psyche of many hitters. Roger Maris, remember, even lost some hair when he hit 61 home runs in 1961, breaking Babe Ruth's season record. But somehow Henry Aaron retained his dignity and his poise. In both Cincinnati and Atlanta he was surrounded by dozens of newspapermen, magazine writers, TV and radio people, photographers and cameramen—many more than either Babe Ruth or Roger Maris had to cope with. All that media coverage increased the "tremendous weight" on Henry Aaron, but by cooperating with the media instead of resisting them, he minimized the burden.

If only more athletes would realize that. But not everybody has Henry Aaron's instincts—with or without a bat.

Henry Aaron hit 40 more home runs for the Braves and the Milwaukee Brewers before he retired after the 1976 season. But during his last spring training, in Sun City, Ariz., a retirement community for people who grew up cheering for Babe Ruth, he told me, "Some of that adrenaline has left me. It hasn't been the same ever since the Babe Ruth thing." And at forty-two, some of his gifts had left him. He mentioned that for more than two years he had been wearing glasses when he reads.

"But it's not that you don't see the ball," he insisted. "It's that your mind and your hands don't react like they used to. And the ball you used to hit out of the ballpark lands at the base of the fence."

He was waiting to go into the batting cage and he talked about how Curt Simmons had been the toughest pitcher for him to read because "he hid the ball so long behind his hip," that of all the good pitchers he had faced, he hit Don Gullett the best because "he didn't change speeds on me, everything was fast," that the fastest pitchers he had faced were Sandy Koufax, Jim Maloney, Nolan Ryan and Bob Gibson, that Robin Roberts had the best control.

"Excuse me," he then said. "I hit now."

In the batting cage he hit a few sharp grounders, then he hit a high drive to left field that had the look of a Henry Aaron home run. But it landed at the base of the fence.

"I wonder," he had said earlier, "if my power's gone."

But that June his power returned briefly. Over seven games he hit five homers. His career total was 752 and he was smiling again as he arrived in New York for a weekend series. He was lodged with the Brewers in the New York Sheraton and he invited me up to his room to talk. But when he got to his door, he realized that he had left his room key in his room. Rather than go down to the front desk, he asked a chambermaid in the hall to let him in with her key.

"I can't do that," the chambermaid said.

"I'm one of the baseball players," he said.

One of the baseball players. That's how Henry Aaron described himself. His gentle sincerity eventually persuaded the chambermaid to use her passkey. But she never recognized Henry Aaron, who hit more home runs than anybody in major league history. Perhaps a chambermaid shouldn't be expected to recognize somebody who describes himself as one of the baseball players.

The only one with 755 home runs.

3 · Football

Long before pro football was popular, I preferred it to college football. I still do.

I'm not knocking college football. I can understand why people who root for Ohio State or Alabama or Texas or U.S.C. favor college football. And if I had grown up or worked in any of those areas, I probably would too. In those environments, college football is popular. But it's never been that popular in New York. Back when I was growing up, there might occasionally be a big college game in New York, like that famous 0–0 tie between Army and Notre Dame at Yankee Stadium in 1946, when Glenn Davis and Doc Blanchard and Johnny Lujack were playing. But that was about it, except for those who thought Ivy League football was big. I never did. I had gravitated to the National Football League at an early age.

My first memory of the N.F.L. was a score—73–0, the Chicago Bears' rout of the Washington Redskins in the 1940 championship game, the score that made the T-formation famous. I heard that 73–0 game on the big, round wooden Philco radio with the orange dial in our Bay Ridge apartment. Nearly a year later I was listening to another N.F.L. game, the Brooklyn Dodgers (who were in the league then) against the New York Giants at the Polo Grounds when a station announcer broke in with a news bulletin.

"Japanese planes," he said, "have bombed Pearl Harbor."

I hurried to tell my parents. I can still see my father looking up and saying, "That means war." When the Dodgers' coach, Jock Sutherland, and their Hall of Fame tailback, Ace Parker, went into service during World War II, the Dodgers' franchise deteriorated. By 1944 even the nickname was changed to Tigers, which alienated the few fans that were left. In those years in Brooklyn, if the team wasn't known as the Dodgers, forget it. As it turned out, 1944 was the last year that Brooklyn was in the league. I wasn't surprised. I had gone to a few games at Ebbets Field, but always alone. I could never get any of the other kids to go with me.

"How come," one of them asked me, "you like pros."

"They don't graduate," I said. "They keep playing."

To me, that continuity has always been one of pro football's basic appeals. When the N.F.L. boom developed a decade later, the appeal of the Giants was a nucleus of players that their rooters developed an attachment for—Charley Conerly, Frank Gifford, Alex Webster and Kyle Rote on offense; Andy Robustelli, Jim Katcavage, Sam Huff and Jim Patton on defense. When the Giants won the 1956 N.F.L. title, they suddenly were everybody's "college team" in the New York area. And the defensive unit was even more popular than the offensive. Not only did it inspire the fans' chant of "Dee-fense, dee-fense" that is heard in other sports now, but it also was the first to be presented in the pre-game introductions rather than in the offensive unit.

"The offensive unit had been getting booed when they were introduced," Sam Huff once told me. "I remember Frank Gifford saying, 'That's all right, Sam, you get the cheers, I'll get the money.' That was Frank."

But in 1964 Sam Huff was traded to the Washington Redskins in a deal that shocked New York as much as it shocked him and his teammates. In retrospect, that trade was the beginning of the end for the great Giant teams. I had been Sam's ghostwriter the previous season in a column that appeared in the *Journal-American,* and after the trade was announced, I phoned him.

"Let's do a goodbye column," I said. "Tell the people what it's like to be traded."

Sam started talking, but soon he was crying. Sobbing, really, sobbing hard. Eventually he regained his composure, but obviously the middle linebacker who symbolized the toughness of the Giants' defensive unit had been emotionally shaken by the trade. Sam's column started on page one the next day:

I cried last night over being traded by the Giants.

And from what I'm told, there are a lot of Giant fans disappointed at my being traded, but none of them is more disappointed than I am. Somehow, I thought I'd never be traded. I know I never wanted to be.

The way I feel right now, I don't know if I'll ever recover from the shock. I know football never will be quite the same for me again.

I know I'll never come running through the goal posts at Yankee Stadium with sixty-four thousand people cheering when they see my blue jersey with the big 70 on it and the public-address announcer saying, ". . . at middle linebacker, number seventy, Sam Huff."

Those introductions develop a sense of pride. And they never failed to give me my biggest thrill in football.

Now, in my final article in the *Journal-American,* I'd like to thank everybody who contributed to that thrill: the Maras, the coaches, all the great players I've been privileged to play with, and especially the fans who stuck with us, win or lose.

When I joined the Giants in 1956, I was just a rookie out of a mining town in West Virginia. But I was lucky enough to have joined a great team, the team that won six Eastern N.F.L. championships in eight years . . . a team with football's greatest fans.

Now it's all over. It ended Thursday night. I was out in Cleveland on a business trip for the J. P. Stevens Fabrics Co. That afternoon, I happened to run into Don Smith, the Giant publicity man, who was there for a league meeting, and I told him:

"Smitty, I'm going to be the one player that if I'm ever traded, I'll bring you along as my personal publicity man."

I was just kidding. I knew nothing about the deal then. Actually, it had not been completed. Later I was having dinner in Dick Modzelewski's restaurant when my wife called me and told me that Al Sherman had called to say that I really had been traded.

She told Al where I was, but for some reason Al didn't want to call me at Mo's restaurant; I guess because the Giants had traded Mo last month.

So I got on the phone and called Don Smith and asked him to call Al and have him call me. And a little later, Al called. Even when I heard it from him, I didn't really believe I'd been traded. I guess that was because I just didn't want to believe it.

Yesterday afternoon, I got off a plane from Cleveland and I saw the big front-page headlines in the *Journal-American*. That's when it began to sink in. That's when I started to think back to all the glorious moments in my career with the Giants.

Strangely enough, the most glorious team moment occurred last season when we beat the Browns, 33–6, in Cleveland. Before that game some people were saying we were too old to win anymore.

We weren't too old. We were just old enough to appreciate the heritage of victory which surrounds the Giant organization. I thought I'd be part of that heritage for another three or four seasons. But the Giants preferred to make a deal for me.

That's their privilege. I'm disappointed. But I'm not angry. These things happen to professional athletes.

Many friends have asked me if I think it will be a good trade for the Giants. I don't know the answer. But I can't see that it will. Possibly the trade that'll hurt even more is the one that sent Mo to the Browns. I'd never have traded Mo.

But by trading Mo, the Giants opened up a spot on the defensive line which resulted in my being traded for the player the Giants hope will fill that spot: Andy Stynchula. He's a good player. So is Dick James, the little halfback in the deal.

In my mind, though, three Stynchulas couldn't take Mo's place. But maybe he'll be a great one. For the Giants' sake, I hope he is.

What about me? I'm not sure yet. I don't know if I'll report to the Redskins. I'm going to have to sit down and talk it over with my wife. Somehow, I can't see myself putting on the Redskins' maroon helmet with the white feather up the back of it.

To me, pro football has always meant a blue helmet with a red stripe down the middle.

(April 11, 1964)

As good as those Giant teams were, a game they lost at Yankee Stadium established pro football as a major league sport—their 23–17 loss to the Baltimore Colts in sudden-death overtime for the 1958 N.F.L. title. On the play before Alan Ameche scored the winning touchdown, John Unitas had thrown a dangerous third-down sideline pass to Jim Mutscheller for a 6-yard gain to the 1-yard line.

"Wasn't that pass risky?" I asked Unitas later. "Suppose the Giants had intercepted?"

"When you know what you're doing," John said firmly, "you don't get intercepted."

Some writers didn't like to talk to John Unitas after a game, but I always did. I liked his no-nonsense manner. He was like that in the huddle too, as his Colt teammates told me in 1971:

Two weeks ago, early in the game between the Baltimore Colts and the Miami Dolphins, Johnny Unitas flipped a short pass to Tom Matte, the experienced running back who was all alone near the sideline. Matte dropped it. As he returned to the huddle, he noticed Unitas glaring at him from inside his face mask.

"Catch the ball, Matte," the quarterback growled.

Significantly, none of Unitas's next ten passes was dropped as the Colts took command of the victory that assured their appearance in the American Conference playoffs. They will oppose the Browns in Cleveland today with Johnny Unitas lowering his white helmet with the blue horseshoes on it into the huddle and snapping orders in his icy, sharp tone.

"As soon as he drops his head, it's quiet," says Bob Vogel, the Colts' left tackle. "He does all the talking."

At the age of thirty-eight, Johnny Unitas is a quarterback with National Football League passing statistics measured in miles instead of yards. He has total respect from his teammate.

"It's like being in the huddle with God," says John Mackey, one of the Colts' tight ends.

When the Colts are gathering for the huddle, Unitas is thinking of the next play. He also is seeking information from his teammates to influence his decision.

"What have you got?" he might ask Eddie Hinton, a wide receiver.

The temptation for a pass receiver is to believe that he can get open on any pattern, but Hinton knows he must be specific. Unitas is interested only in the pattern most likely to succeed. From his linemen, he is interested in their blocking problems.

"Do you need help?" he might ask John Williams, a guard.

Unitas wants to know if an opposing pass rusher should be double-teamed by employing a running back as a blocker. It is not a time for a lineman to be proud.

"If you're having trouble blocking your man," Williams says, "tell John the truth. Don't con him."

His mind made up, Unitas crouches into the huddle. He calls the play quickly, as if it were the only sensible selection for the situation.

"You just believe," says Glenn Ressler, a guard, "that if anybody can call a play that's certain to work, it's him."

Ressler is twenty-eight, in his seventh season with the Colts, but his respect for Unitas is typical. He acknowledged that "it's still a thrill for me" to be in the huddle with him. The defensive unit is aware of Unitas's stature. Once, in the final minutes of a game with the Colts far ahead, Unitas threw an incomplete pass on third down that stopped the clock.

"Hey," one of the Colts' defensive players shouted as Unitas came off the field, "let's run the clock out."

"I'll call the game," Unitas replied. "If you want to be the quarterback, go ahead. Otherwise, shut up."

Bill Curry, the center who was once with the Green Bay Packers, recalled that Bart Starr never criticized a teammate on the field.

"If I made a mistake, Bart would stare at me, that's all," Curry says. "But with John, I can expect to be reprimanded."

Occasionally a laugh occurs in the huddle, but only when the Colts are comfortably ahead. One of his teammates once motioned Unitas to move slightly out of his line of vision toward the stand.

"There's a blonde over there," he explained. "You're blocking my view."

Unitas enjoyed the gag, just as he enjoys teasing rookies occasionally at training camp. In the huddle he will use double-talk without ever calling a specific play. When the rookies line up, each believes that he has missed the play until Unitas, smiling, re-forms the huddle.

Rookies are in awe of him. Eddie Hinton was eleven when Unitas directed the Colts to their sudden-death overtime victory over the New York Giants for the 1958 N.F.L. title. Three years ago, Hinton was the Colts' first-round draft choice. In a game with the Chicago Bears, he dropped two passes from Unitas on identical patterns. But when Hinton returned to the huddle, Unitas called the same pattern again. This time Hinton held the pass for an important gain in a 21–20 victory. In the locker room, Hinton approached the quarterback.

"I love you for that, man," the young wide receiver said, "but why did you call that same pattern the third time?"

"I knew you'd catch it," Johnny Unitas said.

(December 26, 1971)

The next season the Miami Dolphins went 17–0, one of the most remarkable accomplishments in sports history. But in the years since then, it strangely has been one of the most forgettable. Hardly anybody mentions it anymore. And now that each N.F.L. team has sixteen games on its regular-season schedule instead of fourteen, a 19–0 record through the Super Bowl is virtually impossible.

All of which should enhance what the Dolphins did, except that even when they did it, they didn't get the recognition that they deserved:

Instead of believing it, most people seem to be trying to pretend that 17–0 must be a typographical error. Instead of accepting the Miami Dolphins' achievement, they're waiting for a correction. Outside of the loyalists in Miami, most people don't seem willing to acknowledge that the Dolphins are the best team in National Football League history. Nick Buoniconti has a theory.

"If we were the Giants or the Jets doing this in New York," the middle linebacker says, "imagine the recognition we'd get."

If the Giants or the Jets had done it, Tiffany's would be selling pins with seventeen diamonds. There would be seventeen parades, seventeen magazine covers and seventeen agents talking about $17 million in endorsements. There would be seventeen TV shows, seventeen luncheons and seventeen books being written. But the Dolphins did it—a team that's only seven years old, that wears aqua-and-orange uniforms, that has a funny fish on the players' helmets.

"Or if we were from a diehard N.F.L. city," says Jim Kiick, the running back, "we'd be getting more recognition."

If the Washington Redskins had done it, President Nixon might have declared a national holiday. If the Chicago Bears had done it, George Halas might have been put in the Smithsonian Institution, alive. But the Dolphins were in that "other league" before the merger. So there's no way the Dolphins can be the best team ever. Not enough tradition. The weather is too nice there, too. Not like Green Bay, where you've got to play in snow and ice and zero temperatures. That's real football. And the Dolphins' schedule was easy.

"But if you played the Houston Oilers seventeen times," one realist said, "you probably wouldn't go 17–0."

The Oilers are the N.F.L.'s worst team. But the Jets played them only once, and lost. Maybe the Dolphins' schedule looks easy now, but that's because they made it look easy. And when they lose a game next season, it won't dilute what they accomplished this season. They went 17–0, and it won't happen again. It's not the same psychology as when Roger Bannister broke the four-minute mile. Even though it now has been done, other teams won't be able to do it. The chemistry is too involved, and impossible to repeat, as if the test tube shattered before Don Shula had time to analyze the formula.

The chemistry involves a good coach and good players. It also involves planning, timing and luck.

Two of those elements surrounded Bob Griese's ankle injury. When he got hurt, he had guided the Dolphins through the most difficult stretch of their schedule—road games against the Kansas City Chiefs, Minnesota Vikings and Jets in the first four weeks. For just such an emergency, Shula had acquired Earl Morrall as a stand-in. That's planning. But if Griese had been injured a month later, he wouldn't have recuperated in time for the Super Bowl when the Dolphins needed him most. That's timing. Their only other serious injury was Tim Foley's shoulder separation, which kept the left cornerback out of the Super Bowl, but with Lloyd Mumphord, once a regular, the Dolphins were more fortified at that position than at any other on defense. That's luck.

But the basic element of the Dolphin chemistry, and one that will endure, is the togetherness of the players.

When the Packers were winning, Jerry Kramer called it "love." Whatever it is, the Dolphins have it now. Shula generates it, as Vince Lombardi did, by guiding his players with humane values that they respond to in a crisis. It's also something the Redskins don't have. George Allen, the man and the methods, generates distrust instead. He trades draft choices he doesn't own. He defies the N.F.L. rules on announcing injuries. For all his genius, his slinky manner produces a slinky atmosphere.

In a crisis, it's often the difference, as it has been for the Oakland Raiders under Al Davis, another man of intrigue.

"Al Davis has put the Raiders where they are," one of his players has said, "but he's kept them from where they should be."

The Raiders have been in the playoffs five times, making the Super Bowl once and losing. Allen's teams, the Redskins and the Los Angeles Rams, have been in the playoffs four times, making the Super Bowl once and losing. Their only hope is to meet in the Super Bowl someday. Then one has to win. But no matter which teams win the Super Bowl games in the future, none will be 17–0. The Dolphins belong in a time capsule. Treasure them.

"It wasn't much of a game last Sunday," people keep saying. "Not very exciting."

Not unless you realize that it produced something you'll never see again. 17–0.

(January 20, 1973)

•   •   •

The closest the Packers had come to a perfect season under Vince Lombardi was their 14–1 record in 1962, including a 16–7 victory over the Giants at Yankee Stadium in the N.F.L. championship game. I saw that one, but not from the press box. At the time the *Journal-American* was on strike, along with all the other New York newspapers. Jim Kensil, now the Jets' president but then the N.F.L.'s public relations director, asked me if I would be his spotter on the Packers' bench—check injuries, check who recovered a fumble or who created a fumble with a hard tackle.

"I'd like that," I told him. "I'll get a new perspective."

I almost got frostbite instead. The day of the game, winds of up to 50 mph howled through temperatures that dropped to 10 degrees in the dusk of the fourth quarter. The chill factor, I learned later, was down around 15 degrees *below* zero. I had dressed for the weather —thermal underwear, flannel shirt, corduroy suit, heavy woolen socks, storm boots, a big fur-lined storm coat with a fur collar, earmuffs, stocking cap, fur-lined gloves. But I've never been colder. Neither have the players. When the Packers won the 1967 N.F.L. title in 13-below-zero weather in Green Bay, many of them agreed that the wind had made it colder in Yankee Stadium five years earlier. It was so cold there that when Jerry Kramer kicked the clinching field goal, Bart Starr, who had been his ball holder, trotted to the sideline without any emotion but with his index fingers in the earholes of his helmet.

"I think," he said, "my ears are frozen."

Another memory on that bench was watching Jim Taylor spit blood. In a pileup, he had bitten his tongue. When the Packers had to punt, he sat on the bench facing away from the field and kept spitting blood onto the frozen field. But when the Giants were about to punt, I heard Vince Lombardi's voice.

"Taylor," the coach barked. "Taylor, Taylor."

With another quick spit of blood, the fullback got up, turned, put on his green-and-gold helmet and trotted back into the game. None of the Packers questioned their coach. At least not publicly. But privately, Paul Hornung once got the last word. When he was reinstated in 1964 by Commissioner Pete Rozelle after a year's suspension for gambling, the next voice he heard was Vince Lombardi's ordering him to Green Bay to get in shape. Day after day, Hornung ran the steps of Lambeau Stadium to get ready for training camp. But then the coach granted him a day off.

"We're playing golf tomorrow," the coach said. "We tee off at ten o'clock."

That was an order, not an invitation. But the next morning, as the tee-off time approached, Hornung had not appeared. At the stroke of ten, the coach teed off. As two of his Packer teammates, Max McGee and Jerry Kramer, were teeing off, Hornung arrived just in time to hit his drive. As they walked down the first fairway, Lombardi glanced at his watch and glanced at Hornung.

"You just made it," the coach growled. "If you hadn't shown up, we were gone."

"You waited a year for me, Coach," said Hornung. "Couldn't you wait ten minutes?"

About a month later, I visited the Packers' training camp in Green Bay to do a piece for *Sport* magazine on Hornung's return. I heard that golf story and checked it with Paul, who confirmed it.

"But don't use it," he said. "*Please* don't use it."

I had others. After practice one day, Hornung and McGee dawdled in the trainer's room and were late for six o'clock dinner at St. Norbert College in nearby West De Pere where the Packers were lodged. When they finally strolled into the dining hall with their trays of food and sat down, the coach was standing over them. He was pointing to the big clock on the wall.

"You're supposed to be on line for dinner at six o'clock," he roared. "Not ten after."

Hornung and McGee each hunched their shoulders, as if wishing they could disappear. But after morning practice the next day, McGee again was dawdling. Hornung shook his head.

"Let's go," Paul said impatiently. "Let's not be late for *lunch.*"

In those years the Packers joked about "Lombardi time," which was always five minutes earlier than necessary. If the players were to be on a team bus at eleven o'clock, the wise ones were there no later than five minutes to eleven. On other occasions, Lombardi time was whenever Vince declared he was ready to go. I know. At a practice once, he had offered me a ride back to the Packers' hotel with him. While he changed into his street clothes, I was out in the locker room chatting with Jerry Kramer when his voice boomed.

"Dave, Dave," I heard him calling, "let's go."

"You better go," Jerry suggested. "Right now."

I went. Obeyed, really. And that's the aura that Vince Lombardi projected with his players—an aura of command and obedience. In a word, discipline. It worked then and it would work now. There's a theory that Vince Lombardi would not be a successful coach today because a coach no longer can be a dictator. Don't believe it. Vince Lombardi would always be a success, as he was with the Packers, as he was with the Washington Redskins briefly. He had stopped coaching the Packers after they won the first two Super Bowl games. But watching the Packers from his general manager's box in 1968 was not for him.

"I miss the fire on Sunday," he said.

He meant the fire on the sideline. The next season he was back in the fire as the Redskins' coach. But then cancer hit him. He was dead before the 1970 season began. When the Redskins emerged as a Super Bowl contender under George Allen later on, many of Lombardi's players, notably running Larry Brown, formed the nucleus of the team.

"What," somebody once asked Brown, "has George Allen done for you?"

"Vince Lombardi made me," Larry Brown said sharply, "not George Allen."

But as good as Larry Brown was in those years, O.J. Simpson was emerging as *the* running back. During the 1973 season he rushed for a record 2,003 yards, surpassing Jim Brown's total of 1,863 yards in 1963. The day O.J. set the record in the snow against the New York Jets at Shea Stadium he was brought into a big room afterwards for a separate interview in order to avoid a mob scene in the Buffalo Bills' locker room. But when O.J. arrived, he had ten teammates with him. One by one, he introduced the other members of the Bills' offensive unit.

"These are the cats," O.J. said, "who did the job all year long. It's their record as much as mine."

Now that's a *team* player. And that's O.J. Simpson, whose style as a person equals his style as a runner. During the 1975 season I wrote what he was like off the field:

Weary and dripping with perspiration, O. J. Simpson calls to a clubhouse boy in Atlanta Stadium for a Coke after having galloped through the Falcons for 137 yards, a somewhat routine performance for the Buffalo Bills' running back two seasons ago when he set a National Football League record with 2,003 yards. Before the clubhouse boy returned with the soft drink, O.J. was surrounded by newsmen. Patiently, the youngster waited outside the circle of newsmen for more than half an hour as O.J. answered questions. When the newsmen began to drift away, O.J. remembered the Coke and thanked the youngster. But on the first swallow, O.J. shook his head.

"Hey, this is warm," he said.

"Sure, it's warm," said the youngster's father, the clubhouse custodian. "My son's been holding it for you for half an hour."

"In that case, this is just fine."

The youngster smiled. His father nodded slowly. "O. J. Simpson showed me something," the youngster's father said later. "He's got class. You can't coach that." O. J. Simpson just might be the classiest runner in N.F.L. history. With 911 yards this season prior to opposing the New York Jets at Shea Stadium today, he has an opportunity to surpass his 2,003-yard record this season. But the class under O.J.'s helmet is equally impressive. About two dozen members of the Bills wear 14-karat gold bracelets to commemorate his 2,003-yard season. Each bracelet is inscribed with 2,003, 3,088 (the team rushing total that year) and a short personal message. Each is signed, "Juice."

"I had mine appraised at one thousand dollars," says one recipient. "It must have cost him twenty-five thousand for all of them."

O.J. also gives his teammates his time. He appears at the gatherings for Bills' fans that Reggie McKenzie, Walt Patulski and J. D. Hill host at various Buffalo watering holes in connection with the Monday night TV game. Among his teammates, O.J. is literally an untouchable in practice sessions. But during training camp, he was unaccountably jostled on successive plays by Neil Craig, now in his fifth N.F.L. season, and Glen Lott, a rookie defensive back. The second time, O.J. turned on Lott and flung the ball at him. When the rookie said something, O.J. jarred him with a quick left jab. Lott, almost sobbing in sorrow, didn't retaliate. O.J. also was sorry.

"Don't ever let anybody punch you like that," O.J. told him moments later, "without punching back."

To answer his fan letters, O.J. uses a printed reply with an autographed picture. Hundreds go out each week. Requests for appearances are screened by Budd Thalman, the Bills' public relations director. Not long ago Thalman accompanied O.J. on a visit to the Eastman Kodak plant in Rochester, where O.J. displayed his public relations instincts. When it was time to leave, Thalman, from the side of the stage, was waving to O.J. to answer only two more questions. But in the audience at least a dozen hands were raised.

"You can't see him," O.J. announced. "But my public relations man is telling me to answer only two more questions. Just for that I'm going to let him pick the last two people with questions."

O.J. had escaped, subtly and with a smile. Jack Horrigan would have been proud of him. Six seasons ago, when O.J. was a rookie, he was met at the Buffalo airport by the late Jack Horrigan, then the Bills' public relations director. On the short drive to training camp, Horrigan established his rules.

"I'll screen your calls," Horrigan said, "but when I decide which ones you should answer, don't let me down."

O.J. hasn't forgotten Jack Horrigan's advice. His weekday schedule includes time to return calls from out-of-town sportswriters. Thalman screens O.J.'s interviews. He also handles quick questions. Not long ago a magazine writer requested Thalman to ask O.J. if he had been left-handed originally. The writer was preparing an article on people who, as small children, had been forced to become right-handed. Thalman dutifully asked the question.

"I'm right-handed," O.J. replied. "All the way."

"But," said Thalman, "were you ever left-handed before you were right-handed?"

"That," said O.J., "is the bonehead question of the week."

O.J. needled Thalman good-naturedly for several days about the bonehead question. But when Thalman's wife recently had a baby daughter, O.J. sent flowers. He even went into the florist shop himself.

"The florist was so shook up, there was no card with the flowers," Thalman says. "The florist had to call to say he forgot to put it in."

With his wife, Marguerite, remaining in California with their two school-age children, O.J. lives in a $100,000 home in Amherst, a Buffalo suburb. Each day he waters more than a dozen plants. His magazines are stacked neatly. His cardinal-and-gold University of Southern California blanket is draped over his TV chair. Often he stops in small neighborhood restaurants for dinner. He was in the Creekside Inn with Bob Chandler, a teammate, not long ago when a stranger, a Buffalo teacher named Jack Duffy, recognized him. Duffy was having dinner with his wife, Alice, and their two small children. On his way out, Duffy passed O.J.'s table.

"Good luck in the game tomorrow," Duffy said.

"Thank you," O.J. said, "and you have a lovely family."

Duffy was stunned by O.J.'s thoughtfulness.

"He didn't even know me," Duffy says now, "and he went out of his way to say that to a stranger."

You can't coach that.

(December 2, 1975)

And you can't coach what makes Art Rooney perhaps the most cherished N.F.L. club owner—certainly the most frustrated until his Pittsburgh Steelers won Super Bowl IX from the Minnesota Vikings, 16–6. Instead of a column that day, I had to write what the *Times* calls a "Man in the News" but the identity of that man would depend on the outcome. Because of deadline problems, I suggested that I prepare the bulk of background copy on the primary personality on each team—Art Rooney for the Steelers, quarterback Fran Tarkenton for the Vikings.

When the Steelers won, I hurried to their locker room for the trophy presentation, then hurried back to the press box in old Tulane Stadium to write what turned out to be the first seven paragraphs:

NEW ORLEANS—When the Pittsburgh Steelers won the National Football League championship today for the first time in their forty-two-year history, Andy Russell, their defensive captain, presented Art Rooney with a game ball. "This one's for the Chief," the linebacker said. "It's a long time coming." The seventy-three-year-old Steeler owner reacted almost impassively.

"Thank you," he told the players. "I'm proud of you, and I'm grateful to you."

But inside, his emotions were churning. He had been in the locker room several minutes before the Steelers completed their 16–6 triumph.

"I just want to make sure my hair is combed," he said.

After the locker-room presentation, he was led to a green-and-white tent where he and several Steelers stood on small platforms, as if they were on display in a circus sideshow. As he unwrapped a cigar, he talked of his emotions.

"This is the biggest win of my life," he said. "I don't think I could top it even if we won next year again. The fans in Pittsburgh didn't think it would be a contest, but anytime you go out there you're eligible to lose."

Art Rooney knows. Of all the N.F.L. owners, he had been the most famous loser until today—also the most loved and the most legendary.

Arthur Joseph Rooney was born January 27, 1907, the oldest of six sons and two daughters of a Pittsburgh saloonkeeper.

"It was a good saloon," says an old-timer familiar with the Old Allegheny neighborhood of that era. "No women allowed."

He and his wife, Kathleen, have lived in the old Victorian house at 940 North Lincoln in the same neighborhood for the last four decades. Their home is across the street from the one where he grew up. It is a neighborhood of old rooming houses and parking lots now, but the Rooney home resembles a restoration showcase of another time.

Art and his brother Dan, now a Franciscan missionary, grew up in sports. They played semipro football and baseball, they boxed, they attended college at Duquesne, Georgetown, and Washington and Jefferson, and Art later managed semipro football and baseball teams and promoted boxing. And he was a celebrated horseplayer.

"You bet with bookmakers then," he said. "Racing's not the same now. The romance is gone."

The romance of the Rooney legend blossomed in 1936, three years after he had obtained an N.F.L. franchise for Pittsburgh for $2,500. On a Saturday at Empire City and a Monday at Saratoga, he turned a $20 bet into an estimated $380,000 killing. He has never publicly disclosed the amount, but on his return home he emptied his pockets.

"We don't ever," he told his wife, "have to worry about money again."

But he had to worry about the Steelers, seldom a contender. One year at training camp he was watching a workout when he was asked what he thought of his team's chances that season.

"Those new uniforms threw me off for a bit," he said, "but they look like the same old Steelers to me."

That phrase "the Same Old Steelers" became a byword of the team's frustration. But the team never tarnished Rooney's image as a man who lived by the old values, who depended on handshakes instead of contracts, who understood integrity. When a traveling companion often bet $50 on a Steeler game, Rooney took him aside.

"I know you're all right," the owner told him, "but gambling and football don't mix. If you don't stop, I'm going to have to ask you not to travel with us anymore."

Even though the Steelers usually were losers, Rooney continued to be a winner at the race tracks. On the way out of Bowie once, he stopped to pick up a priest who was waiting for a bus. When the priest mentioned that he needed $7,500 to rebuild an orphanage, Rooney peeled the money from his winnings that day. Another time he surprised another priest with a $10,000 hospital donation.

"I hope you came by this money honestly," said the priest.

"Oh, sure," Rooney said. "I won it playing the horses."

As the N.F.L. prospered, Rooney and his five sons created a family sports empire. Dan and Arthur Jr., known as Artie, are Steeler vice presidents. Tim operates Yonkers Raceway, and the twins, Pat and John, operate Green Mountain Racetrack and the William Penn meeting at the Liberty Bell Racetrack, respectively. The family also owns a Palm Beach kennel club in Florida.

"My boys have borrowed about sixty million dollars," Rooney says with a laugh. "I always thought you had to have the money in your pocket to buy something."

He jokes about his millionaire status now, adding, "My wife always wonders where all the money is." But he never enjoyed his image as a gracious loser.

"I was supposed to be the guy who just walked away from his defeats without so much as a second thought—that's a bunch of nonsense," he said two years ago. "Every loss in those days got me right here and I took it home with me and it stayed here until the next week when I went back for another dose of the same.

"I had this standing rule in my house when our five boys were growing up—nobody was allowed to mention the Steelers for two days after we'd lost. That's how much it bothered me. I didn't want to read about it. I didn't want to see the films. I didn't want to have anybody tell me we gave it a good try.

"Losing to me will always be losing. After many years of this, I've learned one thing: it doesn't get any easier. No sir, no easier at all. In fact it bothers me more now. I'm on the other side of seventy now and I want to be around to see us win a championship. So every time we lose I see my chances getting slimmer."

He was around to see the Steelers finally win the N.F.L. championship today.

(January 13, 1975)

•   •   •

Once upon a time, losing was Tom Landry's burden, particularly when the Dallas Cowboys were losing big games—to the Packers in the 1966 and 1967 N.F.L. championship games, to the Cleveland Browns in the opening round of the N.F.L. playoffs in 1968 and 1969, to the Baltimore Colts in Super Bowl V.

But then the Cowboys won Super Bowl VI, 24–3 over the Dolphins, and the monkey was off their backs. When they also won Super Bowl XII, their coach suddenly attained the stature that he had long deserved—the stature that put him up there with Don Shula as one of the N.F.L.'s two best coaches.

NEW ORLEANS—For one embarrassing moment in Super Bowl XII last night, the Dallas Cowboys were penalized for having twelve men on the field. That's not like the computerized Cowboys, but that twelfth man was more symbolic than embarrassing. Some people in the National Football League believe that the Cowboys always have a twelfth man on the field, that Tom Landry provides more of an invisible presence among more of his players than any other coach. Now that Tom Landry has joined Vince Lombardi, Don Shula, and Chuck Noll as the only coaches with two Super Bowl victories, perhaps he will be appreciated more for what he is than for what he is not. With a face that could not possibly be folded, spindled or mutilated, Tom Landry is not colorful. Instead, he is organized, inventive, decisive and dependable. And perhaps more than anything else, he is consistent. His record proves that. His team has qualified for the playoffs eleven of the last twelve seasons. And the year the Cowboys didn't make the playoffs, they still had an 8–6 won-lost record. The Cowboys never need to rebuild. Retool perhaps, but never rebuild.

Give the Cowboys' organization credit too. Consistently good scouting and drafting provides consistently good material.

But when that consistently good material is presented to Tom Landry, he develops consistently good results. The other three coaches with two Super Bowl victories each accomplished them in consecutive seasons with basically the same team. Tom Landry has done it over a span of six seasons with virtually two different teams. Only four starters in the 27–10 triumph over the Denver Broncos also started in the 24–3 defeat of the Miami Dolphins in Super Bowl VI—Roger Staubach and Ralph Neely on offense, Cliff Harris and Jethro Pugh on defense.

"The thing about Tom Landry," says Cliff Harris, "is that he projects security. When he gives you the game plan, you know it's the best possible game plan that you could have."

Tom Landry also might be more involved with both offense and defense than the other two-time Super Bowl winners. Vince Lombardi delegated the basic defensive game plan to Phil Bengtson, as Don Shula does to Bill Arnsparger and Chuck Noll to Bud Carson, their defensive coordinators. Tom Landry designs the offensive game plan and supervises the defensive game plan that is structured on the "flex defense" that he invented, just as he invented the 4–3 defense when he was a player-coach with the New York Giants a quarter of a century ago.

"I suggested the 4–3 to stop Paul Brown's offense at Cleveland," Tom Landry recalls. "To stop Otto Graham and Marion Motley."

And last night, the 4–3 defense stopped Craig Morton, the quarterback whom Tom Landry traded to the New York Giants during the 1974 season for a first-round draft choice that turned out to be Randy White, the defensive tackle who was always around the Broncos' passer.

"The Cowboys were always in the right defense for us," Craig Morton said later. "It was like they knew every play."

In a sense, they did. Tom Landry always seems to know what will happen in football. Sometimes his players will question him, asking, "But suppose that doesn't happen, suppose that receiver isn't there?" Without a smile, Tom Landry will reply, "He'll be there." And invariably that receiver will be precisely where Tom Landry anticipated he would be. Some people wonder why Tom Landry doesn't smile more, especially on the sideline. But if he did, he wouldn't be Tom Landry.

"The reason I take on the appearance of being unemotional," he once explained, "is that I don't believe you can be emotional and concentrate the way you must to be effective. When I see a great play from the sideline, I can't cheer it. As a team, we win by concentrating, by thinking. The players don't want to see me rushing around and screaming. They want to believe I know what I'm doing."

The Cowboy players believe in him as a fifty-three-year-old coach who is considered to be a football genius. And they believe in him as a man, perhaps more than they once did because he acknowledges that he has improved in "handling" his players. Duane Thomas once branded Tom Landry as a "plastic man" but that was Duane Thomas's mistake in not understanding the coach, not the coach's mistake in not understanding the moody running back who seldom spoke to his coaches or teammates during the 1971 season that generated the Super Bowl VI champions.

"When the first group of players arrived from the affluent society of the sixties, I realized I had to handle them differently than I did the players who had grown up during the Depression and the war," the coach says. "Duane Thomas made me realize it. You don't need anything more than that."

Under his Mount Rushmore profile, Tom Landry is probably as emotional as any other coach. He just doesn't show it. Not even in the fourth quarter, which was supposed to belong to the Broncos according to Red Miller's commandments. But not yesterday. In the fourth quarter, the Cowboys blanked the Broncos while scoring a 29-yard touchdown on Robert Newhouse's surprise option pass to Golden Richards.

"Denver made a big thing about the fourth quarter belonging to them," Tom Landry said later. "But we decided it would belong to us and it did."

For the Cowboys' coach, that was a rare flash of emotion. He showed another flash in talking today about how much he likes Craig Morton, about how he "would've been rooting" for the Broncos' quarterback if his Cowboys had not been the opponent. But during the week another flash occurred when he was asked to comment on Morton's statement that football was "no fun" under Tom Landry, certainly not as much fun as it is in Denver.

"The Broncos' situation is unique," Tom Landry replied. "And they better enjoy it while they can, because it won't last forever."

In pro football, nothing lasts forever except the Dallas Cowboys, who just keep winning. But with twelve men on the field, they should keep winning.

(January 17, 1978)

But some of pro football's popularity has been chipped away by its ugly labor disputes, particularly the problems which closed the training camps briefly in both 1970 and 1974 and which threatened the opening of the 1975 season.

Call him Ishmael, call him the last of the pro-footballniks. After nearly ten years in a coma, he awoke in 1984. He had gone into shock in 1975, when it appeared that the National Football League would not open its season because of a labor dispute. Throughout his coma, his body rejected nourishment except for a mysterious serum melted down from N.F.L. highlight films and fed to him intravenously. Offense for breakfast, defense for lunch, special teams for dinner. When he awoke with his doctor at his bedside, he didn't realize that he had been in a coma.

"Are they playing this Sunday?" he asked.

"Oh yes," his doctor said. "All six teams."

"You mean all twenty-six teams, not six teams."

"No, this is 1984, you've been in a coma a long time. There are only six teams now—Canton, Akron, Dayton, Rock Island, Hammond and Decatur."

"But they were charter teams back in 1920."

"Ashes to ashes, Rock Island to Rock Island."

"What happened to all the teams I knew?"

"The fans finally went on strike. They picketed the stadiums. They broke the TV cameras. They boycotted the TV sponsors. They burned all the products with the N.F.L. shield."

"But didn't Pete Rozelle do anything to prevent that?"

"Pete Rozelle is the mayor of New York now," his doctor explained. "He got elected after he arranged a one-hundred-billion-dollar deal for the TV rights to everything that happens in the city. All the citizens had to sign a contract that let the TV cameras go anyplace. It really got the city out of hock but it created some problems. With all that money around, most of the good teachers have agents now. The teachers also are complaining about being transferred from one school to another. They're threatening to take the Rozelle Reign to the courts. Even the cops and firemen have agents now. One detective just signed a one-year contract for four hundred and fifty thousand dollars and only a few years ago he had to sell his bar because alleged undesirables were frequenting it."

"Who won the Super Bowl last season?"

"Oh, the Super Bowl is a soccer game now."

"What about Ed Garvey, the union leader?"

"He's trying to organize the players in the National Handball League."

"What's happened to contact sports?"

"Too many injuries. What really turned the fans off was when the owners passed a rule to let Joe Namath pass from behind sandbags to keep him around as an attraction. Joe's back in Beaver Falls now. He's a gymnastics coach. He just got sued by three kids because he ordered them to get crew cuts."

"Did the Giants ever get to play in that New Jersey stadium?"

"One game. One quarter really. From the weight of the sellout crowd, the stadium sank slowly into the swamp. Slowly enough that everybody got out alive. Wellington Mara wanted to go back to Yankee Stadium, but he couldn't get it Sunday afternoons. That's when they have the OTB bingo games."

"Where's O. J. Simpson now?"

"Playing baseball. It only took him five seasons to break Henry Aaron's home-run record."

"What about Mean Joe Greene?"

"He's the heavyweight champion. He knocked out Muhammad Ali with his first punch, a left slap. Hit him on the side of the head like he used to hit offensive linemen on the helmet and knocked Ali clear out of the ring. Any other place, Ali would've had time to get back, but Don King put the ring on top of Mount Everest because this was his first one-hundred-million-dollar promotion. Ali fell three thousand feet before he landed on a ledge. Landed on his feet doing the Ali Shuffle, but the referee had counted him out by then."

"Who was the referee?"

"Don Shula," his doctor said. "He needs the money now. Most of the time he's a cook in a Hungarian restaurant. Larry Csonka owns it."

"What about George Allen?"

"He owns nursing homes for old N.F.L. players, but he only lets in defensive players."

"What about Al Davis?"

"He runs the C.I.A., but the agents don't like him. He makes them all wear black suits with silver ties."

"What's on TV on Monday night now?"

"Monday Night Tennis, and it's on every Monday night."

"Is Howard still on?"

"Howard and Frank and Jimmy Connors, the first player-announcer. He plays a different opponent every week for one million dollars, winner-take-all. But he has a hard time getting a word in because Howard keeps talking about how he wants to run for President again."

"Again?"

"He ran against Frank last time, and Frank won."

(September 21, 1975)

There are two Howard Cosells—the private Howard is quiet and sensitive; the public Howard is noisy and sensitive. But for somebody who criticizes so many others, Howard can't accept criticism of himself, even when it's obviously in fun. I once wrote that Frank Gifford deserved an asterisk on his plaque in the Pro Football Hall of Fame for "coexisting with Howard Cosell all those years" on Monday Night Football.

I assumed that Howard would accept that line as a gag, but ABC people told me later that he was disturbed by it.

Howard often takes things too seriously, especially himself. The difference between the private Howard and the public Howard became apparent to me in 1972, when he invited me to ride in the limousine that had been sent to the Reno, Nev., airport for him by the Sahara Tahoe hotel, where the Muhammad Ali–Bob Foster fight would be held. Throughout the hour's ride, Howard was a pleasant conversationalist. But when the limo pulled up in front of the Sahara Tahoe, he hopped out, strode into the lobby and stared at the three clerks behind the reservation desk.

"This," announced Howard in a loud nasal voice, "is the moment you've been waiting for all your lives."

The private Howard had vanished, the public Howard was on stage. I enjoy one. I don't enjoy the other.

4 · Namath

There must be two Joe Namaths—the one some other sportswriters don't like and the one I do like. I've liked him from the first time I met him. He had come to New York for his first knee operation in 1965 shortly after having signed his $427,000 contract. Sonny Werblin, then the Jets' president, arranged a get-together with the New York writers in the upstairs room at Toots Shor's old restaurant. Not a news conference, just stop by, meet the rookie quarterback and have a drink. After a while, I was sitting at a small table with Lou Effrat, a *Times* sportswriter who had covered pro football for years, when Joe slouched over with a drink in his hand. Lou stared up at him.

"Joe," he said, "suppose you don't make it, Joe, what happens to the money?"

Joe never blinked. He looked at Lou and replied easily, "I'll make it."

I liked that. No false modesty. No hedging. No song and dance. No boasting either; just flat confidence. And the more I was around Joe Namath, the more I liked him. At his first training camp, I was talking to the Jets' two other quarterbacks—Mike Taliaferro, the holdover, and John Huarte, the Heisman Trophy rookie from Notre Dame who had a $200,000 contract. One of them mentioned that Joe had been classified 1-A in the military draft. I had stumbled on a big story but I didn't want to overreact. When Joe came by, I mentioned it casually and he confirmed it casually.

"Why don't you get married?" I suggested. "They're not taking married guys."

"I'd rather go to Vietnam," he answered with a grin, "than get married."

The next day I checked with his Beaver Falls, Pa., draft board. After the lady who answered the phone confirmed that he was 1-A, I thanked her and said, "Joe is big in New York."

"Joe," she said, "is big everywhere."

Bigger than even she and I thought, as it turned out. The next day, to my surprise, my story was across the top of the *Journal-American*'s front page. All hell broke loose because the Jets had been trying to keep Joe's draft status quiet. He had to endure "one of those days," as he later called them, when newsmen were all around. That night I was in the Jets' press room at training camp when Joe strolled in, picked up a copy of the *Journal-American* and read my story. At one point he shook his head and said quietly, "I wish you hadn't used that line about Vietnam," but he knew he hadn't been misquoted. When he finished, he said, "I was a phys. ed. major at Alabama, not a business major."

"Sorry about that," I said. "I thought you took business."

He put the *Journal-American* down, said, "See you tomorrow," and strolled out of the press room as casually as he had entered. Other athletes of my acquaintance might have complained that the story had been "blown out of proportion," which perhaps it had been with the front-page treatment. Others might have griped that with so much publicity now, the Selective Service doctors would be tougher. But not Joe Namath; all he seemed concerned about was his quote about Vietnam and being incorrectly identified as a business major.

About a month later he was classified 4-F because of his wobbly right knee. He needed another operation on that knee following the 1967 season. That's when I liked Joe even more.

The week before Christmas that year, the Jets announced that Joe's surgery would be performed December 28, so I phoned him in Beaver Falls to get his reaction. As soon as I told him about the Jets' announcement, he snapped, "Damn it, I asked them not to announce anything until after Christmas because I didn't want my mother worrying over the holidays." We talked for a few more minutes, wished each other a Merry Christmas and I started writing. Half an hour later, Phil Pepe of the *Daily News* phoned me.

"I was just talking to Namath," said Phil, "and he told me to call you and say that he didn't realize it was going to be one of those days when everybody was calling him, that he thought he was quick with you and if you need anything else, he's still at that number."

I didn't need anything else, but I phoned Joe anyway. When he answered, I told him, "Now I know why all those broads think you're a helluva guy." I also told him that I had all the quotes I needed and that I didn't think he had been quick with me but that I appreciated his thoughtfulness.

"All right," he said. "I just wanted to make sure."

In my more than twenty-five years in the newspaper business, nobody else has ever done anything quite that thoughtful. Or quite that professional either. Joe Namath was a professional, on and off the field. It just took him more time on the field. Rookie quarterbacks don't make it instantly, not even in the old American Football League, which the Jets belonged to then. But like most rookie quarterbacks, he believed his arm was enough. In those years the Jets' training camp was at the Peekskill (N.Y.) Military Academy, a decrepit prep school in its last years. In one of Joe's first workouts, wide receiver Don Maynard streaked downfield on a deep pattern. Joe let go a long pass that looked as if it might land in Vermont and it might as well have. He overthrew Maynard by at least ten yards. Coach Weeb Ewbank walked over to his rookie quarterback.

"You don't have to show me your arm," Weeb said softly. "If you couldn't throw, you wouldn't be here."

What the rookie quarterback had to learn was what Weeb always preached—it's one thing to throw a football, it's another to complete passes. But in his third season, Joe Namath completed 258 of 491 passes for 4,007 yards, the only quarterback ever to go over 4,000 yards in a season. Even so, those 4,007 yards did not change the skeptics' view that Joe Namath was merely a product of the A.F.L., that he wouldn't make it big in the N.F.L.—but the N.F.L.'s principal authority at the time, Vince Lombardi, was not among the skeptics.

"Joe Namath," the Green Bay Packers' coach told me early in 1968, "is an almost perfect passer."

In his 1968 opener, the almost perfect passer preserved a 20–19 victory in Kansas City by moving the Jets out from their own 4-yard line and controlling the ball for the last six minutes. But earlier in that game he was being dragged down by two Chiefs when he chose to throw anyway. Willie Lanier intercepted the short wobbly pass. Far down in my *Times* game story, I described it as a "foolish" pass. I soon forgot about that line but Joe didn't. Five weeks later in Houston he moved the Jets to the winning touchdown in the closing minutes for a 20–14 victory. On the Jets' charter home that night, Joe slid into a seat across the aisle and turned to me. "Well, David," he said with a grin, "did I throw any foolish passes today?"

Like most people, I usually think of a comeback about three days later. But for once, as I recalled that line about the "foolish" pass in Kansas City, I had an answer.

"I'm flattered, Joseph," I said. "I didn't think you read me that closely."

"That was a bad pass I threw," he insisted, "but it wasn't a foolish pass."

I laughed, he laughed, and that ended the semantics. About two months later, we had a much longer conversation on a Jets' charter, but this time we were going to Super Bowl III, where the Jets had been installed as 17-point underdogs. Much of what he said appeared in the *Times* the next Sunday, a week before the game:

FORT LAUDERDALE—Joe Namath had been lobbing passes on the practice field when Emerson Boozer appeared, the last of the New York Jets to emerge from the locker room.

"I told you, Weeb," yelled Namath, grinning. "I told you Emerson would practice this week."

"Well," said the coach, Weeb Ewbank, "it's nice of you to do us a favor today, Emerson."

The three of them laughed. The halfback had been delayed in the trainer's room, where his surgical knee required taping. Ironically, the true humor of the situation was that Namath, who is excused from the team calisthenics because of his surgical knees, usually is the last Jet out to practice. But not these days.

Joe Namath is preparing to challenge the superiority of the National Football League next Sunday in the Super Bowl game with the Baltimore Colts.

And when Joe Namath is confronted with a challenge, beware. As a $400,000 rookie he challenged the salary structure of pro football, but he proved to be a bargain. With his Fu Manchu mustache, he challenged the tonsorial tradition of American athletics, but he shaved it off for a $10,000 fee.

As the symbol of the American Football League, he is confronted with the challenge of penetrating the Colt defense.

His attitude is significant. Occasionally he presents a droopy appearance, but not now. He's alive and alert. When he saw the Jets' white uniforms, which they will wear in the Super Bowl, hanging in their lockers here, he reacted immediately.

"We're wearing the white uniforms," he shouted to his teammates. "That must mean we're the good guys."

He's anxious to face his moment of truth. But he's not awed by it or by the Colts.

"When the Colts lost to the Browns at midseason," he was saying on the Jets' chartered flight last Thursday night, "they didn't get beat by any powerhouse. I'm not going to take what I read about their defense. I'm going to go with what the one-eyed monster shows me."

The one-eyed monster is the projector that shows films of the Colts.

"The one-eyed monster doesn't lie," he said. "He shows it like it is."

In his blue turtleneck shirt and maroon corduroy slacks, he was sitting, as he usually does, on the left side of the aisle. That way he can extend his tender right leg into the aisle. But on this flight the seat in front of him was empty. He had folded the back rest and his right leg was stretched across it.

"When we won our title last Sunday, I said that Daryle Lamonica of the Raiders was a better quarterback than Earl Morrall, and now that's supposed to fire up the Colts.

"I said it and I meant it. Lamonica is better. If the Colts use newspaper clippings to get up for a game, they're in trouble. And if they're football players they know Lamonica can throw better than Morrall. I watch quarterbacks, I watch what they do.

"You put Babe Parilli with Baltimore," he continued, referring to the Jets' backup quarterback, "and Baltimore might have been better. Babe throws better than Morrall.

"There are more teams in the N.F.L. so they should have more good teams, but you put their good teams and our good teams together, or their bad teams and our bad teams together, and it's fifty-fifty, flip a coin. And we've got better quarterbacks in our league—John Hadl, Lamonica, myself and Bob Griese."

Hadl directs the San Diego Chargers, while Griese is with the Miami Dolphins.

"I read where some N.F.L. guy joked about Lamonica and me throwing one hundred passes last Sunday," he said. "We threw ninety-seven, but what's so terrible about that? How many N.F.L. teams have a quarterback who could complete as many passes to their wide receivers? In our league, we throw much more to our wide receivers.

"I completed forty-nine percent of my passes this season, but I could have completed eighty percent if I dropped the ball off to my backs like they do in their league. For wide receivers the Jets have the best. George Sauer has the best moves, nobody can cover him one on one, and Don Maynard is the smartest.

"The best thrower in the N.F.L. is Sonny Jurgensen of the Redskins. I've said that if Jurgensen had been with the Packers or the Colts or the Rams the last few years, he would have won the championship for any of them. But if you put any pro quarterback on our team, only a few would not be on third string.

"That's my opinion, and I don't care how people value my opinion. But I value it very highly, especially when I'm talking about football."

In his fourth season, Namath is considered to have matured as a quarterback, notably after two early-season games when the Buffalo Bills and the Denver Broncos each intercepted five of his passes to achieve upset victories. During his last ten games, including the title game, he had six interceptions.

"But after those games with the five interceptions," he acknowledged, "I disciplined myself as to throwing the ball. I was overcautious at times. I remembered an old rule: The only way to win is to keep from losing."

In the league title game an interception positioned the touchdown that put the Oakland Raiders ahead, 23–20, midway in the final quarter. But it did not deter Namath from connecting for three consecutive completions in moving the Jets 68 yards in fifty-five seconds for the winning touchdown of the 27–23 triumph.

"After that interception," he said, "I just told myself, 'you got eight minutes and you got to score.' That's all."

His arm has been his great gift, but he mentioned the luck factor for an athlete.

"Any player has to be lucky," he said. "Take our kicker, Jim Turner—suppose he had to have an operation on his right knee when he was playing quarterback at Utah State. If he did, he'd never be kicking now. I was lucky because I was trained good by my brothers, Bob and Frank, and I've had good coaches.

"Larry Bruno, my coach at Beaver Falls High School, he was terrific. We had thirteen guys go on scholarships to college, thirteen guys from one team. And to go from a coach like that to Coach Bear Bryant at Alabama, a kid has to be lucky. He made me feel proud to be a part of his team. I learned a lot from Coach Bryant.

"And then coming here, with Weeb, was lucky for me. Until this season, I don't think I really appreciated Weeb, but now I realize how hard he works.

"Something the trainer, Jeff Snedeker, said one day made me realize it. He told me that when he got to the locker room at eight o'clock one morning, Weeb already was there taking a whirlpool bath. I mean Weeb's an old man, he's about sixty, and he was in the locker room before eight o'clock in the morning.

"And the day we came back from San Diego after just about clinching our division, Weeb and the coaches got off the plane at seven in the morning and went straight to the stadium. They could have taken a break, but they didn't.

"I've had my disagreements with Weeb, I probably always will. I'm that kind. Like last Sunday, after we won the championship, there's a league rule that you're not supposed to have champagne in the clubhouse. But I told Weeb to break it out, and that all of us were three times seven and that I'd pay the fine out of my pocket.

"And later Mr. [Milt] Woodard, the league president, came over to talk to me about it and I told him that I thought it's a stupid rule, that all of us were three times seven and that it was the biggest day of our lives.

"Mr. Woodard tried to tell me that it was bad for the image of football, that it was bad for the kids to see it. You know what the real image of football is, it's brutality. Why don't they tell the kids like it is? Tell the kids that this guy is trying to hurt that guy and knock him out of the football game.

"Like the letters I get from people who hope some guy cripples me because of my mustache."

Namath swirled the ice in his plastic cup and glanced at his right knee across the folded seat.

"Some of those letters," he said, "I read for entertainment because those people are sick. Or maybe I'm the sick one, but I'm happy the way I'm sick."

(January 5, 1969)

• • •

On the Thursday night before the game, Joe was to be honored by the Miami Touchdown Club as pro football's outstanding player that season. That morning I asked him if he needed a ride. "No," he said, "they're sending somebody to pick me up. Ride with me." As it developed, I was the only other person in the turquoise Cadillac driven by Joe Facile, a used-car-lot manager who had been assigned to pick him up. Before leaving the Galt Ocean Mile in Fort Lauderdale, where the Jets were lodged, Joe stopped in the bar for a big paper cup of scotch and ice. As he sipped his drink all the way down Interstate 95 to the Miami Springs Villas, we talked of why we thought the Jets would win. It didn't surprise me when, during his acceptance speech, he said:

"And we're going to win Sunday, I'll guarantee you."

He didn't say it boastfully or loudly. He said it as casually as he had said "I'll make it" that first night I met him. He said it so casually, in fact, that I didn't react to it until his "guarantee" was in headlines in the Miami *Herald* the next morning. In big bold type his "guarantee" suddenly had much more impact than it had the night before, probably much more than Joe had intended. But when the headline appeared, he didn't back off. Neither did Weeb Ewbank.

"That's the way Joe feels about it," the coach said, "and I'm for him. I wouldn't give a darn for him if he didn't think we could win. I don't think Joe's whistling Dixie at all."

The psychology of the "guarantee" seemed to lift the Jets, but the Colts were annoyed. Their coach, Don Shula, agreed that Namath's prediction had created a "challenge" for the Colt players. Shula's use of that word was interesting. Originally, the challenge of Super Bowl III had confronted the Jets in challenging the N.F.L. establishment. But now the Colts were confronted with the challenge of Joe Namath's "guarantee." Coming down on the charter, remember, he had said, "It's going to be a challenge for us, but it's going to be a challenge for them too."

As it turned out, it was a challenge the Colts did not respond to in the Jets' 16–7 victory. Because of his "guarantee," Joe Namath has been thought of as a prophet, but he had not been trying to be a prophet—he just had been himself. Six months later he again was himself when he retired from football rather than obey Commissioner Pete Rozelle's edict that he sell his share in Bachelors III, an East Side bistro that was frequented by alleged "undesirable" customers. After a few weeks he capitulated to the commissioner and a news conference was hastily called in N.F.L. headquarters. When the reporters and cameramen had assembled, the commissioner and the quarterback sat together behind a table—the commissioner in an expensively tailored blue suit with a white shirt and a striped tie, the quarterback in a sport shirt, jeans and sneakers.

"Are we ready," the commissioner asked, looking around at the newsmen. "All set?"

"Hold it," Howard Cosell barked in his nasal voice as he stared at a cameraman who was fiddling with some wires. "My man's not ready."

"Fuck your man," Joe Namath said.

Howard sneered but the commissioner laughed, the newsmen laughed and Maxine Isenberg laughed. Mrs. Isenberg, one of the N.F.L. secretaries, was there to record the news conference. When somebody motioned to Joe that a lady was in a corner of the room, he glanced at her and winced.

"Excuse me, ma'am," he said softly.

She laughed again, and moments later, when the cameraman was ready, the news conference began. Joe's surrender was official. I've always thought that the Bachelors III episode drained him of some of his enthusiasm for football in 1969 and 1970. But in 1971, after having missed most of the previous season with a broken bone in his passing wrist, his enthusiasm returned. At training camp he even drew a "smile" symbol—a circle surrounding two dots for the eyes and a curved line for the mouth—on the left knee of his white football pants. That knee had required tendon surgery in 1968.

But in the Jets' first exhibition game, the smile was wiped off that left knee.

Against the Detroit Lions, he threw an interception. In trying to tackle Mike Lucci, the Lions' linebacker, he was blocked by Paul Naumoff, another linebacker. Ligaments in his left knee were torn. He needed his fourth knee operation. After the Jets returned to New York that night, I accompanied Dr. James Nicholas, the team orthopedist, to Lenox Hill Hospital where the operation would be performed:

•   •   •

Below, on Park Avenue, the only movement occurred when traffic lights changed in the morning darkness of the empty streets.

On the seventh floor of Lenox Hill Hospital early yesterday, Joe Namath, wearing a blue hospital gown, sat on his bed. His left leg extended, he winced as Dr. James A. Nicholas, the New York Jets' orthopedic surgeon, examined the knee with his fingers, probing the ligaments.

"Here?" the doctor asked.

"Yeah," Namath answered, grimacing sharply.

"Here?"

"Not bad."

"Here?"

"Yeah," said Namath, his voice rising. "Ow."

"There it is," the doctor said.

Namath's kneecap wobbled from side to side, like a door without hinges, as the doctor held it and nodded.

"The anterior cruciate," Nicholas said.

"You mean something's wrong with that?"

The quarterback knows the medical terms. Three surgical scars curved along his right knee, another on his left. He had been in Lenox Hill Hospital for three previous knee operations. Now, as Nicholas arranged for a "seven o'clock incision," Namath winced again at the rate for his private room, for which the Jets pay.

"It's a hundred and forty-eight dollars a day," he said. "It was sixty-five dollars a day the first time I was here, ninety-eight dollars a day the second and third times."

Soon the doctor departed for a couple of hours of sleep. It's his habit to operate as quickly as possible before the knee ligaments lose their elasticity. Namath had been injured about nine o'clock Saturday night in Tampa, Fla., but the operation would be completed here about twelve hours later.

"I feel more comfortable about this one," Namath was saying to Jimmy Walsh, his attorney. "Having been through it before."

Suddenly, the quarterback grabbed his left leg. He had a cramp in it, and he tightened his lips as he rolled onto his side.

"If it just wouldn't cramp," he said. "You can't do anything about it. And the worst is a cramp when it's in a cast. Cramp, cramp, go away, come back in about eight weeks."

By then, the cast will have been removed. But he talked of rejoining the Jets at their training camp while the cast remained.

"I don't know if it'll do me any good physically," he said, "but maybe it'll help them. I want to coach Al Woodall. I'm going to work with him as much as I can. After the way he played last year and with five more exhibitions, he might be able to do it."

Instead of pitying himself, the star quarterback had reacted stoically and fatalistically to his latest injury.

"What am I going to do?" he explained. "If it's supposed to happen, it's supposed to happen. The more you go through these things, the more you learn to adjust. With the exception of my leg, I feel pretty normal. I don't know if it's dawned on me yet."

He searched for the remote-control switch to operate the TV on a raised platform, but he couldn't find it.

"I'm going to get some movies for you," Walsh said. "We can close the blinds to make a screen. We'll charge three dollars a head, half a dozen people, that's eighteen dollars a night."

"It still won't be able to pay for the room," Namath said, grinning. "Damn, a hundred and forty-eight dollars a day, that's one thousand thirty-six dollars a week. But if you bring the films, bring my popcorn popper."

Soon an attendant arrived with a wheelchair to transport Namath to the X-ray room. He hobbled over and sat in it.

Two hours earlier, hobbling off the Jets' chartered airliner at LaGuardia Airport, he had noticed a gray canvas wheelchair in the rampway. He glanced at the skycap behind it and shook his head.

"No," he said firmly.

The left leg of his pink bell-bottom pants had been slit to the thigh in order to permit ice packs to be wrapped to the knee. Ignoring the wheelchair, he hobbled stiffly through the polished corridor of the terminal. Outside, a black limousine sped him across the Triborough Bridge to the hospital.

"He's proud," one of his teammates had said. "He didn't want any of us to see him in the wheelchair, or anybody else."

Now, after his return from the X-ray room, Namath rolled over as a nurse poised a hypodermic needle above his rump.

"Pick a soft spot," he said, smiling.

"Ain't no soft spot here," she said.

Not long after that, she returned with another needle. He glared at her and winked.

"If you hurt me again," he said, rolling over, "I'm going to slap your hand."

Outside, dawn filtered through the nearby apartment houses and office buildings. Pigeons soared across the rooftops. Below, a few cars moved along Park Avenue as the city began to stir with sun glittering on windows.

"It's a nice day," Walsh said.

Dozing now, his operation about an hour away, Joe Namath stirred, then grimaced as he turned his left leg. He glanced out the window at the daylight. Thinking of a phrase he remembered from *Little Big Man*, the movie, he smiled.

"It's a good day to die," he said.

(August 9, 1971)

But he was alive again late that season, returning to throw three touchdown passes against the San Francisco 49ers that almost pulled out a 24–21 loss. Early in the 1972 season at Baltimore he had his most productive game as a passer. I had stayed in New York that day to watch the Giants lose but I found Joe late that night:

In the dim light, Joe Namath swirled the ice in his glass. He was drinking vodka on the rocks with a splash of Kahlua, a Black Russian, and he was grinning.

"At the airport in Baltimore, waiting for the plane, Gerry Philbin came over to me," he said, referring to the New York Jets' defensive end. "He said, 'Damn it, we come out of the game after they score, but when you score on the first play, we have to go right back in. Damn it, give us a rest.' And he laughed. Everybody laughed."

On the jukebox at Bachelors III early yesterday morning, Tom Jones was singing "She's a Lady." At a table in the rear, Joe Namath had on a turtleneck shirt, jeans and sneakers. He was sitting with a few friends, and every so often he would sign an autograph for a stranger as he waited for a steak, French fries and salad.

"I'm hungry," he said. "I ain't eaten all day. I didn't have but two bites of steak at the pre-game meal down there."

With two bites of steak for nourishment, he had passed for six touchdowns and 496 yards as the Jets outscored the Colts, 44–34, in the most outstanding performance by a passer in National Football League history. Two other quarterbacks accumulated more yardage, but each did it against inferior teams. Norm Van Brocklin of the Los Angeles Rams totaled 554 yards in 1951 against the New York Yanks, who won one game that season. Y. A. Tittle of the New York Giants threw for 505 yards in 1962 against the Washington Redskins, who had a 5–7 won-lost record. But on Sunday, the Jets' quarterback dissected one of the N.F.L.'s most respected defensive units.

"That's amazing, it really is," he was saying now. "I was lucky. Some days you got it and some days you don't, and some days you can spit in a swinging jug. But if a good quarterback has time, he can do well against a zone. If you have time, all you do is send one or two people deep in one area and another deep underneath, and that man underneath should be open. I had good time, but Bubba Smith not being in there for the Colts was a factor in me having time, a titantic factor. I'm not taking anything away from their defensive ends, they're outstanding players. But our interior line was giving me the time I needed to look at that zone."

In the final quarter he collaborated with Rich Caster, the tight end, for a 79-yard touchdown but then Johnny Unitas's second touchdown pass had narrowed the Jets' lead to 37–34 with about six minutes remaining.

"Waiting for the kickoff," he was saying now, "I was thinking about another long pass to Caster on the first play, but I wasn't sure if I should risk it, only three points ahead. But then I said to myself, 'If you ain't confident, you don't belong here,' so I decided to try to score again quick because I knew there ain't no way we're going to use up the clock running the ball in that situation. I knew the Colts would be storming the walls, and the first play, they were blitzing, but I had it picked up. I knew Caster had to be one-on-one so I just hustled the hell back there, set up, let it go and it was just right."

He acknowledged that his new $500,000 contract over two years is his new motivation.

"I got paid for it, I'm supposed to do the job. It's cut and dried. I want to be convinced myself that I earned that money. I am so far, I always have been anyway. Comparatively speaking, wage-wise, it's way out of balance with the rest of the team. But situation-wise, it's not out of balance. Contract is business. Then after the business part comes the playing part. And that's still a business, but it's physical, it's a game, it's fun, it's emotional."

His performance Sunday should convince the skeptics that he belongs with all the great quarterbacks—not that he had to be convinced.

"I'm convinced I'm better than anybody else," he said. "I've been convinced of that for quite a while. I haven't seen anything out there that I couldn't do and do well. When you go back to Sammy Baugh, guys like that, they were great, sure, but it wasn't the game it is now. Johnny Unitas is great, but I just like to believe I'm better. Out there playing, I get annoyed at myself for doing something wrong. Sometimes I tell myself, 'You ain't too good,' and that helps me play better because then I tell myself, 'You're the best, damn it, do it right.' "

Another drink arrived. The quarterback mixed the Kahlúa with the vodka, and smiled.

"You want to take a sauna with me out at Shea tomorrow?" he said to Mickey Kearney, one of the people with him. "By the time I'm finished tonight, I'll need a sauna."

(September 26, 1976)

When he went to Baltimore the next season, he needed another hospital room. Stan White, the Colts' linebacker, had blitzed and pounced on him, slamming him into the hard brown dirt of Memorial Stadium's leveled pitcher's mound. His right shoulder was separated. But he didn't complain. He never did. Once he was talking with Bob Oates of the Los Angeles *Times* about whether the N.F.L. should create stricter rules to protect quarterbacks.

"I hope they don't do that," Joe said firmly.

"Why not?" Bob wondered. "It would help you."

"Nothing should be done to detract from the essence of the game —the fight to get at the quarterback, the fight between the offensive line and the defensive line. If the defense wins, you've got to give them their trophy."

"Their trophy?" Bob asked.

"Me," Joe Namath answered.

Sometimes he was a battered trophy. I was in Oakland the day in 1967 when Ben Davidson, the Raiders' huge defensive end, assaulted him with a taped right hand, spinning Joe's helmet across the sideline as if he had been beheaded. Joe's cheekbone had been fractured. That evening his face was swollen and he couldn't talk without wincing. But the Jets had a couple of days off before they were to regroup in San Diego for the final game of the season. In the lobby of their Oakland motel he appeared in a tuxedo with a glass of scotch in one hand.

"Where are you going?" somebody asked him.

"I'm catching a plane for Vegas," he said.

The next Sunday, with a protective mask over his cheekbone, he completed his 4,007-yard season, then celebrated with a few more glasses of scotch. But by 1973 he had switched to vodka, and in 1975, when he turned down an allegedly guaranteed $5 million offer from the Chicago Fire of the World Football League, he was drinking blackberry brandy.

"I wouldn't feel comfortable there," he said of that W.F.L. offer. "It was too big a chance."

He realized that if the W.F.L. didn't succeed, much of his stature would be tarnished, no matter how successful he might have been personally. He realized that his stature affected his future as a commodity in business ventures and in his ambition to be an actor. And that indeed was too big a chance to take. But when his Jet contract expired after the 1976 season, he took a big chance. He joined the Los Angeles Rams for his last hurrah—to prove that Joe Namath was still Joe Namath.

"Some people don't think I can play anymore," he told me the day before the season opener in Atlanta, "but they're wrong and I'm going to prove them wrong."

He didn't. After four games in 1977, the Rams were 2–2 and he had a bruised knee; also a bruised ego. On a rainy Monday night against the Chicago Bears in Soldier Field, he had completed only 16 of 40 passes, with four interceptions, in a 24–23 loss. Late in that game Pat Haden took over as the Rams' quarterback and Joe never played another down. I've always thought that the reason Joe threw so often that night in the rain was that he wanted to prove on prime-time national television that he was as good as ever. I mentioned my theory to Joe when he was at Super Bowl XII to do a TV show.

"No," he said. "Our game plan that night was to throw."

During the rehearsal, I also asked him if he planned to retire. "I have a pretty good idea of what I'm going to do," he said, "but I don't want to talk about it until I talk to the Rams about it." Later that month I phoned him in Fort Lauderdale, Fla., to do a question-and-answer piece for our Sports Monday section. I wanted to get him to look back at his career and also to look ahead. I was sure he was going to retire, but I expected him to repeat that he didn't want to talk about it yet.

"Have you decided anything?" I asked him.

"I'm not going to play next year," he said.

"We can't hold that until Monday," I said.

He knew that as well as I did. His retirement story started on the

Times' front page. He soon signed to do a movie and a TV situation comedy. I happened to be in Los Angeles when he went into re-hearsal for the TV series:

BEVERLY HILLS—Out on the patio, palm trees filtered the glow of sunset. In the pastel elegance of the Polo Lounge at the Beverly Hills Hotel, the beautiful people paraded to their tables for a drink before dinner. Sitting near the door, Joe Namath was gazing at a blonde walking by when a gray-haired waiter leaned over and whispered, "I hear you're Joe now instead of Harry."

"Yeah," he said., "we've got to reshoot a couple of scenes that were in the pilot."

Joe Namath has begun rehearsing a TV situation comedy, *The Waverly Wonders,* in which he portrays a former pro basketball player hired to coach a high school team that has never won a game. In the original script, his name was Harry Casey but now he's Joe Casey.

"They decided," he explained, "that I'm a Joe, not a Harry."

He passed up a tray of dip and crackers as he sipped iced Sanka.

"I haven't had a drink in two months," he said. "I just decided to stop drinking, just like when I stopped smoking ten years ago."

Joe Namath had begun rehearsing *The Waverly Wonders* at a Sunset Boulevard studio on Thursday.

"It's a long day," he said. "It's like training camp with two-a-day workouts."

Training camp. For the first time since before he was in high school, Joe Namath is not in a football training camp. Instead, he is in a TV studio from 9 A.M. to 5 P.M. five days a week. Dick Martin, once a *Laugh-In* comic, is his director. The sitcom will be shown on the NBC-TV network on Friday evenings this fall.

"Doing those lines," Joe Namath asked during the rehearsal, "was I supposed to be sitting down?"

"No, no," Dick Martin said. "I like the way you were pacing up and down. That was fine."

Joe Namath rehearses his TV show as seriously as he rehearsed as a quarterback. He's no stranger to show business. He has been a guest host of the *Tonight Show* and appeared in several TV variety shows. And he's now made four movies, including *Avalanche Express* with Lee Marvin and Robert Shaw in which he's an intelligence agent. He was on location in West Germany for three months for the espionage film that is scheduled to be released later this year.

"People tell me you're great, Joe," a Hollywood agent named Mike Greenfield had said to him earlier. "A natural."

Joe Namath never even smiled. He just stared at Mike Greenfield as if he had never heard him. In a way, he hadn't.

"All this talk about how good I am in the movie, how good I'm going to be in the TV show, all this talk doesn't mean a thing," he was saying now. "All this is before the race has started. I remember at Alabama when we were ranked number one before the season, Coach Bryant told us it didn't mean a thing. What counted was where we were at the end of the season. That's how I'm treating this. I don't care what other shows are in our time slot, I don't even know. But when the movie comes out and the TV series is over, then we'll find out how good it is, how good I am."

Suddenly a slim brunette was standing at his shoulder, whispering to him.

"Well, yes," Joe Namath said to her, "I'd like to see you again, too. Let's do that."

Over in Europe, hardly anybody had recognized him. Football players are not known there.

"It was wonderful," he was saying now. "I like to blend in, but I can't really accept blending in. I have to excel. And if you excel, you're known."

Joe Namath has been known ever since he excelled in Super Bowl III for the New York Jets.

"The only thing I really have been down on about the Jets," he said, annoyance in his voice, "is how they changed their letterhead. They took '1968 World Champions' off it. I know they wanted to change their image, but I'm disappointed they would go to that degree. I can understand they don't want to live in the past but that Super Bowl happened."

"Do you think the Jets will retire your number twelve this season?" he was asked.

"I don't know," he said. "In one respect, it would be a great honor. But in another respect, I don't give a damn one way or another."

Soon he was joined by Ray Abruzzese, once a Jet teammate, and Bobby Van, his longtime restaurant partner.

"I can't believe the hours you're working," Ray Abruzzese told him. "They're worse than football. But this place is better than living in those dorms at training camp."

"This is the only place," Joe Namath said.

"All that trouble Reggie Jackson is having," Ray Abruzzese said. "Doesn't that remind you of all the trouble you used to have. But at least Reggie got a candy bar named for him."

"In that case," Joe Namath said, "I'll stick with panty hose."

Much of Joe Namath's trouble involved his Bachelors III restaurant in New York and now those same three bachelors had gathered in the Polo Lounge before going out.

"You know," Joe Namath said, "that something's up."

(July 23, 1978)

But his TV show was a flop. After only four weeks, NBC canceled it because of bad ratings. Joe Namath had been cut as an actor, something he never had to worry about as a quarterback. I remember John Dockery, now a television sportscaster but then a Jets' cornerback out of Harvard, talking once about the emotion involved in anticipating the roster cut each week at training camp. "It's exciting," he said. "In a way, I feel sorry for somebody like Joe Namath who never knows what it's like—good or bad."

Joe knows now.

But whenever I write about Joe Namath now, I always wonder how good a quarterback he would have been if he had been blessed with even adequate mobility. I also wonder how arthritic his knees will be in a few years. I always remember the time we were caught in traffic near his East Side apartment. The traffic had backed up while an elderly man was being helped out of a double-parked car. Steadying himself on the fenders, the gray-haired man hobbled painfully to the sidewalk as Joe Namath watched patiently.

"Must be an old quarterback," he said.

5 · Tennis

I covered the first tennis match I ever saw. I was working then at the *Journal-American.* Max Kase, the sports editor, dispatched me to the Merion Cricket Club outside Philadelphia for the 1956 Pennsylvania Grass Court championships. In those years that was a big tournament, the opener of what was known as the Eastern grass-court circuit leading to the Nationals at Forest Hills, but tennis had nowhere near the popularity and stature it does now. In those years before open tournaments, tennis also had no prize money. Appearance money, yes; maybe as much as $500 a week for the top players, but no prize money as such. Tennis was a society game then and Merion was the bastion of Main Line society. Old trees and high hedges surrounded the old clubhouse, a red-brick fortress. And the grass courts were as manicured as the members. If the ladies had worn hoop skirts, Merion would have resembled a sketch of an English lawn party a century earlier.

It was nice duty. Watch the matches, talk to a few players, write a story. That first day I wrote about Vic Scixas—when in doubt, Vic Seixas always was a good subject then. I didn't know tennis but I knew enough to listen to what the other sportswriters were talking about.

Allison Danzig of the *Times* and Al Laney of the New York *Herald-Tribune* did most of the talking about tennis, but Jim Burchard of the New York *World-Telegram and Sun* did most of the laughing and drinking. He had a hearty "Har, har, har" laugh that got louder with each drink. Jim was always in his best form at Southampton, the society playground out on Long Island that was the second stop on the grass-court circuit. The tournament there was played at the Meadow Club, which had a nice little bar off the porch. One night there Jim picked up the tab for the group of strangers he had been drinking with.

"That's not necessary," one of them said.

"I insist," another said. "Let me sign that."

"Give me that tab," the third demanded.

They didn't know Jim Burchard, who whipped out his money and paid the tab. The three strangers shrugged, thanked him and departed. The next day, the bartender drew Jim aside.

"You know those guys you picked up the tab for last night?" the bartender said. "You know who *they* are?"

Jim didn't have the foggiest other than they had been three good guys to drink with. That's all he cared about.

"That was Mr. Ford, Mr. Firestone and Mr. Hearst," the bartender said. "And *you* paid the bar tab for *them.* "

Jim laughed a hearty "Har, har, har" and went for a swim at the nearby Southampton Beach Club, another millionaires' retreat. The week of the tournament, the tennis writers and their families also had the use of the Beach Club during the day. I seldom went over, but my wife Maureen did, along with Stephen, Mark and Mary Jo, who were still small then. The other young children on the beach usually were supervised by nannies or teenage sitters while their mothers played bridge in the clubhouse or swam in the pool. One day a Southampton dowager noticed our children playing in the sand. She turned to Maureen and said, "What lovely children! Whose are they?"

"Mine," my wife said, not too sweetly.

But there's no tennis tournament at the Meadow Club anymore. Open tournaments changed tennis from a society game to a commercial game. As blatantly commercial as some tournaments are now, at least the best players are playing for the best titles. If somebody like Jimmy Connors or Bjorn Borg or Guillermo Vilas wins at Wimbledon or the U.S. Open, he deserves to be recognized as the world's best player. In the years before open tennis, the best players were never recognized as such. The best players, then as now, were the touring pros. But the tennis world then was dominated by amateur officials in blazers and striped ties, who were more interested in maintaining their feudal authority than in the popularity of the game. The pros were outcasts. Golf had jumped far ahead of tennis in prestige, especially in the United States.

Golf had Arnold Palmer, but tennis had no symbolic player that the public could identify with.

Richard (Pancho) Gonzales should have been that symbol. In the two decades I've watched tennis, he has been the best player I've seen. But by the time the tennis lords sanctioned open tournaments in 1968, he was nearly forty years old. He had spent nearly half his life performing in obscurity. He would open the pro tour in Madison Square Garden against Lew Hoad or Ken Rosewall or Tony Trabert and then virtually vanish into a series of one-night stands in little arenas and high school gyms all over the country. He was the world's best tennis player for a decade, but he never received the acclaim he deserved. In the newspapers, he was fortunate to get a small paragraph reporting that he had defeated Hoad or Rosewall or Trabert in Omaha or Albuquerque or Dayton, while an amateur nowhere near as skilled would receive much more attention.

From 1954 to 1961 Pancho Gonzales reigned as the undisputed champion of pro tennis. More than anyone else, *he* was the tour. When he retired in 1962, there was no tour. And when the tour was revived by Jack Kramer in 1963 without him, not many people cared.

In May of that year, Rod Laver, then a rookie pro, had emerged as the challenger to Rosewall for Pancho's vacated title in a playoff series that opened at the Garden before only 4,612 customers. After the match the workmen were rolling up the green canvas court. Rosewall, the tour manager as well as its star, looked on.

"What," the Garden foreman asked him, "should we do with the court?"

In the Garden catacombs, a truck was chugging up a ramp. The court would be tossed inside it to be driven to the next stop. But preoccupied with the lack of interest in the tour, Rosewall wasn't paying attention. The foreman had to ask him again what to do with the court. This time Rosewall looked up.

"Burn it." he said.

That's how low pro tennis had sunk. But the pros were still the best players. My favorite tennis tournament was not at Wimbledon or Forest Hills; it was at the White Plains (N.Y.) County Center in 1964 when Pancho Gonzales, with the glowering rage of an old lion, made a comeback at thirty-six and knocked off, in order, Mal Anderson, Rod Laver, Lew Hoad and Ken Rosewall for the $3,000 first prize. And against Rosewall, he was down, 5–7, 3–6 and 1–4, before he won the last three sets, 10–8, 11–9, 10–8—long before the tie-breaker was introduced. Typical of pro tennis then, only 732 spectators saw the final.

Ironically, when open tennis arrived, Pancho was the first pro to lose to an amateur. In the first open tournament, the British Hard Court championships in Bournemouth, England, he lost to Mark Cox, now an obscure touring pro. But he didn't complain.

"It had to be one of the pros," he said, "so I guess it might as well be me."

And he didn't complain that open tennis had arrived too late to project him.

"I don't feel cheated," he said at the first U.S. Open in 1968 at Forest Hills after defeating Tony Roche in a memorable five-set match. "I'm just glad open tennis is here. It's great for the game. That's more important."

Then he had to play Tom Okker in the quarter-finals:

Outside, the umpire was droning, "Mr. Okker leads, two sets to one. There will be a ten-minute intermission."

Underneath the concrete stadium, in the little oak-paneled room where Pancho Gonzales would rest, his younger brother, Ralph, had lit a cigarette and the forty-year-old warrior snatched at it and took a quick puff.

"Get me a relaxing pill," Pancho ordered, rubbing his left thigh, "I'm starting to get a cramp."

His brother disappeared and Gonzales leaned against the white-sheeted rubbing table. On a table was a plate with two oranges, two lemons and a knife on it, but he took a can of Teem out of an ice pail and snapped it open.

After another puff on the cigarette, he plugged in the air conditioner.

"Do you want a cup of tea," an official asked, "a hot cup of tea?"

Gonzales shook his head. He sipped the tea as he undressed for a shower.

"My eye's bothering me," he told Robert J. Kelleher, the president of the United States Lawn Tennis Association. "My right eye. I've had a blur in it all day. And that's my focusing eye. I can't focus properly."

He was cramping, and his vision was blurred. He really was forty after all.

In the seventy-six-minute first set yesterday, he had been magnificent, perhaps superior to his straight-set conquest of Tony Roche on Wednesday, but after the first set he had begun to act his age. When he emerged, in clean white clothes, onto his grass stage for the fourth set, he was making his last stand.

His brother returned with a relaxing pill, but by then he had lost his serve and was trailing, 0–2.

"We didn't have enough time anyway," his brother, who is thirty-four, would say later. "You need a half-hour."

In less than half an hour, the match was over. He walked to the net and shook hands with Tom Okker, to the accompaniment of sad, almost mourning, applause. Moments later he departed, lifting his head like a racehorse halfway to the marquee as more applause surrounded him.

"Nobody ever gave it a better go," his old promoter, Jack Kramer, consoled him behind the marquee.

"My legs were not up to moving for the return of serve," he told Kramer. "My legs gave out on me."

Alone, with a can of Teem in one hand, he walked to the Tudor clubhouse. Upstairs, in the locker room, he sat on a gray wooden bench and smiled.

"He didn't miss any shot that I remember," he said. "Those little guys are harder than they look."

When he was asked where he goes from here, he glanced at his grass-stained sneakers and looked up.

"That's a good question," he said. "Where do I go from here? I'll probably play another year, just to play. Conceivably, this might be my last serious tournament."

But maybe not. Returning to the stadium later, he passed Okker, who was on his way to the clubhouse.

Gonzales glanced at him and nodded but he did not smile, and he did not speak, almost as if he were beginning to prepare for a rematch somewhere sometime—at 41.

(September 6, 1968)

• • •

The next year, at forty-one, he played an even more memorable match at Wimbledon, a 22–24, 1–6, 16–14, 6–3, 11–9 triumph over Charlie Pasarell, then twenty-five years old. It set Wimbledon records for games played, 112; for time consumed, 5 hours and 20 minutes over two days; and for what might have been if Wimbledon had been open to Pancho Gonzales all those years.

In the twilight of his career, Pancho had shown the world something of what he had been like at high noon.

I didn't see that Wimbledon match, but I finally got to Wimbledon in 1972, when Chris Evert played Evonne Goolagong for the first time. Wimbledon is the stiff upper lip of tennis. Somewhat inconspicuously, it has a military atmosphere. Near the polished wooden doors of the clubhouse, British army officers peer intently under their cap visors. Atop the high outside walls, three strands of barbed wire discourage intruders. As a newcomer, I was given a tour of the clubhouse by an elderly member with a walrus mustache. To join the All-England Lawn Tennis and Croquet Club, he explained, a candidate must be proposed and seconded.

"And then," he added, "he must be vetted."

"I beg your pardon," I said. "What does 'vetted' mean?"

"Vetted," he said. "Very carefully examined."

As he spoke, I had the feeling that *I* was being vetted. I'm still not sure if I passed inspection, but I was permitted to cover that first Evert-Goolagong match.

WIMBLEDON, England—Under the stands, Chris Evert and Evonne Goolagong were about to walk onto the center court today when the seventeen-year-old American turned to the twenty-year-old Australian aborigine.

"How do you curtsy?" Chris asked.

"Just bob, that's all," Evonne said.

Moments later they were strolling onto their grass stage, the American in her prim little steps, the Australian in her casual stride. Suddenly they turned toward the royal box and curtsied quickly, as if embarrassed.

"The worst two curtsies I've ever seen," a man grumbled. "Who's that in the royal box, anyway?"

"I thought it was Lady Churchill," a woman said. "But then I saw she was chewing gum. I know she wouldn't."

It was Princess Alice, the Countess of Athlone—not chewing gum, incidentally. But the long-awaited confrontation between the two precocious young players deserved kings and queens, pomp and ceremony. And when it was over, each deserved a Rolls-Royce to return to her lodgings.

Until this year, each would have had one. Over the years Wimbledon has hired black Rolls-Royces with chauffeurs to transport competitors to and from the matches. But influenced by a saving of $35,000, tournament officials rented a fleet of small white British Leylands this time, with attractive girls as drivers.

Slowly, so as not to disturb those strolling past the red and blue hydrangeas, Miss Evert and Miss Goolagong arrived separately in small white cars that purred to the main gate of the All-England Lawn Tennis and Croquet Club. Quickly, each hurried inside the ivy-covered enclosure, oblivious to the quiet stares of men in blazers and women in tailored coats.

Quickly, too, Mrs. Billie Jean King cleared the stage with a 6–2, 6–3 victory over Miss Rosie Casals in the other women's semifinal match. And now, on the famous center court, under the peering eyes of fourteen thousand aficionados, Miss Evert and Miss Goolagong were about to oppose each other for the first time.

Above the black-roofed enclosure gray clouds moved slowly. Beyond, two high-rise apartments infringed on the atmosphere. So did an occasional aroma of hamburgers cooking in a nearby "Wimpy" stand.

When the match began, it created the tension of a heavyweight-title fight: Miss Evert with the red-trimmed dress, blond hair tied in a long ponytail, her strokes somewhat stiff, a poodle on parade; Miss Goolagong with the small red figures on her skirt, curly hair bouncing carelessly, her movement and strokes more natural than most men's, a jaguar about to pounce.

In retrospect there were two matches. Miss Evert won the first, 6–4, 3–0; then Miss Goolagong fought back, 6–0, 6–4.

When the Australian, the defending champion, began to play well, the spectators betrayed their loyalty to her. Whenever she produced an artful stroke, applause crackled through the enclosure as quickly as a lightning bolt. Miss Evert's best shots provoked polite, slower applause.

"I think the crowd was behind her," Miss Evert said later, "because she's the defending champion and when she was losing, she never got mad. British crowds like that."

Miss Goolagong's slow start might have been prompted by the intrusion of strategy. Her mentor, Vic Edwards, never before had outlined a battle plan. But for this match, the most famous first meeting in women's tennis since Suzanne Lenglen and Helen Wills at Cannes, France, in 1926, he had two thoughts.

"He told me to come in to the net as much as possible," Evonne said, "and second, he told me to cut them short on her backhand side, so that Chris would have to come up."

The weakness of the Florida teenager is that she's content to remain at the base line. It didn't work against a competitor with the speed and fluidity of the Australian. But it must be remembered that Chris is only seventeen, a child in a women's world. She'll develop a stronger serve-and-volley game as she matures.

Evonne realizes that, because when the match ended, she told her rival: "I can't believe the match is finally over. It seemed like we were out there forever today."

And even though she lost, Chris wasn't discouraged by her failure to hold the lead.

"I enjoyed the match," she said. "I know Evonne and I will be playing many more matches in the future."

Next time, Rolls-Royces, please.

(July 6, 1972)

The next time for me at Wimbledon was in 1975 on the way home from the Muhammad Ali–Joe Bugner fight in Kuala Lumpur; our all-night flight from Malaysia landed at Heathrow Airport the morning of the women's final:

WIMBLEDON, England—As if possessed in her final Wimbledon singles match by the inner strength of all her causes, Billie Jean King needed only thirty-nine minutes today in winning her sixth championship. Some women need more time than that to get dressed. Quickly again, Billie Jean the competitor had changed into Billie Jean the woman in a green sweater over a green flowered blouse and green slacks. She sat down with a can of Tab at a classroom-type desk and a tape recorder was politely slid toward her. "Stick it right up here," Billie Jean suggested. "Go after it." Go after it. Chisel that in the marble of Wimbledon champions instead of her name. Going after it has been her life. And today she was rewarded, 6–0, 6–1, over Evonne Goolagong Cawley, her easiest important victory. From either side of the net, the court was downhill. The net seldom was too high. The chalk lines seldom were too close. After all the controversy that has swirled around perhaps the most persistent women's libber of all, her dominance today was a reminder that she deserves to be remembered among the genuinely great players in tennis history. The old-timers treasure Suzanne Lenglen and Helen Wills Moody and Maureen Connolly Brinker, but the now-timers treasure Billie Jean King, as she will be treasured forever. Not just for winning, but for winning her way. And for living her way.

"I think I played out of my brain," she was saying now. "I don't think Evonne knew what hit her. Everything was close to the net, she couldn't read it, she couldn't see it. I told myself if I got ahead, I wasn't going to let up. Don't let her get back in the match. Watch the ball and play the ball and not think of who I'm playing. I know Evonne is so dangerous when she's behind and when she won that game, I told myself, Oh, no!"

Not until the fifth game of the second set did Mrs. Cawley, the recent bride of a London metals salesman, get on the scoreboard.

"I told myself to keep a sense of urgency in me and not let up," Billie Jean continued. "I kept telling myself, This is another World Team Tennis set. I've been dreaming and thinking about Wimbledon and it really makes you play."

"What was your feeling," somebody asked, "when the match ended?"

"Relief," she said. "I was just so happy it's over. What a way to end my career."

She has announced this was her last major singles tournament.

"When I was young, I dreamed about coming to Wimbledon and now I've won it six times. When I was with the Sets in New York or on the road, I'd wake up thinking I was in the Wimbledon final that day; that's how much I've been thinking about it. And today when I woke up, I realized, Oh, no, it's for real. But now it's cemented even more."

But she has been a woman of history, not merely tennis history.

"I think I've been the most fortunate woman athlete who ever lived up to this time. I hope some younger player can say that eventually, but I was able to see a lot of firsts. Anytime you're a leader or try to change anything, you're held up to ridicule. But you're still a person. Fight for equality. Fight for prize money. But there's no way an athlete plays for anything but to win."

She sniffled, took out a handkerchief and blew her nose.

"I've got a virus and hay fever," she said. "I took a cortisone shot, antibiotics, nose drops, eye drops, but I couldn't take antihistamines."

"If you'd been well," somebody suggested, "perhaps you wouldn't have dropped that game."

"In your career," somebody asked, "did you ever get beaten the way you beat Evonne today?"

"I lost to Chrissie [Evert] in Fort Lauderdale, love and one; I got annihilated. I lost to Margaret [Court], one and two, but that was a long time ago. I wasn't a player then."

"How much did you really prepare to win your final Wimbledon?"

"I prepared the best I could prepare. I never worked harder. I never trained harder. I told myself if somebody plays better, fair enough; if you have a bad day, that was fair enough, too, because I had prepared the best I could. I sacrificed my time with friends, I sacrificed movies and plays. This fortnight, I went back to my hotel and had room service because I wanted to save all my energy for the matches. That's not the way I like to live. But now I can have beer and ice cream."

"Will you change your mind about retirement?" somebody asked, perhaps aware that Muhammad Ali's retirement lasted eight days.

"Not me. When I tell you guys something I mean it. I'd like to help the Sets to win World Team Tennis. That means a lot to me. I want to get totally involved in television and my *womenSports* magazine. That takes a lot of work like everything else."

"What did you tell Evonne after the match?"

"I told her what everybody used to tell me when I was her age—'You got a lot of years left.' But winning today was like reliving fifteen years in one wonderful moment. The training was worth it, but I hate it. I hate it. Blood and guts. I hate every moment."

"How are you going to celebrate your title?"

"I don't know. I remember in 1961, when I won my first doubles title here, Bud Collins treated Karen Hantze and me to a spaghetti dinner," she said, referring to the TV commentator and Boston *Globe* columnist. "That was the first time I hadn't eaten at Wimpy's Hamburger Place. I love that junk stuff."

Billie Jean King laughed and her eyes laughed behind her glasses.

"But tonight I know one thing. I'll have some beer and ice cream."

(July 5, 1975)

With only a few hours of sitting-up sleep on the plane from Malaysia in the last two days, I didn't even have dinner afterwards. I went back to my hotel and conked out. I felt as if my body were still over the Arabian Sea somewhere. But the next day I took the underground to Wimbledon again for the men's final:

WIMBLEDON, England—Everything here is proper, if not genteel. At the nearby Southfields stop on the London underground, the sign reminds,

"Alight Here for Wimbledon." Roses bloom on the balconies of mod apartments and in the gardens of old gingerbread homes along the narrow leafy streets. Among the flowers outside the historic center-court enclosure are porticos where strawberries and cream, champagne and bonbons are sold. Wimbledon is tennis. And tennis propriety. Not even Alfred Hitchcock would use Wimbledon as the backdrop for a murder. Unthinkable. But today Arthur Ashe stabbed Jimmy Connors in four sets and in cold blood for the men's singles championship. The traditionalists cheered.

Seldom, if ever, has there been a tennis match with such silent passion. Two weeks ago Connors announced a $5 million libel suit against Ashe for having criticized Connors's refusal to join the United States Davis Cup team. Connors previously had filed three other suits for a total of $20 million against the Association of Tennis Professionals, of which Ashe is the president.

Throughout the tournament, as Ashe advanced inexorably on a collision course with Connors, who won the title last year, each publicly minimized the significance of the lawsuits. Neither was thinking about it. Or so they said. But if that were true, they were the only ones who weren't. And when they walked onto the grass court that is more brown than green, Arthur Ashe was wearing a blue warm-up jacket with "USA" in red on the chest. Just in case Jimmy Connors had forgotten about the Davis Cup controversy.

Connors, in contrast, wore a green, red and white sweater designed by Sergio Tacchini, once a leading Italian player.

The other contrasts were obvious. Arthur Ashe—cool, thirty-two years old next week, with a reputation of never having fulfilled his potential because of his laconic style. Jimmy Connors—fiery, only twenty-two years old, with a reputation as a spoiled brat and a cinch for the undisputed world's No. 1 ranking. In the William Hill betting tent next to the champagne bar, Connors was a 3-to-20 favorite, Ashe a 23-to-5 underdog. Connors was a 9-to-10 choice to win in straight sets; Ashe was 40 to 1 to win in straight sets, 16 to 1 to win in four sets.

Now that his romance with Chris Evert has ended, Connors had a new girlfriend, Susan George, the English actress, sitting next to his mother and Bill Riordan, his adviser. Ashe had his attorney, Donald Dell, and the A.T.P. executives and players rooting for him.

Almost immediately, the third game of the first set, Ashe broke Connors's serve on the discreet jurisprudence of George Armstrong, the umpire. Connors's shot clearly floated beyond the base line, but the linesman indicated the ball was good. Ashe stared as the fourteen thousand devotees groaned in disbelief. Armstrong turned to the linesman. Moments later Armstrong announced, "The linesman has deferred his call, the ball was out, game to Ashe," and across the net Connors reacted typically. He thrust a finger toward the gray sky.

Ashe whipped through the first set 6–1, and took a 3–0 lead in the second set.

Moments later, as Connors failed to chase down an angled cross-court volley, a voice from underneath the black tar roof of the green wooden stadium broke the silence. "C'mon, Connors," the voice yelled.

"I'm trying, for Chrissake," he replied.

Connors indeed was trying. With each serve, he was grunting like Joe Frazier throwing a left hook. And after losing nine consecutive games, he finally held his serve in that fourth game. But that would be his only winning game in the 6–1 second set. He hadn't lost a set in his six previous matches and now he had lost two sets. He was grunting and hunching his shoulders and shaking his hair and slapping himself on the right thigh. And in the third set he broke Ashe's serve in the final game to win, 7–5.

Connors even took a 3–0 lead in the fourth set, but Ashe, performing with a poised purpose, lost only one more game for the 6–4 set that completed his triumph.

On winning, Ashe turned to where Dell and his other friends were sitting and held up a clenched fist. He and Connors quickly shook hands at the net, but they avoided each other during the presentation ceremony.

"He didn't say anything," Ashe was saying now, "and I didn't say anything."

As outwardly cool as ever, Ashe was wearing his blue jacket with "USA" on it in the interview room. When he was asked if this was his most memorable triumph, he shook his head.

"No, winning the Davis Cup in '68 would be first," he said. "And winning Forest Hills in '68 was second until this one."

Every so often, Ashe would stab Connors subtly. It was as if he were using an icicle so that no murder weapon would exist, such as when he was asked if he was surprised at his easy victory.

"If you're a good player," he said softly, "and you find yourself winning easily, you're not surprised."

When he was asked about Connors's performance, Ashe mentioned how the dethroned champion had put about 70 percent of his errors "into the middle of the net, he hardly ever put the ball beyond the base line—that's a sign of choking." But he remained in character, taking his triumph with the ultimate in cool.

"Are you happy, Arthur?" wondered Dell with a smile.

"Yeah," said the first black man to win Wimbledon.

Moments later, after Ashe had departed, Connors appeared in his Italian sweater. He was polite, saying that he had lost to a "better Arthur Ashe," but he also stayed in character, making it clear that he felt he was still the superior player.

"Any guy has to play out of his mind to beat me," Connors said. "I'm not going to lose the match. Got to beat me. And he beat me today." He paused. "Today."

Asked about Ashe's reference to his choking, Connors snapped, "I don't choke, my friend, I've been playing too long to choke." He talked about his independence in the Davis Cup and the A.T.P. situation, recalling how when he was growing up, "I listened to my parents but if I didn't agree, I wouldn't do it." And then he was asked jokingly if he was going to the Wimbledon Ball tonight.

"If I can have the first dance."

"With Arthur?" somebody suggested.

Jimmy Connors scowled. But somewhere Arthur Ashe was smiling. In cold blood.

(July 6, 1975)

I cherish those Wimbledon visits but I also cherish Forest Hills— the West Side Tennis Club, to be exact, the site of the tournament known as the Nationals before the U.S. Open evolved. Now the U.S. Open is played at the new National Tennis Center in nearby Flushing Meadow, but some tennis people still refer to it, forgetfully, as "Forest Hills." Some probably always will. It's understandable. For more than half a century Forest Hills was synonymous with tennis.

But the world turns. Even the tennis world. The last U.S. Open at Forest Hills was played in 1977, with Jimmy Connors again at center stage:

Jimmy Connors had hit balls for a few minutes, had a massage, took a shower, used a hair dryer and put on his usual tennis clothes with the blue-and-red stripes across the shoulders of his white shirt. Now, wearing a blue jacket with "United States" on the back, he appeared outside the upstairs door to the men's locker room at the West Side Tennis Club and hurried down the winding green staircase. Suddenly, the people on the veranda of the old Tudor clubhouse stopped talking and drinking. "Go get 'em, Jimmy," some said. "Good luck," others said, and a few applauded. Jimmy Connors hopped onto the old grass courts in front of the clubhouse, and with a retinue that included his mother, Gloria, and his guru, Pancho Segura, he walked quickly toward Forest Hills Stadium, where the flags were snapping in the chilly wind blowing out of a sunny blue sky. People were taking his picture and whispering, "There he is," and they swarmed around him until he entered the marquee. And on the last day of the last United States Open at Forest Hills, a tennis player had walked down from the clubhouse to the stadium for the last time.

But the last was not first. Jimmy Connors was dethroned as the Open champion by Guillermo Vilas, 2–6, 6–3, 7–6, 6–0.

In the years to come, when tennis aficionados reflect on the charm of Forest Hills, they will remember how the players used to walk down from the clubhouse to the stadium and back again. That's where the people could see them up close. That walk won't exist next year at Flushing Meadow, where the stadium court will be adjacent to the locker room. But such charm was not enough to keep the Open at Forest Hills, where the tournament had outgrown the facilities and where tennis had outgrown the West Side members.

When the Open moves to Flushing Meadow next year, the stadium will accommodate 20,000 spectators, compared with yesterday's 12,644 sell-out.

"And even twenty thousand is too small," Pancho Segura says. "They should be thinking about a stadium for thirty thousand people, or forty thousand people."

In the tennis boom, perhaps someday the Open finals will be held in Giants Stadium before 75,000 spectators. But for now the Flushing Meadow blueprints are an improvement over Forest Hills, where there were not enough seats, not enough parking, not enough rest rooms but, mostly, not enough foresight. In recent years, West Side officials might have expanded and modernized the stadium—and thereby assured the retention of the Open on a long-term contract. But typical of their resistance to change, they ignored the suggestions. And now the Open has departed, less than a decade after the approval of open competition between pros and amateurs created the boom.

On the last day of the last Open at Forest Hills, the West Side members still didn't seem to realize that it could have been avoided. Some of them didn't even seem to care. Some sat silently in the upstairs lounge watching the matches on television, as they have for years, as they will next year. Others played bridge. Others had lunch on the veranda. They won't realize the Open has departed until their club dues increase because of the loss of $125,000 in revenue from the tournament.

And on the last day of the last Open at Forest Hills, there was a first—an organized demonstration outside the stadium.

On the corner of 69th Avenue and Clyde Street, across from the turn-stiles, about two hundred people were chanting, "Sports, yes; apartheid, no;

tennis with South Africa's got to go." The demonstrators from the American Coordinating Committee for Equality in Sports and Society were trying to persuade the United States Tennis Association to break off tennis relations with South Africa, notably in the Davis Cup competition. But as the chant drifted into the stadium, only two or three people in the top row could be seen turning around. The others continued watching the mixed-doubles final, which Frew McMillan of South Africa and Betty Stove would win.

In the men's final, Jimmy Connors's strategy was "to play our game," as Pancho Segura had said. "Hit deep, hoping he comes back with short shots, then move in on him with strength shots." And for a set the strategy worked. Even after he lost the second set, it worked as Jimmy Connors attained two set points. But then the poet, Guillermo Vilas, found the pentameter of his game, to the cheers of those who obviously preferred the poet to the punk.

When it ended there was another demonstration, this time by Jimmy Connors who stalked out of the stadium without waiting for the presentation ceremony. At the last ceremony on the last day of the last Open at Forest Hills, nobody missed him.

(September 12, 1977)

Jimmy Connors doesn't remember what tennis was like before open tournaments but I do. I remember the hypocrisy of the amateur tournaments, with the players receiving their "appearance" fees in white envelopes. And always in cash, so that the IRS couldn't trace it. But mostly I remember the pros like Pancho Gonzales and Lew Hoad and Ken Rosewall and Rod Laver when they were the world's best players but virtually nobody appreciated them because they had to appear in little places like the South Mountain Arena in West Orange, N.J.

I went back to the South Mountain Arena in 1977 to see Rod Laver, who was there to play Bjorn Borg in an exhibition.

In the quiet of a dreary cement-block locker room, I asked the red-haired Australian if he had played at South Mountain Arena before. Over the years the small arenas tended to blend together in his mind.

"I think I played in here," he was saying now. "I must have. I remember the bar across the street."

6 · Adversaries

Doing a sports column I've naturally developed some adversary relationships. But some are more adversary than others. And in their own way, the adversaries are fascinating subjects. Some are likable; some are not. My favorite is Al Davis, the managing general partner of the Oakland Raiders—managing general genius I like to call him. "Genius" is one of Al's favorite words.

"When you're writing about me," he once told a Raiders' public relations man, "be sure to use the word 'genius.'"

That order apparently still applies. In the Raiders' media guide for the 1978 season, the word "genius" appeared twice in Al's profile. He also is described there as "astute," a "driving force" and having an "inventive mind." All those words are justified. Al Davis is a brilliant operator. He has constructed the Raiders into a "dynamic organization" of "pride and poise," the winner of Super Bowl XI, a perennial American Conference contender. But among pro football people, he also has a reputation for being ruthless, sinister and obsessed with winning—a reputation he quietly revels in. Once we were talking on the telephone when he paused and said, "I've been meaning to ask you—when you're writing about me, why do you always use that word?"

"What word is that, Al?" I asked.

"Sinister," he said. "You always refer to me as sinister."

"I thought you'd consider that a compliment," I said.

"Well, yeah," he said, "but my mother reads the *Times.*"

Now you know why Al Davis is a likable adversary, but I doubt if he enjoys me as much as I enjoy him. When we see each other, he always says hello but not too enthusiastically. I can understand that. Doing a column, I have to write what I believe. I'm bound to offend somebody sometime. If it's Al Davis one day, so be it. If it's Charles O. Finley another day, so be it. Back in 1973, after the Oakland A's had won their second of three consecutive World Series and three years before the Raiders would finally win a Super Bowl game, I coupled them in the same column:

His cold sniper's eyes almost disappeared between narrow lids. Charles O. Finley was in Baseball Commissioner Bowie Kuhn's office yesterday to appeal fines totaling $7,000 and probation for his conduct during the World Series, notably the exile of Mike Andrews, a second baseman who made the mistake of making two errors. But the Oakland A's owner wasn't wearing his green blazer. He had on a black pin-striped suit and a silver tie. Those are the colors of the Oakland Raiders, not the A's, who prefer green and gold. The proponent of the black-and-silver color scheme is Al Davis, the Raiders' major-domo. Strange that Oakland should attract both Charles O. Finley and Al Davis, two of a kind. Each is a man of intrigue. Each is part tyrant, part rebel. Each appears to be putting others on the carpet, just as each appears to enjoy being on the carpet himself.

"I don't know what the commissioner means by probation," Finley said, his eyes narrowing even more. "It's not in the rule book."

If it's not in the rule book, don't expect Charles O. Finley or Al Davis to comply with the pleasantries of tradition. They prefer to live by their own rules. But they don't publish them. That way, they can change them to fit their whims.

Each is an escape artist, too. Charles O. Finley yesterday obtained a promise from Kuhn of a reevaluation. Earlier in the week, Pete Rozelle, commissioner of the National Football League, cleared the Raiders of alleged "dirty tricks" against the Pittsburgh Steelers in last Sunday's game. But things seem to happen in Oakland that happen nowhere else, or at least that surface nowhere else. Such as Andrews's exile. Such as Mean Joe Greene, the Steelers' most respected pass rusher, hurrying back to the defensive huddle as he stared at his hands.

"I got Vaseline on my hands," Mean Joe blurted. "That man must have Vaseline on his jersey."

Mean Joe meant George Buehler, the Raiders' guard whose assignment was to prevent Mean Joe from dismembering the quarterback. Throughout the N.F.L., some players have been smearing Vaseline-type substances on their uniforms for years. Running backs and wide receivers use it on their pants and stockings, to make it more difficult for a tackler's hands to grip them. Offensive linemen use it on the shoulders of their jerseys, to make it more difficult for a pass rusher to toss them aside. But when Mean Joe accused George Buehler of doing it, Al Davis was considered the ultimate villain. Al Davis can thank his reputation for that.

Later in the game, Ray Mansfield, the Steelers' center, was about to snap for a field-goal attempt.

"Hey," he said to the nearest official, after having handled the ball. "It's underinflated. Another ball."

The official complied. The ball might've been defective, but students of Al Davis preferred to believe it was another of his plots. They also suspected him in a controversy over an alleged slow clock that provided the Raiders time to kick a field goal moments before half-time. But the Raiders lost, 17–9. The week before, when the New York Giants visited Oakland, their 45-page defensive plans mysteriously disappeared. The plans reportedly were examined by gamblers in Lake Tahoe before they were discovered by a stranger in an Oakland telephone booth. Coincidentally or not, the Giants' defense was virtually nonexistent in a 42–0 loss. Again, the Al Davis mystique was under suspicion.

"Let me say this, as God is my judge," Al Davis said, "I didn't know about the Giants' missing plans until after they got them back."

But the circumstances were enough to create suspicion of his involvement. Not that Al Davis is, has been, or will be the only superspy in pro football. As an assistant coach with the San Diego Chargers more than a decade ago, he studied under a master, Sid Gillman, whose first decision in taking over the Houston Oilers this year was to build a high fence around their practice field so that the Oilers couldn't be spied upon. In the years when Gillman was coaching the Los Angeles Rams, the Chicago Bears somehow lost their kickoff tee during a game.

"Can we borrow yours?" a Bear asked him.

"No," said Gillman sharply. "No chance."

At first glance, Gillman appeared unsympathetic. Actually, the Rams' tee was oversized, therefore illegal. He didn't want the Bears to realize that. Al Davis studied well. He hardly introduced intrigue to pro football, but he polished its use. As a member of the N.F.L.'s competition committee, he is involved in recommending rule changes. He enjoys that. It enables him to examine the loopholes first. But the frustration of Al Davis is that the Raiders never have won the Super Bowl game.

"Winning the big one," Al Davis often says. "That's what it's all about. That's why we play this game."

And that's where Charles O. Finley is 2 up on him. Charles O. even has the nerve to wear black and silver.

(November 17, 1973)

Charles O. Finley also deserves to be called a genius. He not only assembled the A's that won three consecutive World Series—the best baseball team since the Yankee dynasty—but he did it with the smallest front-office staff in baseball, if not in big-league sports. Most other clubs have twenty people on their front-office staffs, but the A's listed only seven in 1974, the last year of their World Series reign. And the main man, Charles O. himself, usually was in Chicago instead of in the Oakland offices. One day the A's entire front-office staff happened to be together in an Oakland Coliseum elevator.

"Name me another team," one said, "that can put its front office in one elevator."

But even a genius makes mistakes. Charles O. Finley made a mistake in not paying $50,000 to a deferred-income plan chosen by Jim (Catfish) Hunter because it created an unfavorable tax situation for the A's owner. That breach of contract led to the then twenty-eight-year-old right-handed pitcher being declared a free agent; he subsequently joined the Yankees for a $3.75 million contract. Another mistake was antagonizing many of his best players in salary negotiations. When a federal arbiter, Peter Seitz, ruled the next year that baseball players could exercise the option clause in their contracts, many members of the A's preferred to become free agents.

Suddenly the A's were in ruins.

M. Donald Grant, the New York Mets' chairman of the board, made a similar mistake. He did not understand that baseball is different now, that a "franchise" player, such as Tom Seaver, must be embraced rather than embarrassed. In what Red Smith called "the Midnight Massacre," the Mets dealt off both Tom Seaver and Dave Kingman at the June 15, 1977, trading deadline:

•   •   •

In time, perhaps, the New York Mets' front office will be able to justify the banishment of Tom Seaver and Dave Kingman from M. Donald Grant's plantation.

In time, perhaps, Pat Zachry, Doug Flynn, Steve Henderson, Dan Norman, Bobby Valentine and Paul Siebert will be worth collectively to the Mets what Tom Seaver and Dave Kingman have been worth. Perhaps not, too. But don't demean the potential value of those six new names simply because they're new names. New names never are as impressive as old names. But the eventual judgment of the trades with the Cincinnati Reds and the San Diego Padres is not the real issue. The real issue is that the Mets' front office does not yet understand the baseball revolution that transferred the power to the players. Worse, it might never understand.

More than anyone else, the six new players should be concerned. If one or two approach the stature of Tom Seaver or Dave Kingman and demand that they be paid for it, they can expect to be treated with the same contempt that M. Donald Grant leveled at a Hall of Fame pitcher and the only home-run slugger in Mets history.

In a sense, the Mets are now a major league farm team for any pennant contender that wants to strengthen itself by acquiring players of stature that M. Donald Grant no longer can tolerate, or vice versa.

If the Mets will trade Tom Seaver, they will trade anybody that does not fit M. Donald Grant's definition of a proper baseball slave. When the chairman of the board's ego must be placated rather than that of the pitcher known for nearly a decade as "The Franchise," then the franchise is crumbling.

Of the millions who have watched the Mets through the years, good or bad or comic, nobody ever bought a ticket to see M. Donald Grant.

Those millions have now been alerted not to become too attached to any of the Mets players; the chairman's ego won't permit it anymore.

Those millions have also learned to distrust M. Donald Grant's pronouncements.

The chairman put out a statement last Monday that Tom Seaver "now wishes to renegotiate his contract that he was so happy with a year ago. Our board of directors voted unanimously against renegotiation. The contract is the fundamental cornerstone of our country and baseball as well." And the implicit contract of trust is the fundamental cornerstone of the relationship between a sports franchise and its fans.

Tom Seaver denied that he had attempted to renegotiate his current three-year contract that expires after next season. Instead, he insisted that he merely was willing to negotiate beyond the 1978 season.

Judging by the Mets' propaganda regarding their "excellent offer" to Gary Matthews, the outfielder now of the Atlanta Braves, during the free-agent auction last year, Tom Seaver is more trustworthy than M. Donald Grant's pronouncement. The "excellent offer" to Gary Matthews was not even an offer.

It was merely a vague suggestion that the Mets "would be willing to negotiate" a contract worth somewhere between $1 million and $1.2 million —nearly $600,000 less than Gary Matthews received from the Braves.

The Mets' propaganda also blared for months that Tom Seaver had asked to be traded when he had merely challenged the front office to trade him.

But the Cincinnati Reds didn't care about the semantics, they cared only about acquiring Tom Seaver in their obsession to overtake the Los Angeles Dodgers in the National League West and become the first National League team to win three consecutive World Series.

Bob Howsam, the Reds' president and disciple of Branch Rickey, has now obtained Tom Seaver, Joe Morgan, George Foster and Cesar Geronimo in trades.

To appreciate what Bob Howsam has accomplished, consider that Tom Seaver was acquired in exchange for a pitcher who has been struggling in his second year, an infielder who didn't play and two minor-leaguers. If the Mets' front office were to have pulled a comparable coup with the Reds, they would have acquired the slugger they need, George Foster, in return for Nino Espinosa, Roy Staiger and two minor-leaguers.

The Padres also conned the Mets out of Dave Kingman, even though he's unsigned, in return for an outfielder and a pitcher they don't need.

But for Tom Seaver, the trade puts September back on his calendar. He learned to appreciate September in 1969 and 1973 when the Mets surged to their two pennants.

"September is the best month for baseball," Tom Seaver once said, "if there is a pennant race."

With the Reds, there will be a pennant race, beginning Friday night when Tom Seaver opposes the Dodgers at Cincinnati in the opener of a weekend series. For the first time in his career, he is pitching for a team that is capable of supplying him with runs.

With the Mets, he knew he virtually had to pitch a shutout to win. Now a bad inning is not fatal. Tom Seaver finally has a luxury he deserves.

And just as followers of Joe Namath and Julius Erving have transferred their interest to the Los Angeles Rams and the Philadelphia 76ers, respectively, many Mets' followers now will be rooting for the Reds—an indictment of how the Jets, the Nets, and the Mets have deteriorated. No wonder the tennis team changed its name from the Sets to the Apples.

But the shame of the trading of Tom Seaver is put in perspective by a scene involving M. Donald Grant a few years ago.

Several new players had joined the team that season and Joan Payson, then the Mets' owner, was waiting to enter the clubhouse to meet them while M. Donald Grant alerted the players as a *Roots* slavemaster might.

"New boys, new boys," M. Donald Grant said. "New boys over here."

M. Donald Grant prefers new boys. They're not as expensive as old boys.

(June 19, 1977)

The strangest twist to the Seaver situation developed early the next season. I was sitting in the Mets' media lounge with Joe McDonald, the Mets' general manager, when he mentioned that the "41" uniform that Tom had worn with the Mets was stashed in the big steel safe in the club offices.

"I put it there," Joe explained, "to keep some souvenir hunter from snatching it."

How ironic. At the same time the Mets were hoping to justify the trade, they realized that Tom Seaver's empty uniform was now, in a sense, buried treasure. And yet M. Donald Grant can't seem to understand why he was under fire not only from me but from several other New York sportswriters before he was eased out as board chairman shortly after the 1978 season. His type always think they're being persecuted when they're merely being perceived for what they are.

Bob Arum, the boxing promoter, reacted the same way after the Travesty in Tokyo—the boxer (Muhammad Ali) against the wrestler (Antonio Inoki), perhaps the ultimate non-event in sports his tory.

The next day Arum traveled to Bangkok on business. Perhaps he thought he would be out of range there from whatever criticism might develop. But he forgot that the sun never sets on *The New York Times* News Service that supplies about four hundred clients throughout the world.

"When he was in Bangkok," a man close to Arum told me, "he bought a Singapore paper and there was your column."

Anytime I've written a column about Ali, a world subject, it appears in newspapers all over the world. This is the column that not only Bob Arum found in a Singapore newspaper, but also the one that found him in Bangkok:

In the ring, Muhammad Ali was standing over Antonio Inoki and waving his right glove at his opponent, alias his fellow conspirator. Ali was waving for the Japanese wrestler to get up and do something, anything. To those students of Ali lore, the pose resembled that in Lewiston, Me., in 1965 when Ali was standing over Sonny Liston and waving for him to get up. The pose is not coincidental. When that world heavyweight title bout in Lewiston ended in the first round, the chant of "Fix, fix" could be heard on lobster boats outside the twelve-mile limit. But whatever happened in Lewiston, the bout there was the essence of ethics compared with the Travesty in Tokyo that was seen, if not smelled, here Friday night on closed-circuit TV at Shea Stadium.

What was billed as "the Martial Arts World Championship Fight" emerged as The "Farcial" Arts World Championship Ripoff.

For throwing four harmless left jabs in fifteen rounds, Ali allegedly will receive $6 million—that's $1.5 million per jab. And for sitting down and tripping Ali harmlessly with a toehold three times in fifteen rounds, Inoki allegedly will receive $2 million. Neither deserves a dime. If the Tokyo district attorney wants to save face, he should put them both in jail along with Bob Arum, the Top Rank, Inc., promoter.

Yes, the Travesty was brought to you by the same people who brought you Evel Knievel vs. The Snake River Canyon nearly two years ago. "Got to be a winner or a loser," Evel Knievel kept saying, alluding to the specter of death. "Can't be no draw." But it was a draw. Even so, at least Evel's rocket, with Evel in it, bounced down the rocks of the canyon. Evel survived. The rocks provided a sense of honesty for the occasion. Rocks can't be fixed.

And on Friday night, the Travesty in Tokyo was announced as a draw. It really was no contest. It should have been scored on a o-point must system.

But for those familiar with Bob Arum's theatrical flair, there is some hope of justice, or maybe injustice. Bob Arum also announced that Evel Knievel would receive $6 million, but the daredevil is whispered to have received only $200,000—the $6 million was a number Bob Arum used in order to top the $5 million that Ali and George Foreman each had been guaranteed by Don King for their Zaire bout. Bob Arum also had to jump on a train for Switzerland to escape financial questions after the recent Ali–Richard Dunn bout in Munich.

"I didn't know how good a promoter I was," Don King says now, "until I saw some of these other promotions."

Although the reputable Madison Square Garden promoters have organized Ali's next appearance, his September 28 title defense against Ken Norton at Yankee Stadium, be forewarned that Bob Arum is part of that promotion, too. But that only adds to the odor of the Travesty in Tokyo. With another alleged $6 million at stake, Muhammad Ali was not about to break a bone. He did not even break a sweat.

On the live card at Shea Stadium, another boxer, Chuck Wepner, and a wrestler, Andre the Giant, at least earned their money by entertaining the 32,897 spectators. Chuck Wepner tried to punch and Andre the Giant tried to grab him. In the third round, Andre butted Wepner, scooped him up and tossed him out of the ring. Andre was declared the winner when Wepner did not return to the ring within twenty seconds.

The ethics there were suspect too. Chuck Wepner, the Bayonne Bleeder, has been known to bleed when kissed on the forehead by small children. But when Andre the Giant butted him there, Chuck did not bleed. That's entertainment.

But there was nothing entertaining about the Travesty in Tokyo that even offended the wrestlers, past and present, gathered at Shea Stadium for the occasion. Antonino Rocca, Bruno Sammartino and Gorilla Monsoon were ashamed of Inoki's reluctance to attack Ali and thereby defend the honor of wrestlers everywhere.

"It is big gar-bahge," Antonino Rocca thundered. "You've got to take chances. If he don't come to you, go to him. Don't sit there. Nobody worth a penny."

"When people pay money, you've obligated to bust your butt," Bruno Sammartino said. "Ali threw four jabs in fifteen rounds and Inoki just sat there. He's finished in Japan now. All he had to do was rush him, take a few punches and grab him. Once you hook his arms in the middle of the ring and get him down, he's at your mercy."

"In order for there to be action," Gorilla Monsoon said, "the wrestler has to move in there, he has got to take that chance."

Antonio Inoki either didn't have the guts to take that chance or he was under orders not to. In years to come, Antonio Inoki won't be remembered other than as the wrestler who opposed Muhammad Ali, but the "Farcial" Arts match is now part of Muhammad Ali's lore. With that in mind, another scene in Lewiston, Me., is worth recalling.

In the days before the bout there, James J. Braddock, once the world heavyweight champion, was talking about the new champion.

"He's good," James J. Braddock said, "but he don't have the dignity a champion should have."

That assessment of Muhammad Ali was never more apparent than in the Travesty in Tokyo.

(June 27, 1977)

About ten days later my phone rang. Bob Arum had returned to New York and he was calling to complain about the column. But during our conversation he acknowledged that the $6 million guarantee to Evel Knievel had been a publicity stunt.

"I shouldn't have done that," he said.

As it developed, Arum's alleged $6 million guarantee to Ali also did not materialize. Of that $6 million, $3 million was to come from the *first* $3 million that Top Rank, Inc., collected; the other $3 million was to come from two Japanese promotional firms. But of that $3 million from the Japanese firms, only $1.8 million was assured by a letter of credit; the other $1.2 million represented a tax credit. In the ripoff, Ali's role suddenly had changed from ripper to rippee.

"It confirms my principle," Ali's manager, Herbert Muhammad, told me at the time, "of getting all the money in the bank ahead of time. I didn't do it this time."

Ali eventually collected about $2 million from the Travesty in Tokyo—not bad, but not the $6 million that Bob Arum had advertised. But the day Arum phoned me, the thrust of his argument was that he couldn't understand why I had knocked his Ali-Inoki promotion.

"What," he complained, "are you doing to me?"

"What," I said, "are you doing to the public?"

Using the "buyer beware" theory, promoters often treat the public with disdain. And more than most sports, boxing is infamous for its shameless villains. One of them surfaced in 1978:

One of boxing's most notorious scoundrels, Francis (Blinky) Palermo, has filed an application with the Pennsylvania Athletic Commission for a manager's license. Instead of Blinky, perhaps Brazen would now be a better nickname. For the Pennsylvania commission to grant Blinky Palermo a manager's license would be like a law school hiring Richard Nixon as an ethics professor. But strangely, the commission chairman, Howard McCall, sounds sympathetic to Blinky's case.

"Back when I was a trainer," Howard McCall told Tom Cushman of the Philadelphia *Daily News,* who broke the story yesterday, "I never had any trouble with Blinky."

Perhaps he never had trouble with Blinky because he did not have any boxers worthy of Blinky's attention, or perhaps Howard McCall is not much of a student of boxing history. For every responsible citizen in Pennsylvania, beginning with Governor Milton Shapp, who has the ultimate control of the commission, a refresher course in Blinky history is suggested before the meeting on January 23 in Philadelphia when his application is scheduled to be considered.

Nicknamed for his fluttering eyelids, Blinky Palermo was a Philadelphia numbers racketeer who graduated into being a henchman of the late Frankie Carbo in the underworld control of boxing two decades ago. He was convicted with Carbo in 1961 of conspiracy and extortion after trying to muscle in on the earnings of Don Jordan, then a welterweight champion. Sentenced to fifteen years, he was paroled in 1971 from the Lewisburg (Pa.) Federal Penitentiary.

Through the years, boxing has never been known for attracting seminarians as managers. But that conviction should be enough to eliminate Blinky Palermo from consideration as a licensed boxing manager. It is one thing for a boxing commissioner to license a promoter, such as Don King, or a boxer, such as the late Sonny Liston, who has done time in the slammer for crimes not connected to boxing. That's rehabilitation. It is quite another to license a manager who was once convicted for a crime against boxing. That's scandalous.

Not that Blinky has necessarily been waiting for a license. In recent months he has been suspected of manipulating the career of Jimmy Young, although the Philadelphia heavyweight's licensed co-managers, Jack Levin and Ray Kelly, have denied that Blinky is anything more than a social acquaintance in Joe Frazier's gym, where Jimmy Young trains, and a customer in Jack Levin's electrical-supply store.

"He comes in my store," Jack Levin acknowledged before the Young–Ken Norton fight two months ago, "to buy lighting fixtures."

At the store yesterday, Jack Levin's son told a caller that his father had departed Sunday night for Rio de Janeiro on vacation. Ray Kelly also was not available.

"Ray Kelly is elusive," Jack Levin's son said. "I never know where to find him. He is Mr. Elusive. He's never around."

At the age of seventy-three, it is not likely that Blinky Palermo suddenly has a whim to be a licensed manager again. It is much more likely that he has a fighter in mind, if not in hand.

According to some Philadelphia boxing people, Blinky has more than half a dozen fighters in hand, including Jimmy Young, one of the heavyweight contenders. Blinky's control of Jimmy Young has been suspect ever since Jack Levin and Ray Kelly purchased the heavyweight's contract from Frank Gelb, another Philadelphia manager, more than two years ago for what Gelb called "much, much, much more money" than he expected.

Several months ago Jack Levin met with Ben Thompson, a California promoter who is hoping to arrange a Muhammad Ali–Young bout.

"There were two other strange guys at that meeting, two guys Thompson didn't know, two guys that Levin didn't introduce," one boxing man says. "The two guys kept saying that they would have to get back to somebody else before a deal could be made. Thompson finally asked, 'Well, who's the manager?' And one of the two guys said, 'None of your business who the manager is.' "

Equally mysterious, Blinky's application was filed with the Pennsylvania Athletic Commission last Friday by a lawyer who somehow has remained unidentified thus far by the commission. But perhaps the commission was fooled by the name on the application. Not everybody would recognize the name Francis Palermo or Frank Palermo; not even the late Sonny Liston recognized it at a Senate hearing investigating underworld control of boxing. At the time Frank Palermo was suspected of being Sonny Liston's guardian angel.

"Do you know a Frank Palermo?" Sonny Liston was asked.

"No," the boxer said. "I never heard of Frank Palermo."

After several similar questions and answers, Sonny Liston finally said, "You mean Blinky, yeah, I know Blinky, everybody knows him."

And just about everybody in boxing did know him. Sugar Ray Robinson once told about an incident early in his career when Blinky was handling numbers and fights on a Philadelphia street corner. Sugar Ray was in town to box Al Nettlow when Blinky motioned to him to join him near the newsstand on the street corner.

"Is it all set?" Blinky said.

"Is what all set?" Sugar Ray said.

"You'll find out," Blinky said.

Unknown to him, Sugar Ray discovered that it had been arranged for him to carry Al Nettlow for the scheduled ten rounds. "Al was a nice little guy," Sugar Ray recalled. "I didn't have any reason to measure him. For two rounds he was no trouble but in the third he swatted me with a good right hand and I let go a left hook." Nettlow was counted out. At the newsstand later that night, Sugar Ray tried to explain to Blinky.

"It was an accident," Sugar Ray said. "I just happened to catch him."

"It's all right," Blinky Palermo said. "Nothin' we can do about it now."

But the Pennsylvania Athletic Commission can do something about Blinky Palermo's application.

(January 10, 1978)

Shuffling out of the shadows, Blinky appeared before the commission and pleaded his case. He talked of how he wanted a license to "help the kids at the Montgomery County Boys Club stay out of trouble." Such benevolence, of course, does not require a manager's license. Blinky also contended he had "no financial interest in no fighter, none." But when Jimmy Young's co-manager, Jack Levin, testified that Blinky had been present at the meeting with Ben Thompson regarding an Ali-Young bout, Blinky obviously had been one of "two other strange guys there" that I had mentioned in the column. I phoned Bill Caplan, who had been in that meeting as Thompson's associate and had been my source for the anonymous quote I had used in the column.

"Remember the two strange guys at that meeting," I told him. "Levin testified that one of them was Blinky."

"The old guy was Blinky!" Bill said, almost in shock. "I'd seen the other guy [identified by Levin as Sandy Sands] around before in boxing offices but he didn't say much. I never realized until now that the old guy was Blinky, and he was doing most of the talking."

Bill told me that Levin had been offered a $25,000 nonreturnable option bonus to sign the contract but that Blinky had demanded a $100,000 bonus.

"We were flabbergasted that they were turning us down," Bill told me. "The two million dollars [offered to Young] was ten times what Young got for the George Foreman fight. At one point Ben reminded Blinky that Levin had told him everything was all set, but Blinky said, 'Yeah, but Jack doesn't make all the decisions.' That's when I said, 'Well, who does then? If he's not the manager, who is?' And that's when Blinky said, 'None of your business who the manager is.'

I didn't pursue the manager thing after that. I mean, I got guts, but I don't have that much guts. I mean, we were in Philly."

And now I was wondering if Bill Caplan had the guts to be quoted this time.

"By the way, Bill," I said, "I want to make sure that I spell your name right when I use these quotes in the column. Is it C-a-?"

"That's right," he said. "C-a-p-l-a-n."

At a commission meeting a month later, Blinky withdrew his application for a manager's license, whining that he had been harassed by the media because of his background. Tom Cushman of the Philadelphia *Daily News* and Robert J. Boyle of *Sports Illustrated* also had denounced him. "I think," Blinky said, "the media is very unfair."

Adversaries always think that.

7 · Hockey

I believe I'm the only sportswriter ever to pay a fine to the National Hockey League; not that *I* was fined, but I once shared a $500 fine with Andy Bathgate of the New York Rangers for a magazine piece that we had done together. His by-line, my grammar. The article, which appeared in the Canadian insert of *True* magazine in its January 1960 issue, warned that "spearing," which is hockey's version of the fixed bayonet, "is going to kill somebody." The title was "Atrocities on Ice," and when Milt Dunnell, the Toronto *Star* sports columnist, devoted his column to the piece, his newspaper put it on top of page one under a red headline: "Jungle Law in NHL—Bathgate." The headline was justified.

"Jungle law rules hockey," the article explained. "If somebody gets you, then you get him. Maybe it takes a while—a year, two years, maybe as long as five years. But someday you know you'll get your chance. I'm waiting for a shot at a few guys myself—with my fists."

Andy Bathgate had intended the article to be constructive criticism of a dangerous situation. But instead of accepting it that way from the N.H.L.'s most valuable player the previous season, Clarence Campbell, then the N.H.L. president, ruled it "inflammatory" and fined Andy the $500 he had been paid by the magazine—not a bad fee in those days. I also had received $500 as my share of the total $1,000 payment. I was covering the Rangers for the *Journal-*

American then, and the next time I saw Andy I handed him my personal check for $250.

"We split the fee," I told him. "We'll split the fine."

Andy smiled, folded the check and put it in his wallet. "Thanks," he said. But he didn't have to thank me. He already had thanked me by standing behind every word in the article. Through all the controversy that had swirled around him for nearly two weeks before the fine, he never complained that he had been misquoted, he never backed down on a comma. That's class. And it provided the article with even more credibility.

"Yes," he told the other sportswriters, "I would do it all over again."

In a sense, he did. Several days after all the newspaper headlines that the fine had generated, the *True* editors decided to reprint the piece in their March issue with its full United States circulation as one of the leading men's monthly magazines then. For the reprint, Andy and I each received another $500 fee, which meant that we each netted $750 instead of our original $500, all because of the headlines created by the fine.

I've always meant to thank Clarence Campbell for the fine that turned out to be worth an extra $250 to me.

At the time the N.H.L. lumped spearing with cross-checking and butt-ending among its violations that called for a two-minute minor penalty or a five-minute major penalty at the discretion of the referee, along with an automatic $25 fine if injury resulted. And the N.H.L. was not about to make any changes. That would justify Bathgate's warning. But quietly, eighteen months later, spearing suddenly was isolated in the rule book. And eventually the N.H.L. decreed that spearing now called for a five-minute major penalty and an automatic $50 fine if injury resulted—still a wrist slap.

In retrospect, Andy Bathgate's warning was more intelligent than inflammatory.

But the N.H.L. has been invariably slow in recognizing unnecessary violence. By its nature, hockey is a violent game. Its speed makes it a collision sport, not a contact sport. And unlike most other games, each competitor has a stick in his hands—a weapon, if the player prefers. Too many players do. In the nine seasons I covered the Rangers for the *Journal-American,* I enjoyed the fury of hockey but I abhorred the unnecessary tactics which inspired the article Andy

Bathgate and I did. When the Philadelphia Flyers won the Stanley Cup in both 1974 and 1975 by intimidating other teams, I didn't accept it as part of the game. Early in the 1975–76 season, Bobby Hull didn't accept it either:

After only three weeks of the season, hockey already has its man of the year. Bobby Hull sat down to be counted.

In protesting the degrading violence that keeps spreading deeper into the hockey psyche, Bobby Hull went on strike. He didn't play for the Winnipeg Jets in their World Hockey Association game against the Denver Spurs last Friday night. Missing one game was enough. "I accomplished," he says, "what I wanted to." He had embarrassed hockey with his sitdown strike. Hockey doesn't blush easily but it did this time. If somebody such as Bobby Hull, a left wing of muscle and conscience, is angry enough not to play in protest, perhaps something really is wrong—not only in the W.H.A. but also in the National Hockey League, where the Philadelphia Flyers have popularized mugging. Violence permeates all hockey today, from small boys to men presumably old enough to know better. What incensed Bobby Hull involved small boys as well as men presumably old enough to know better.

"The incident last week that provoked me not to play," Hull says, "was only the last straw."

After a Jets' goal by Veli Ketola, two members of the Cincinnati Stingers assaulted the Finnish center behind the net and Perry Miller went to his teammate's rescue. In the scuffle, another Stinger blind-sided Miller in the left eye. Miller missed two games with cloudy vision. When the Jets oppose the Stingers in Winnipeg tonight, Miller probably will be wearing a protective mask. Hull had been burdened by another straw since last winter when his twelve-year-old son, Blake, was involved in a bench-clearing brawl in a neighborhood game. Blake later was scolded by his father but Blake wasn't that contrite.

"I'm the Dave Schultz of my team," Blake said.

"Is that the type you want to emulate?" his father said of the Flyers' licensed thug who served a record 472 penalty minutes last season. "If you want a model don't take Dave Schultz, he's not a hockey player. Take somebody like Gil Perreault or Stan Mikita."

Or somebody like Bobby Hull.

"Schultz doesn't play hockey," Hull was saying now over the telephone from his Winnipeg home. "When the Flyers were in Montreal not long ago, all Schultz did was to try to goad Guy Lafleur into a fight. That's not hockey. I never saw the film of the Dave Forbes–Henry Boucha thing in Minnesota last season, but last Saturday night when the Bruins and the Canadiens had a bench-clearing, I saw Forbes and Ken Hodge and Wayne Cashman at mid-ice laughing and snickering as if that had been the right thing to do. Kids see that and they think that's hockey. It seems like nobody is teaching kids how to skate, how to shoot, how to position themselves. The imagination of the game doesn't seem to count anymore."

Bobby Hull's imagination and scorching shot have produced 787 goals in nineteen seasons in the N.H.L. and the W.H.A., second only to Gordie Howe's two-league total of 852 goals. Howe is forty-seven years old; Hull will be thirty-seven in January.

"Setting an example for kids should be hockey's main theme," Hull continued. "Body-checking and aggressiveness is part of hockey. So is the odd fight because of the tempo. But not the stuff that's going on. The intimidation. The stick-swinging, flailing it like an ax. The high stick. The spear. That's not hockey. Intimidation isn't hockey."

Intimidation has increased with N.H.L. expansion and the formation of the W.H.A., which Hull stabilized by accepting a reported $2.5 million contract from the Jets to leave the Chicago Black Hawks.

"I've been part of it," Hull acknowledged. "But if there were the proper people in the front offices and the proper people coaching, this wouldn't be going on. Don't tell me there aren't enough guys around who want to play hockey the way it should be played. Some of the new coaches were little guys who got the hell kicked out of them in the minor leagues and now they're getting even by putting together a team of tough guys to kick the hell out of everybody else.

"Hockey also doesn't give the referee an iron hand. Give him the power to assess a stiffer penalty for the aggressor in a fight and for the third man in. Make it something that will hurt the team. Just a ten-minute penalty and a fine isn't enough. The team pays the fine anyway. And crack down quickly. If a guy gets away with a cross-check, he'll cross-check higher the next time. There are too many guys now who just hack and bang out there."

Bobby Hull has been accused of an ulterior motive in protesting violence because the Jets' roster includes nine European players who thrive on artistry.

"But these Europeans are showing us how the game should be played," Hull said. "It's no secret that the Europeans have gone ahead of the Canadians in textbook hockey—the Soviets, the Czechs, even the Swedes and Finns. But instead of learning from what they've developed, and making hockey a better game, we're tolerating people and things that are forcing a deterioration of the game."

Bobby Hull is trying to help hockey, if anyone will listen before it's too late.

"Before," he said, "something happens that will end a career or cause death."

(October 31, 1975)

Not long after that two Soviet teams, the Central Army and the Wings, toured eight N.H.L. cities. While the Wings were winning three of their four games (losing only to the Buffalo Sabres, 12–6), the Army team won two and tied the Montreal Canadiens before skating into the Philadelphia Spectrum in 1976 to oppose the Flyers in a historic confrontation, matching for the first time the league champions of hockey's two worlds.

It was advertised as "an international hockey event." Instead, it was an international incident.

PHILADELPHIA—In their patriotic contribution to the Bicentennial celebration, the Broad Street Bullies, alias the Philadelphia Flyers, alias the Stanley Cup champions, bisected the touring Soviet Central Army hockey team today, 4–1, and upheld the Spectrum's reputation as the cradle of licensed muggings. The triumph of terror over style could not have been more one-sided if Al Capone's mob had ambushed the Bolshoi Ballet dancers. Naturally, it warmed the hearts of the Flyers' followers, who would cheer for Frankenstein's monster if he could skate. Warmth was important because the temperature inside the Spectrum was as chilly as the atmosphere, as if somebody had left a window open in Siberia somewhere. The chill developed into a freeze when the Soviet team returned to its dressing room for sixteen minutes during a scoreless first period in a protest of the Flyers' tendency to use their (a) shoulders, (b) elbows, (c) sticks, (d) all of the above. But the National Hockey League president, Clarence Campbell, persuaded the Soviet delegation to accept detente. As it turned out, they also accepted defeat, the Army team's only loss after two victories and a tie. In international policy, perhaps Clarence Campbell should give Dr. Henry Kissinger a few lessons.

"This is no way to terminate a series of this kind," Campbell advised Vyacheslav Koloskov, the Brezhnev of Soviet hockey. "You must resume."

Koloskov agreed, and he quickly convinced Konstantin Loktev, the Soviet coach who had removed his red-uniformed team from the bench.

Andrei Gromyko never stalked out of the United Nations with more style, or less reason, considering that the Russians knew how the Flyers play before they scheduled this tour. The most honorable thing about the Flyers is that they're not sneaky. Ed Van Impe, an elderly defenseman, proved that when he massaged Valery Kharlamov's brain and the Soviet left wing, who is considered their best player, as a left wing should be, curled up on the ice like caviar on a cracker. Moments later Loktev did his Gromyko imitation.

"I had just come out of the penalty box," said Van Impe, as comfortable there as he is in his easy chair at home. "He was looking down to pick up the puck. And when he looked up, I was there."

To some viewers of the TV replay, it appeared that Van Impe's elbow was mostly there. Some of the Russians later contended that Van Impe had slugged him with his gloved hand. At least nobody indicted his stick.

"It was," Van Impe testified, "my right shoulder."

"Not your elbow," he was asked, "or not your glove?"

"Oh, no," he said with a thin smile, "but I think I hit him, anyway. If he had done that to me, I would've just gone to the bench. It was ridiculous to take the team off the ice. I bumped him pretty good, but not like he was dead. He looked like he was on show-time."

But with the Army team the nucleus of their Olympic squad next month at Innsbruck, the Russians were concerned about injuries.

"In that case," Ed Van Impe said, "they should've played somebody else or they should've stayed home. They know who we are."

In the negotiations the Russians requested that their two-minute penalty for delay of game should be erased, but Campbell remained firm.

"You can't change the rules," said the one-time military attorney at the Nuremberg trials, "in the middle of the game."

Whether the Soviet players had been intimidated is difficult to tell, because only seventeen seconds after the game had resumed the Flyers scored on a goal by Reggie Leach, a right wing who leads the N.H.L. with 27 goals. After that the Russians appeared deflated as the Flyers, persistent forecheckers, anyway, kept them pinned at mid-ice most of the time.

"They do a lot of unnecessary skating," said Fred Shero, the Flyers' coach. "They do a lot of retreating, hoping to get one man to leave his position. But we wouldn't be enticed out of position. It takes patience to beat them. Bobby Clarke knew that from having played for Team Canada against the Soviets in the 1972 series, and he told our forwards."

At his locker Bobby Clarke wore a rosette of blood on his forehead, a souvenir of Viktor Kutergin's stick.

"It was an accident," the Flyers' captain said seriously. "He came right over and apologized when it happened."

That's more than any of the Flyers did, but then they're not hypocrites. They marveled at the Soviet goaltender, Vladislav Tretyak, a spiderman who made forty-five saves, almost all of them spectacular. And when the game ended, the Flyers and Russians shook hands, as they had after the introductions when they exchanged gifts.

"Somebody told me we got little pennants and pins," Clarke said. "I don't know. I haven't looked at them."

In keeping with the N.H.L. tradition, the Soviet Army players each received a lucite plaque with the Flyers' crest on it. They can add it to their collection of plaques with the crests of the New York Rangers, Montreal Canadiens and Boston Bruins, their other opponents. But the Army players had been hoping for a different gift this time. They didn't realize that the Flyers would really give them the business.

(January 12, 1976)

The next day the Philadelphia *Bulletin* printed excerpts from that column, notably the line that the Flyers' followers "would cheer for Frankenstein's monster, if he could skate." Suddenly the City of Brotherly Love had none for me.

That column provoked the most mail I've ever received, about 110 letters, all angry and all from the Philadelphia area except for one thoughtful epistle from a gentleman in Vermont who agreed with me. About two weeks later Joe Kadlec, the Flyers' public relations director, phoned.

"We're doing a TV show on 'The Retreat of the Red Army,' " he said. "We'd like you to be on the panel."

What the hell, I figured, why not, but I had a question—who else would be on the panel with me?

"Fred Shero and Bobby Clarke and Ed Van Impe and Frank Udvari [the N.H.L. supervisor of officials]," Joe said, "and the moderator will be Gene Hart, our TV broadcaster."

"Anybody else on *my* side?" I asked.

"Well, no," Joe said. "Not exactly."

I went anyway. As it turned out, Clarke and Van Impe didn't show up, so I never got elbowed the way Kharlamov did. And about a week later I even got a letter from somebody in the Philadelphia area praising my courage for showing up. But that didn't take any courage. Words are my business. Skating onto the ice against the Flyers, that would have taken courage. But eventually the Flyers went too far. In the Stanley Cup playoffs later that year, three Flyers were arrested in Toronto on five counts of assault and one count of brandishing a dangerous weapon (a hockey stick). The charges were dismissed later, but the Flyers got the message from Roy McMurtry, the Ontario attorney general, who was determined that the next great hockey coach shall not be Angelo Dundee.

In the 1976 Stanley Cup final a few weeks later, the Flyers got another message:

All around him, his players were guzzling champagne or chug-a-lugging beer or singing or laughing or quietly enjoying the moment of having won the Stanley Cup, but Scotty Bowman, the coach of the Montreal Canadiens, wasn't even smiling.

"We've still got to look at our game," Scotty Bowman said. "I hope this series doesn't change the thinking."

For two years, the Philadelphia Flyers had held the Stanley Cup, held it between clenched fists. But now the Montreal Canadiens had dethroned them. The only thing the Canadiens clenched were their teeth. Traditionally, the Canadiens are a hockey team of skill and speed. Style really. They appear to be skating in Pierre Cardin velvet blazers. Not that there aren't some muscles under the velvet. And a few elbows. But basically, the Canadiens play hockey the way it's supposed to be played. By sweeping the Flyers in four games, they recorded a triumph for law and order; a philosophy that the National Hockey League has occasionally winked at. But realists, such as Scotty Bowman, hope that the Canadiens' victory won't erase the embarrassment that the Flyers had created with their brawling intimidation until Roy McMurtry, the Ontario attorney general, intimidated them by arresting four players on assault charges. That's really law and order. Suddenly the Flyers' coach, Fred Shero, told his players, "No more cheap penalties, let's play hockey." And the Flyers played hockey very well, but the Canadiens played it even better.

"We've got to police our game," Scotty Bowman said. "And we've got to do it quickly."

"Quickly" might mean next week. That's when the N.H.L. Rules Committee will meet in Chicago to consider several proposed rule changes in a communique titled "re: alleged violence," following a conference involving Clarence Campbell, the N.H.L. president, and the referees. In the past, Clarence Campbell excused fights as a "safety-valve" release for excitable athletes. But now he has expanded his vocabulary by recognizing such words as "intimidation," "punishment" and even the word "starts," as in "starts a fight." The proposals also include a recommendation that "referees be directed to use every means to stop brawling," which the N.H.L. used to pretend didn't exist. Among the recommendations are:

"If, in the opinion of the referee, any player who persists to continue fisticuffs or who resists stoppage by the linesmen of fisticuffs, shall receive a game-misconduct penalty.

"If, in the opinion of the referee, any player who starts fisticuffs for the intent and purpose of intimidation or punishment, shall receive major and game-misconduct penalties.

"If a player incurs a total of three game-misconduct or gross-misconduct penalties, he shall be suspended for one game. For his fourth misconduct penalty that season, he shall be suspended for two games; for his fifth, three games, etc. In addition, his club shall be fined $1,000 for each suspension."

As radical as these proposals are, Scotty Bowman would prefer a much longer suspension.

"It should be ten games, not one," the Canadiens' coach says. "Make it so powerful that you can't risk having the guy on your team."

Bill Jennings, the New York Rangers' president, also prefers stricter rules for fisticuffs.

"Make it that the instigator of a fight, or a participant if two are to blame," Jennings says, "shall receive a major penalty, a game-misconduct penalty and an automatic one-game suspension. For his second fight, he would be suspended two games; for his third fight, three games and so on. And the club fines should be one thousand dollars for the first fight by any player on its team, two thousand dollars for the second by the same player or another player and so on up to a five-thousand-dollar limit. That way a team can't have player X, player Y and player Z in fights without it costing them more each time."

According to Bill Jennings, even the Flyers' executives agreed with the spirit of the rule changes when he last spoke with them. Apparently, even the Flyers have begun to realize that the N.H.L. must police itself, quickly, before an assault conviction occurs and a player is put in a penalty box by a turnkey instead of a timekeeper.

Until those rule changes occur, hockey aficionados must be content with the memory of the Canadiens' crusade for class. "I hope the little kids," Jean Beliveau, one of the Canadiens' living legends, said, "have watched these games." If they did, they hopefully realized that Guy Lafleur, not Dave Schultz, is a hockey player to emulate. Guy Lafleur is known among his teammates as "the Flower," the English translation of his name. He's a rose with thorns—soft, but dangerous. When he skates, his brown hair flutters in the wind he has created. And when he shoots, he often scores.

He had 56 goals during the regular season and 7 in the playoffs, including the winning goal in Sunday night's 5–3 victory in Philadelphia.

"I think it's good for hockey that we won," Guy Lafleur said quietly. "We play hockey. No brutality. We showed we could win without that."

Now it's up to the N.H.L. to show that any team can win without it, that hockey players just have to clench their teeth, not their fists.

(May 18, 1976)

The new champions and the new rules restored law and order to hockey. There's still an occasional melee. There always will be. But mugging shouldn't be part of a team's strategy. Gordie Howe never mugged anybody. He had his fights, notably a famous brawl in 1959 with Lou Fontinato, a husky Rangers' defenseman. And when provoked, he protected himself with a sneaky stick and a sneaky elbow. But that, too, is part of the game, especially for a player who always was a marked man:

Gordie Howe doesn't count his years or goals. He will be fifty in March and a grandfather in April, but he is still skating easily in the World Hockey Association, and any game now for the New England Whalers he will score his thousandth goal.

"I didn't know about it," he said, "until they told me. Does it include the ones in Omaha?"

No, it does not include the 22 goals he scored for Omaha in the old United States Hockey League during the 1945–46 season, mostly when he was still seventeen years old. But in the next twenty-five seasons with the Detroit Red Wings of the National Hockey League, he scored a record 786 goals and added 67 in the Stanley Cup playoffs. He retired, but when the W.H.A. was formed two years later, he returned to play with his sons, Marty and Mark, now twenty-three and twenty-two, respectively. Now in his fifth W.H.A. season, he has scored 126 goals plus 20 in the playoffs. That's a total of 999 as the Whalers await tonight's game with the Indianapolis Racers at the Hartford Civic Center. In his glory seasons, Gordie Howe inspired hockey people to revere him as perhaps the best athlete of our time. People in other sports scoffed. But nobody scoffs anymore. Gordie Howe surely has been the most durable athlete of our time, especially in such a demanding game. Gordie Howe is more than a superstar; he is a superman.

"I don't know how to explain it," he said over the telephone from his Hartford home, "except that I never gave up."

Even during his two-year retirement, Gordie Howe continued to play hockey in an old-timers' league in the Detroit area.

"Sometimes we'd play against disk jockeys and writers," he said. "I remember Paul Anka, he grew up in Canada, he would call one of the disk jockeys and tell him, 'I'm coming in, get a game.' And we'd be waiting for him. He's so small, if he had high heels he still wouldn't be tall."

"Did you check him?" Gordie Howe was asked.

"No, he always played with me," he replied, laughing. "But when the W.H.A. came along I hadn't really been away. Back when I was younger, when a guy got to be thirty-three, thirty-four, if he had a bad year, the Red Wings would write him off and he'd go home to the prairies. I kept going until I was forty-three and the Red Wings didn't exactly write me off, but they didn't encourage me. My left wrist was really aching. I had to have a bone removed. I scored twenty-three goals that last season, but I'd been a one-armed hockey player. But then I started shooting golf in the seventies, and when the W.H.A. started up I thought I'd give it a try to play with my boys."

That's what he does each year now—give it a try at training camp.

"I saw Al Kaline at a baseball game in Detroit last summer and he asked me what I was going to do, and I told him, 'I think I'll give it a try,' and he said, 'You're really gonna play again?' and he fell off his chair."

Skeptics wonder if Gordie Howe could still be playing in the N.H.L. at his age if the merger had been completed.

"Sure, he could," says John Ferguson, the New York Rangers' general manager, "and he would probably score twenty goals."

As the Whalers won five, lost one and tied one in exhibition games with N.H.L. teams recently, Gordie Howe had five assists.

"Except for Montreal, Boston, Toronto, Philadelphia and the Islanders, when they're going good, the leagues are about the same," Gordie Howe said. "It's too bad the merger didn't go through. I honestly believe a merger would have done away with the negatives we've been hearing about for so long. Anytime you knock anything, some people will believe it even when it isn't true. Like the first year, Ted Lindsay [once his Red Wing linemate and now the Detroit general manager] commented that the W.H.A. must be in bad shape because Gordie Howe is leading the league. That hurt. We spent a lot of time on the ice together. We're not on good speaking terms now. He also said something not long ago that there were only two good players in our leagues, Bobby Hull and Anders Hedberg, but now he has a couple of former W.H.A. players on the Red Wings."

Gordie Howe has produced five goals and fourteen assists this season on a line with his son Mark at left wing and Tom Webster at right wing.

"I'm a center now, not a right winger," he said, laughing again. "I call it the Doughnut Line, no center."

Mark has scored four goals this season while Marty, a defenseman now out with a fractured cheekbone, has scored two.

"I remember when I scored my five-hundredth or six-hundredth goal, Mark asked me how many goals I had, and when I told him, he said, 'I should get there, I got eleven already.' He was maybe seven years old then. Another time Marty was talking to Johnny Bower, the old Toronto goal-tender, and Johnny told him, 'If you want to stay in this game a long time, worry about this end of the ice,' meaning his own end, but Marty said, 'Yeah, but I like scoring goals.' "

Mark's wife, Ginger, is expecting their first child, which would make Gordie Howe a grandfather during the playoffs.

"Imagine that, a grandpa still playing," he said. "But the games aren't as hard as the practices. I push it until about Christmas, but after that I take a day off from practice now and then."

Surprisingly, he doesn't jog or lift weights to keep himself in shape.

"That year I played for Team Canada," said Gordie Howe, "they did some stress tests on the players and the doctor told me I wasn't as old as my age, that I had tested out better than a lot of the younger guys."

Anybody who has ever seen Gordie Howe play hockey over three decades does not need a stress test to know that.

(November 12, 1977)

Gordie Howe eventually scored his thousandth goal. And many more. If he keeps playing into 1980, he will have skated in parts of five decades—the forties, the fifties, the sixties, seventies and eighties. Now, that is a superman.

8·Unforgettables

I don't write much horse racing. I like to talk to athletes, and in horse racing I've found that the actual athletes, the horses, are always unavailable for comment. The jockeys are athletes, of course, and they're good talkers; so are some of the owners and trainers. But the horse is *the* athlete and the horse is unavailable, so I only go to the racetrack occasionally.

And yet one of my favorite moments occurred in 1973, when Secretariat completed his Triple Crown by winning the Belmont Stakes by thirty-one lengths.

Despite his poor vocabulary, Secretariat is one of my unforgettable characters. The day of the Belmont, the horse didn't talk but I knew everyone around him would. I just stayed with the horse as much as I could:

On a tiny portable TV set atop a midnight-green Cadillac parked outside the Meadow Stable barn at Belmont Park yesterday, a voice was saying, ". . . and that horse, named Secretariat. . . ." Minutes later, deep in the shadows of the green-and-white barn, the three-year-old chestnut emerged from his stall.

"Clear it out," somebody was yelling now outside the barn. "Clear it out. The horse is coming."

About ten people, a few newsmen but mostly spectators, had been gathered at the barn for half an hour, the way people wait for a heavyweight champion to come out of his dressing room before a title fight. And now, with a blue bridle contrasting with his glistening chestnut coat, the horse followed a gray lead pony into the warm sun as a breeze fluttered the leaves of the small oak trees. Quickly, with his groom, Eddie Sweat, holding the blue reins, the horse turned down into the tunnel that leads to the paddock.

"Go get that money," somebody yelled.

"You see why everybody has fallen in love with this horse," somebody else said as dozens of people surged into the tunnel behind him. "He's beautiful, he's just beautiful."

"Stop crying," a man said to a child. "While you're crying, you can't see the horse."

Soon, the horse was moving under the tall trees of the paddock. As he circled the walking ring, applause followed him from the spectators who surrounded it. Above, on a balcony of the red-brick-and-glass clubhouse, others peered through binoculars.

"Bravo," somebody called. "Bravo, Secretariat." So large was the crowd on the grass inside the walking ring that when Ron Turcotte was about to be hoisted into the saddle, the trainer, Lucien Laurin, was unable to get through to help him. The assistant trainer, Benny Hoeffner, had to do it. And then, as the horse moved through the darkness of the underpass toward the track, applause and cheers followed him again.

"Triple Crown, baby," a young man yelled. "Triple Crown in New York, baby."

When the horse appeared on the track, a roar from the 69,138 spectators thundered out from under the roof, as if a Super Bowl team had run onto the field.

"Look at those odds," a man said. "One to nine."

But that was only because the odds board doesn't have room for three digits, as the proper odds of 1 to 10 demanded. Soon, the bell clanged in the starting gate and the horses were hurrying toward the first turn, where a red helicopter hung in the air.

"You've got a hole, baby, go," a man yelled.

Moving along the rail, Secretariat accelerated through that hole into the lead. He was in command to stay. On the backstretch, he was lengthening his lead when the Teletimer on the toteboard flashed 1:09 4/5 for six furlongs.

"He's got to come back," a man said.

But he didn't. At the mile, he had a seven-length lead. His time was flashed as 1:34 4/5.

"If he doesn't come back," somebody said, "he's a superhorse."

He didn't, and he is. He won by thirty-one lengths, the roar of the spectators rumbling to a crescendo in accompaniment as Secretariat pounded across the finish line, more alone than Greta Garbo ever was. Soon he was in the winner's circle, the first to sweep racing's Triple Crown in twenty-five years. But just as the names of thoroughbreds relate to their breeding, the names of Secretariat's owner and groom are symbolic, too.

His owner, being photographed with him now, is Mrs. Penny Tweedy, as in herringbone. His groom is Eddie Sweat, as in perspire.

All morning the groom, in a red undershirt, had cared for Secretariat and he had led him to the paddock. Now, the ceremony in the winner's circle over, he began to lead the horse through the underpass and around the paddock toward the tunnel back to the barn.

Again applause followed the horse. Some spectators ran after him, as they might a rock singer. One reached out and touched him.

"He took the heart right out of Sham," a man said. "If that son of a gun ain't an athlete, I don't know what an athlete is."

In about an hour, after the mandatory postrace chemical test and a walk, Secretariat would be back in his barn. But now, in the New York State Racing Commission Test Area, he was having saliva swabbed out of his mouth into a basin.

"To think," a woman said, looking at him, "that they're treating him like any other horse."

(June 10, 1973)

I wasn't able to talk to Pelé at first either—at least not without an interpreter to relay his Portuguese and my English. After he joined the New York Cosmos, his English improved. My Portuguese remained nonexistent. But in the years to come Pelé will not be remembered for what he said in his Jose Ferrer voice as much as for what he did for American soccer. And the way he did it:

The world's most famous soccer player, Edson Arantes do Nascimento, always says, "My nickname means nothing. Pelé. It is just a word." But in American soccer now, Pelé means everything. It is *the* word. Win or lose with the Cosmos in Soccer Bowl '77 at Portland, Ore., today, Pelé's legacy in America is assured. Most of the national television viewers won't really understand the nuances of what they're watching today, but they should be watching because Pelé has made soccer important here. Babe Ruth did that for baseball, Jack Dempsey for boxing, Bobby Jones for golf. And now, half a century later, Pelé has done it for soccer.

"Soccer is much bigger than Pelé," the Brazilian said on joining the Cosmos two years ago. "I can only show the people the game. They will decide."

But in showing the people the game, Pelé also showed them himself. And that helped them decide. Even now, at thirty-six, Pelé radiates a joy and a purity of sport that few other athletes project. At a time when greed seems to dominate many of our games, Pelé is an unspoiled superstar who smiles instead of snarls. Nobody seems to resent his $4 million contract because he has produced and because he has not complained, not sulked, not tried to renegotiate and not feuded with any of his teammates.

Whenever Pelé scores a goal, and he has scored 1,277 in his twenty-two seasons, he reacts as if it were his first, leaping high and thrusting his right fist in celebration.

In retrospect, it's perhaps significant that the Cosmos ascended in popularity this year at a time when the Yankees' egos were at their most obnoxious, when the Mets betrayed their loyalists by trading Tom Seaver, when the Giants and the Jets were reorganizing, when the Knicks and the Rangers were rebuilding, when the Nets were relocating and the Islanders were regrouping. Amid all this, here was soccer, the sport whose time had come, and here was Pelé, an idol whose time was ending. And both were at Giants Stadium, the Tiffany window of New York area sports.

Two years ago, when Pelé joined the Cosmos, they played in Downing Stadium on Randalls Island, which was like displaying the Hope diamond in a Times Square litter basket. But at Giants Stadium, he finally had the setting he deserved.

And the people responded. During the regular season, the Cosmos averaged 35,142 spectators, including a throng of 62,394 for one game. In three playoff games at Giants Stadium, they averaged nearly 70,000, including the magic number of 77,691, the largest assembly in the United States or Canada for a soccer game. That night Pelé had already been excused in the second half and was being massaged when he heard the announcement of the attendance over the public address system that is piped into the dressing room.

"That's it," he said.

Then he hugged Charlie Martinelli, the Cosmos' equipment manager, who was massaging him, and he wept. He knew his role as a missionary had been a success, he knew the people had decided. But only he could have been the missionary. Throughout the world, there are only two genuine sport superstars, Muhammad Ali and Pelé; away from the United States, not many people know or care about Henry Aaron and his 755 home runs in his baseball career or that O.J. Simpson ran for 2,003 yards in a football season. But throughout the world, people know and care what Pelé does.

"Pelé had to be the first," says Clive Toye, now the president of the Chicago Sting but then the Cosmos' president, who persuaded him to come. "The other great players around the world have to say to themselves, 'If he trusts them, I have to trust them.' And because of Pelé, other great players followed him."

George Best left England to join the Los Angeles Aztecs, and Giorgio Chinaglia of Italy and Franz Beckenbauer of West Germany joined the Cosmos.

As for Franz Beckenbauer, the presence of Pelé was among the reasons he joined the Cosmos in midseason this year instead of waiting until next year. He felt that playing with Pelé would be an "honor," as he described it. And he knew he had to do it this year because next year Pelé will not be with the Cosmos, next year would be too late—quite a contrast to how Reggie Jackson and Thurman Munson coexisted when the Yankees were producing more controversies than victories.

Not that Pelé has the North American Soccer League thriving everywhere. That will take more time. But he has made it happen in the New York area, where it had to happen for the nation to be alerted.

"I didn't expect this so quickly," Pelé says of the Cosmos' huge crowd. "I thought it would take a few more years. But everybody wants to come now. The kids bring soccer here. The kids know it is a great game. And without me next year, it will be the same. Everybody will still want to come."

The Cosmos have already announced a sellout for Pelé's farewell on October 1 in Giants Stadium, where he will play for the Cosmos in the first half and for the Santos (Brazil) team in the second half. Already people are phoning the Cosmos about season tickets next year, when Pelé will not be playing. And perhaps that is Pelé's most glorious legacy of all.

(August 28, 1977)

But in sports, Sonny Werblin holds the record for legacies—the Jets, Joe Namath, the A.F.L., Giants Stadium, the Meadowlands racetrack. He's the smartest promoter I know. The hardest-working too; maybe that's why he's the smartest. But when he took command as the Madison Square Garden impresario in 1978, most people were shocked until they thought about it for a moment. And then everything was perfectly clear.

With the Knicks, the Rangers and its boxing department struggling, the Garden was the perfect place for Sonny Werblin to work on another legacy:

One career is enough for most people and one too many for some. But yesterday sixty-seven-year-old David Abraham (Sonny) Werblin, as the new president and chief executive officer of the Madison Square Garden Corporation, began what amounts to his fourth career. His other three, in inverse order, were creating the New Jersey Sports Complex, reorganizing the New York Jets from bankruptcy to the Super Bowl, and lifting the Music Corporation of America's income from packaged TV shows to $100 million annually. But what Sonny Werblin has done in each career was best described once by *Variety,* the show-business weekly. "He is," *Variety* declared, "a master of the time-honored show-biz dodge of starting a war and selling ammunition to both sides." And, it could be added, winning the battles, if not the war, for both sides. That is really what is happening now. Sonny Werblin has been campaigning for an indoor arena in the Meadowlands that would threaten the Garden's reign. And now he's going to work for the Garden in order to beat back the potential challenge of the Meadowlands arena that he inspired. The ammunition he sells is himself.

"Two theaters are better on one block, two restaurants are better on one block," he was saying yesterday at "21," where his appointment was announced. "Gimbels always tries to move closer to Macy's."

Sonny Werblin is thought of as a sports guy now, but he's basically a show-biz guy. Always was. In his early years at MCA, he traveled with the big bands. His wife, Leah Ray, sang with Phil Harris's band. Then he was an agent for Jackie Gleason, Jack Benny and Ed Sullivan, and, in recent years, he negotiated Johnny Carson's contracts. But he sold ammunition to both sides as the president of MCA's television division. He once moved *Wagon Train* to ABC when its NBC contract expired.

"But now," said an NBC official, "we've got an empty time slot."

"Don't worry," Sonny Werblin said. "I've got a show for you."

The show was *The Virginian* and NBC bought it. And in 1964, about a year after Sonny Werblin organized the group that saved the New York franchise in the American Football League, he sold the A.F.L. television contract to NBC for $36 million. That contract was worth about $4 million to the Jets, who were worth virtually nothing when Sonny Werblin met Joe Foss, then the A.F.L. commissioner, at the Bull and Bear bar in the Waldorf-Astoria to discuss the $1.4 million price tag. While they talked, a banker from the Irving Trust Company tapped Sonny Werblin on the shoulder.

"I hope you buy the ball club, Mr. Werblin," he said. "They owe our bank four hundred thousand dollars."

When the banker departed, Sonny Werblin turned to Joe Foss and asked, "What's this about four hundred thousand dollars? Is that part of the $1.4 million price?"

"Yes, it is," Foss said.

"It's not anymore. I'll give you one million flat. I'm not buying a bankrupt ball club to pay off a bank loan. I'm only buying the club's assets, not its liabilities."

And that's all he paid—$1 million.

"It wasn't the principle," Sonny Werblin said long after without a smile. "It was the money."

Then he spent $427,000 for Joe Namath.

"I want the best show," Sonny Werblin said in 1965, when Joe Namath was the most expensive rookie in pro-football history. "And to have the best show, I have to have stars."

His stars won Super Bowl III in 1969, although he had sold his Jets stock nearly a year earlier.

Sonny Werblin, meanwhile, had created a war with the crosstown rival Giants, and soon he was selling ammunition to them—a proposed stadium in the New Jersey swamps. He had won the war for the Jets, but now he had to win the new war as the Giants' landlord, the unsalaried chairman of the New Jersey Sports and Exposition Authority. But as dazzling as Giants Stadium and the Meadowlands racetrack are now, Sonny Werblin's third career came hard. On a cold gray December day in 1972, he was among the dignitaries at a ground-breaking ceremony for the sports complex. It should have been called a water-breaking ceremony. Desolate swamps surrounded the landfill that had been imported for the occasion. Taxpayers surrounded the dignitaries.

"Werbling [sic]," a lady in a mustard-colored coat was yelling that day, "is robbing our land."

Instead of snarling back, Sonny Werblin invited that lady, Mrs. Margaret Hallaway of Kearny, to the ceremonial buffet and arranged a helicopter ride for her. He also quietly explained to her that a bond issue would pay for the complex—not the taxpayers. When the racetrack opened last year, Mrs. Hallaway was among Sonny Werblin's personal guests. And with the success of the racetrack and Giants Stadium, Sonny Werblin was planning a $20 million indoor arena that had the Garden executives worried. But now, suddenly, Sonny Werblin is the chief Garden executive.

"The Garden," he explained yesterday, "is just another spot in the megalopolis."

That's his favorite word. He doesn't believe in borders. He believes in areas. And to him, the entire New York–New Jersey area is a megalopolis, a catchy word that emerged from his show-biz instincts. And his show-biz instincts have always produced a boffo finish—$100 million in TV sales, Super Bowl III, the sports complex in a swamp.

Somehow, someday, Sonny Werblin will produce a boffo finish at Madison Square Garden, and then he'll probably be on the move again, selling ammunition to somebody else.

(December 17, 1977)

Muscle for muscle, my most unforgettable character is Wilt Chamberlain—basketball player, volleyball player, amateur weight lifter. We were waiting for the elevator once in Madison Square Garden when the doors opened and two husky workmen struggled to wheel a heavily loaded dolly into the corridor. On the dolly were ten big cartons of office supplies. The workmen kept pushing and pulling, trying to get the wheels of the dolly across the uneven slit between the elevator and the floor. Huffing and puffing, they finally dropped their hands in frustration.

"You look," Wilt said, "like you need a little help."

His massive arms unencumbered in a chocolate-brown sleeveless shirt, he reached down, grabbed the rope attached to the dolly and lifted the load into the corridor as if it were a baby in a stroller. The workmen stared and thanked him. Wilt smiled, entered the elevator and the doors closed. Pretending that I had forgotten something in a nearby office, I said goodbye to him and hurried to ask the workmen how heavy that load was.

"I never saw anything like that," one said. "These cartons weigh eighty pounds each. This load is eight hundred pounds."

For me, that memory is more unforgettable than anything Wilt ever did on a basketball court. I have another unusual memory of him too, a visit with him before and after a volleyball game in 1973, not long after his Los Angeles Lakers had lost to the New York Knicks in the NBA championship but long before he emerged as the president of the International Volleyball Association:

Outside the Staten Island Community College gym, Wilt Chamberlain emerged in sections from a brown station wagon. Inside, the basketball backboard had swung up out of the way. The seven-foot-one-inch center of the Los Angeles Lakers had arrived as a volleyball player with "The Big Dippers," his touring California team. But now, in the locker room, he was asking about Dave DeBusschere of the New York Knicks.

"What's that new job he's got?" he said.

"He's going to play one more season with the Knicks, then he'll become general manager of the Nets the following season," he was told.

"I wish he'd taken it last season," Wilt said. "He means more to the Knicks than any of their other players."

He sipped some apple juice out of a big jar he had brought with him.

"Ever since the playoffs ended I've been playing volleyball with my team," he said. "We carry six guys, including myself, but we only use four at a time against the other team's six. Volleyball is a rotating game. You have setters, who set the ball up for the hitters, or the spikers. You have your blockers, who block the other team's hits. You have your passers and your defensive players. But with only four men, we've got to have versatile players. I've got to concentrate on passing, hitting and blocking, all phases except setting."

His ambition is to compete with the United States volleyball team in the 1976 Olympics at Montreal.

"I'm an amateur volleyball player," he said, "but because I'm a professional basketball player, I'm ineligible by National Volleyball Association and A.A.U. standards. It's ridiculous. If I want to give up making half a million dollars a year as a basketball player to try out for the Olympic team, why shouldn't I be allowed to? Give me one reason."

Under the Olympic code, a professional in one sport is ineligible to compete as an amateur in another sport.

"These people should be challenged," Wilt continued. "Who gives them the right to make rules like that? If it's the President, I'm going to have to talk to ol' Nixie baby. This kind of thinking is a hundred years old. If a law becomes outdated, the Supreme Court votes to amend or change it. But nobody's doing anything about this rule."

He discovered volleyball about two and a half years ago, when he was recuperating from knee surgery midway in the basketball season.

"I used to run in the sand at Santa Monica Beach. There were guys playing volleyball there all the time. I started fooling around and I really enjoyed it. But I'm not an accomplished player."

At a nearby locker, Rudy Suwara, the captain of the United States team that performed in Cuba in 1971 and a volleyball coach at the University of California at Santa Barbara, looked up.

"You watch him," Suwara said quietly. "Spiking the ball, he's unstoppable. He's as good as anybody who ever spiked a ball. And blocking shots, he's a stonewall."

Would the United States win the Olympic volleyball gold medal if Wilt were eligible?

"I wouldn't say that," Suwara replied, "but we'd have a better chance than we do now."

Wilt's presence had filled the small gym with more than 1,500 spectators for the game against the Radigans, a team based at the Staten Island Y.M.C.A., with its own cult of followers. It is perhaps the East's best team in a game dominated in this country by California teams. The Big Dippers won easily, 15–10, 15–10, 18–20, 15–3, as Wilt produced sixteen of his team's points. Equally efficient was Suwara, Dean Selznick, Larry Rundle and Rich Riffero, but their most spectacular player was Toshi Toyoda, an acrobatic Japanese player who just about came up to the "13" on Wilt's blue-and-white uniform.

Every so often, the most prolific scorer and rebounder in National Basketball Association history smiled. Once he even laughed, his heavy "ha-ha" reaching the nearby bleachers. Another time, when Wilt flubbed a spike, a voice yelled, "We want Willis Reed," but Wilt frowned only momentarily.

Unlike the man who often scowls and sneers on a basketball court, Wilt actually seemed to be enjoying himself.

"It's a lot of fun," he was saying now in the locker room as he put on maroon slacks. "Everything being equal, I like this game more than basketball now, but mainly that's only because I've played twenty-five years of basketball. In basketball, there's a limited amount of fun. When you lose, it's no fun. Volleyball correlates with basketball in that you need a certain power to go along with skill and grace. But in basketball, there's no way to vent your frustrations like there is when you spike a volleyball. Dunking does it in basketball, but there aren't that many chances to dunk."

He took another sip of apple juice and put on a flowered black shirt.

"It's fun being the promoter of this team," he said. "We get our expenses. If we do make anything, it helps to send my girls' team, the Little Dippers, around the country, too. I'm just doing it to promote volleyball. I'd like to see better athletes come into volleyball. But right now, there's no money to be made in it. That's why I play basketball."

(June 3, 1973)

• • •

Wilt never was eligible for the Montreal Olympics, of course, but seeing an athlete like Wilt in another setting is always fun. Mostly, though, I prefer to see an athlete working at his sport. The trouble is, I seldom can get really close to him. Sportswriters aren't allowed in a baseball dugout during a game or in a football huddle. But at an auto race, I can be only a few feet away from a driver when he comes in for a pit stop.

To feel the speed and the smell and the urgency of the Indianapolis 500, I always stand near the pits. That's where I was in 1976, when A.J. Foyt thought he would win:

INDIANAPOLIS—Behind him, some spectators held up a homemade banner with a telephone drawn on it. "Victory Lane," it read, "is calling A.J.—No. 4." When they yelled to him, A.J. Foyt turned and smiled and waved. He was sitting on the low cement wall of his pit at the Indianapolis Speedway today, talking to some friends and signing autographs and watching his pit crew in red-plaid shirts tinker with the red Gilmore Special that he would be driving. A.J. Foyt has won the Indianapolis 500 three times, as did Mauri Rose and Wilbur Shaw, but he's forty-one years old now and if he is going to win it for a record fourth time, he can't wait much longer. But he's going to have to wait at least until next year because he finished second to Johnny Rutherford by 12.8 seconds today in the rain that shortened the race to 255 miles and in the controversy that shortened his fuse. To the competitor named Anthony Joseph Foyt, Jr., this Indianapolis 255 will be remembered as the mystery of the missing 19 seconds.

"I knew we had twenty-three seconds on John when the yellow came on," A.J. Foyt was saying, alluding to the yellow caution light that orders the drivers to maintain their position. "We run three times on the yellow, but when the green came on again, they gave me only four seconds. What the hell."

A.J. Foyt was sitting on the same low cement wall as he had before the race. But now, during the two-and-a-half-hour delay, he was waiting for the race to resume after a light rain. He was wondering where those 19 seconds had gone. But he believed that when the race was resumed, he somehow would win. A.J. Foyt always believes he will win, especially when he's only 12.6 seconds behind the leader. He also knew that the rain had kept him in the race.

"My front swaybar came unhooked," he said. "If it hadn't rained, I would've had to come in."

But during a delay, repairs are permitted. His pit crew installed a new front swaybar.

"It would've taken a long time to fix it," he acknowledged. "At least fifteen, twenty minutes."

"A.J. Foyt was talking optimistically, talking about how the rain might permit him to win.

"Maybe this'll be a storybook," he was saying with a smile. "You get a broken car, but then you get time to fix it and go win. If it's your day, you win. If it's not your day, you don't win. If you're not supposed to finish the race, we'll blow up. If we're supposed to win, something will happen. I believe that, I really do. Luck figures, but sometimes you make your luck."

But it wasn't A. J. Foyt's day. Just as the race was about to be resumed, the rain began falling again. On the public address system, Johnny Rutherford was declared the winner.

When he heard the announcement, A. J. Foyt slapped his right thigh in disgust, grunted "Ah, obscenity," talked to Jim Gilmore, the gray-haired millionaire sportsman who is his sponsor, and then strolled through Gasoline Alley toward his garage. He was wearing a blue baseball-type cap, his white flameproof driver's suit, black shoes with red laces and a tight-lipped scowl. Quickly, he disappeared behind the doors of his garage and huddled privately with Jim Gilmore again. A. J. Foyt remained in the garage, but Jim Gilmore appeared outside soon.

"A. J. doesn't want to say anything right now," Jim Gilmore said. "He's in deep thought about a lot of things."

A. J. Foyt possibly was thinking about an official protest of Johnny Rutherford's victory, but he probably also was thinking about how the rain had saved his swaybar problem and about how his crew goofed shortly after he pulled into his pit during the delay—he chewed out a man named Steve for not having resoldered something and he chewed out a man named Cecil for not having changed tires. He even had to intercede in a dispute in the pits when his father, known as Tony, menaced a newsman.

"Now, Daddy," he had said, pushing his father away, "now, Daddy, you calm yourself."

His father recently underwent open-heart surgery. A.J. Foyt explained that to the newsman and then said firmly, "Now if you keep this up, I'm going to have to step in myself." The newsman did not appear eager for that to happen. And so now, as he smoldered in the garage, A.J. Foyt had many things to think about. But after a few more minutes, Jim Gilmore again appeared as his spokesman.

"He's still thinking," Gilmore said, "about a lot of things."

"Is one of them," a man asked, "an official protest tomorrow about the missing nineteen seconds?"

"It goes beyond that," Gilmore said.

"Does it involve retirement then?"

"Not quite that," Gilmore answered. "I can really say that retirement would be a great surprise to me."

"Did he think the race could've been resumed sooner?"

"We sincerely believe," Jim Gilmore said, "that the officials could've resumed the race thirty-five or forty minutes sooner than they did. And if they had, we think we would've had a chance to get into first place before the rain came again."

Jim Gilmore stepped aside as a trash can of canned beer was ushered into the garage.

"As for the protest," Jim Gilmore repeated, "I doubt very much if A.J. will protest."

Inside the garage, A.J. Foyt was sipping a beer and smiling. He probably was still thinking about the mystery of the missing nineteen seconds, but maybe he also was thinking about something he had said in his pit during the delay.

"I like John Rutherford," he had said. "Hell, if I think I can get away with making up time on the yellow, I'm going to try."

(May 31, 1976)

The next year A.J. won his record fourth Indy but I wasn't near him that day. I was over with Janet Guthrie, the first woman ever to drive in that race. But after A.J. won, I remembered riding with him in midtown New York traffic. He had agreed to be a New York driver while I watched and listened. I met him at the Americana Hotel and he steered a borrowed beige Cadillac down Seventh Avenue, which was pitted from construction.

"You wouldn't have a little foreign car long on this pavement," he said. "It'd be torn up underneath."

In the garment district not far from Penn Station, he noticed a man pushing a rack cart with boxes of clothing on it along the street as if there were no cars there.

"Hey," said A.J., "where's this cat comin' from?"

When he noticed a taxi cutting across several lanes on Eighth

Avenue, he said, "These cabs are something else. Anytime that I been in one here, it's like being in a race with a bunch of rookie drivers, it's wild." Soon he was driving up the 57th Street ramp to the West Side Highway and then moving up a slight incline into the traffic coming from behind. When he put his foot on the gas, his right foot produced a *whoom* of power that moved the Cadillac into that traffic quickly and easily.

And every time I pass that ramp now, I remember that *whoom* of power when A.J. stepped on the gas. Unforgettable.

9 · The Little Names

Most of the time I'm committed to writing about big names, big events and big issues. That's why I like to write about the little names whenever I can. The little names are as much a part of sports as any of the people who make headlines. It's impossible for someone to identify with Muhammad Ali winning the world heavyweight championship, with Joe Namath changing Super Bowl history, with Henry Aaron breaking Babe Ruth's record. But it is possible to identify with people who are struggling.

Some of the little names are just overmatched, as Ron Stander was when he was butchered in 1972 by Joe Frazier, as Mrs. Ron Stander knew he would be:

OMAHA—Now that the fight is over, everybody is willing to acknowledge that it never should have occurred. Unknown to Ron Stander, a hospital room had been reserved for him.

"We were afraid he might get really hurt," one of his friends disclosed over a drink in the hours after the fight. "We knew he was overmatched. He was just part of a TV promotion."

He was just part of a slaughter, too. It belonged in the stockyards here.

"The blood was in his eyes," Joe Frazier said with concern. "He couldn't see."

Had the blood prompted the heavyweight champion to soften his assault?

"The man couldn't see, but the blood didn't bother me. I worked in blood all my life. I was a butcher in a slaughterhouse in Philadelphia for two years. I'm not making fun of it. Blood has been part of my life."

It still is, except that the unbeaten champion never has bled. His victims do.

Ron Stander needed seventeen stitches to close four wounds—two above his nose, one over his right eye, another under it. His bulbous red nose was broken. But somehow he had remained on his chunky legs. His manager, Dick Noland, had told Dr. Jack Lewis that he wouldn't let him come out for the fifth round, and the Nebraska Boxing Commission physician relayed the message to Zack Clayton, the referee.

"You can't jeopardize a man's eyesight," Noland explained.

But his manager had jeopardized Ron Stander's career by letting him come out for the first round in return for a big payday. All through the Omaha Civic Auditorium last night, Ron Stander's loyalists spoke of his "guts," as if that's all that had mattered. Of those who knew him, the only one who seemed to understand the perspective was his ash-blond wife, Darlene, her trim, tiny figure in a pink pants suit with white polka dots, her narrow face in a grim mask.

"I think it was too early for Ron to fight Joe Frazier," she was saying in a gloomy corridor outside her husband's dressing room. "Someone like Ken Norton would have been all right."

She is a realist. The night before the fight, she had come to the Omaha motel where her husband had been quartered while he trained for the title bout. She informed him that their checking account was overdrawn and that she needed $250 to pay a bill. She also knew that her husband's ability was being overdrawn, that a little-known California heavyweight, Ken Norton, sometimes one of Frazier's sparring partners, was a more suitable opponent.

"He's a little boy at heart," she continued. "Boxing made him an instant hero around here. He was an excellent husband until he turned pro. Then his whole lookout on life changed. You can't raise two kids on fantasy."

They met when Ron Stander was a star fullback at Abraham Lincoln High School in Council Bluffs, Iowa, across the Missouri River from Omaha. They've been married eight years. Their six-year-old son, Frankie, was with his mother at ringside. Their three-year-old daughter, Angela, remained at home.

"God only gave him one brain," she said. "I'd like to see him keep it. They've used him. I can't cope with it. The two kids, the dangers, my home.

But when I talk to him about it, he tells me I'm a nagger, that I don't know what I'm talking about. I don't know if he'll even listen to me now."

As the thirty-first ranking heavyweight in the *Boxing Illustrated* magazine ratings, Ron Stander didn't deserve a title bout.

"You don't take a Volkswagen into the Indianapolis Five Hundred," she was saying now, "unless you know of a helluva shortcut."

He had a 23–1 won-lost record, with one draw, but she wasn't deceived by the hometown decisions over obscure foes.

"I thought he lost to Eddie Dembry," she said, "and I thought he lost to Manuel Ramos the first time, when he got a draw. He's been out of shape. He's had his knuckles frozen so that he could fight. And then he celebrated from one fight to the next. But he won't listen to me. I've been shut out of boxing by him and the people around him."

His purse last night will come to nearly $50,000, compared with his previously publicized high of $7,000.

"His best purse was three thousand dollars," she said. "He promised me the last four fights that he'd quit. I'd like to see him finish college and go into coaching football. He likes kids. He wouldn't make much money, but it's a helluva lot easier."

Her husband's "guts" had excited some boxing people who cherish the box-office appeal of that attribute.

"You must be very proud," a stranger told Darlene Stander, interrupting her. "Your husband really has guts. He's got a great future in boxing as a contender, a real contender."

"With what?" she said.

(May 27, 1972)

Ron Stander's marriage didn't have a great future either. He and Darlene are divorced now.

Some little names never seem to get a chance, no matter how hard they try. Roger McCann used to hang around basketball games at Madison Square Garden, telling anybody who would listen that he was a good whistle, good enough to work in the N.B.A. if he only had the opportunity. And then, during a labor dispute in 1977, the whistle finally blew.

Some people spend their lives waiting for a break that never comes. They believe they're as good as almost anybody else in their profession. But they never get an opportunity to prove it. Life was like that for Roger McCann until now. Roger McCann is a basketball referee. All he has ever wanted to do is prove that he's good enough to blow his whistle in the National Basketball Association; all he has ever asked is the opportunity. Now he's got it. Roger McCann is one of the whistles that the N.B.A. has hired to work the playoffs, because almost all its other referees are on strike. Roger McCann is thirty-five years old and he has scuffled along with odd jobs in his obsession to prove he's a good whistle. "I'm so broke," he says with a grin, "I can't pay attention." But last night, when the Washington Bullets played the Cleveland Cavaliers in the opening game of their playoff series, Roger McCann was out there on the glossy court in the Capital Centre with Richie Powers, the N.B.A.'s most respected whistle. One man's strike is another man's chance.

"It's the playoffs, but a game is a game," Roger McCann was saying before it. "Officiating is just common sense and knowing the rules."

And getting a break. Roger McCann thought he had got his opportunity in 1971, when he was invited to the N.B.A. referees' tryout camp. But he was cut.

"I'm eating my heart ever since," he reflected. "My wife, Judy, even called me 'Underdog' because that's what I was."

Roger McCann has been a referee since 1964, when Abe Saperstein handed him a whistle in Europe on the Harlem Globetrotters tour. He had played for the Globetrotters stooge team, the Washington Generals, while in the Army there. In the years since, he has traveled with the Globetrotters, he has worked in the European basketball league, in the summer pro leagues in the New York metropolitan area and he was awaiting the Eastern League playoffs early last week when John Nucatola, the N.B.A. supervisor of officials, put him on standby at $300 a game, $40 per diem, plus transportation expenses. After a lifetime of waiting, Roger McCann reacted with the poise that any sports official requires.

"I've already got the title of my book—'If I Knew Where I Was Going, I'd Be on the Way Back'—because I got confidence," he said.

Roger McCann was in Chicago Stadium as a standby last Tuesday night, in the Capital Centre last Wednesday night, in Madison Square Garden last Thursday night and in Boston Garden last Friday night.

"Stay in Boston for the Celtics-Cavaliers game Sunday afternoon," Nucatola told him. "The referees might strike Sunday."

When the referees did strike, Roger McCann and Paul Campbell, a twenty-five-year-old referee with international experience from the Boston area, suddenly were wearing N.B.A. uniforms. In the moments before the opening tap, Bill Fitch, the Cavalier coach, walked over to them.

"Are you," Fitch asked McCann, "really a referee?"

"I've officiated in twenty-four countries and fifty states," Roger McCann said. "Not to be facetious, Coach, but I've been embarrassed by nicer people in better places."

Fitch smiled and walked away. During the game, Fitch did not smile. Coaches never do, especially when their team loses, as the Cavaliers did. But when the game ended, Austin Carr of the Cavaliers told the two rookie referees, "You guys did a great job." John Havlicek, the Celtics' captain, told them, "Great game." But to Roger McCann, the nicest compliment came from Dave Cowens in the closing moments.

"You're the first referee," the Celtics' center said, "I've seen sweat all year."

There's plenty there to sweat. Roger McCann knows he's a little heavier than he should be. But ever since he realized he might be on display in the playoffs, he has been on a diet.

"I've got a forty-eight-inch chest and twenty-seven-inch thighs," he said. "It's hard to hide that on a basketball court, but I'm not fat. I've always been built like this."

Roger McCann lives now in Wood Ridge, N.J., but he grew up in the Park Slope neighborhood of Brooklyn, not far from Ebbets Field, where he worked as the clubhouse boy for the visiting teams. When he was younger, he often sneaked into the left-field stands early or hung around outside on Bedford Avenue behind the right-field wall and collected baseballs hit over the fence during batting practice.

"I got five hundred and eighty-three of 'em one year," he recalled. "Sold them for a dollar each, sometimes for a dollar fifty if they weren't scuffed much."

The fifth of seven children, he dropped out of St. Francis Prep after two years when his father died. He was a Knicks' ball boy around the time that his brother Brendan, a college star at St. Bonaventure, was with them.

"If my brother could shoot like me, he would have been in the league ten years," Roger said. "They called him Blinky, he couldn't see."

Roger McCann has had several odd jobs—shooting baskets in a Santa Claus costume at half-time during Holiday Festival games and parading around the city in a tiger costume to promote the Dick Tiger–Joey Archer middleweight title fight. In recent years he was a sales manager for a plastic pipe company—briefly.

"It wasn't me," Roger McCann said. "I'm a basketball referee."

He was in N.B.A. headquarters Tuesday when Larry O'Brien, the commissioner, complimented him on his work in Sunday's game. If he continues to make the most of his opportunity, perhaps Roger McCann will be an N.B.A. staff referee someday.

"It's the first time I ever felt wanted," Roger McCann was saying now. "I'm available on any day that ends in 'y.' "

(April 14, 1977)

About sixteen months later my telephone rang. Roger McCann was calling.

"I just wanted to tell you," he said, "that the N.B.A. hired me today."

Some little names force their own opportunity, as Bobby Hall did. I had never seen the Boston Marathon until 1977 and I still haven't really seen one. That year I didn't see the start or many of the runners. I went there and sat in the back of a van to write about Bobby Hall, who started fifteen minutes early—in a wheelchair:

BOSTON—After about sixteen miles of the Boston Marathon today, a man on a Wellesley Hills street corner called, "Who's leading?" From inside a beige van, a voice replied, "Drayton, but Bobby Hall is leading the whole thing." Bobby Hall was in a wheelchair. And soon Bobby Hall appeared, his arms pumping his wheels along, a white visor over his blond hair, a white track shirt with "Greater Boston Track Club" in red over his muscular torso, his polio-crippled legs inside blue sweatpants, his feet in blue sneakers, the right crossed over the left. With the fifteen-minute jump he and six other wheelchair athletes had received to avert the crush at the starting line in Hopkinton, he would stay ahead of the runners through nearly eighteen miles of the 26-mile-385-yard course along the blacktop roads and streets. Jerome Drayton, the event winner, finally caught him, but rolling down a Commonwealth Avenue hill Bobby Hall regained the lead briefly until the Canadian passed him again. From there, about thirty other runners passed him through the corridor of spectators leading to the downtown finish line. But some of the loudest applause surrounded Bobby Hall, the wheelchair athlete.

"The people were great," he would say later. "I wish I could've seen them eyeball to eyeball, but all I could see were legs and knees and backsides."

But twenty-five-year-old Bobby Hall heard the applause and he waved every so often and he smiled. He seemed to be smiling even when he was laboring to pump his wheelchair up the hills. About the only time he didn't smile was when he had to slow down momentarily because he couldn't get around the van that accompanied him.

"Hey," somebody called from the van, "you need anything?"

"Yeah," he yelled back with that great smile, "a beer!"

Bobby Hall sounded like any other athlete when he said that. And that's all he wants to be known as—an athlete. He just happens to be an athlete with a wheelchair instead of legs. And according to Dr. Cairbre McCann of the National Wheelchair Athletic Association, pumping a wheelchair with your arms for 26 miles and 385 yards is more difficult than running that distance with your legs.

"Arms were never meant to propel your body," Dr. McCann says. "Running is natural, but propelling yourself in a wheelchair is an unnatural phenomenon. People never realize what a wheelchair athlete is capable of. This is a breakthrough in man's limits."

It also was a breakthrough in Bobby Hall's limits. He was in the Boston Marathon two years ago and finished in 2 hours 58 minutes unofficially. "He's not part of the race," an official barked that day. "We don't count him." But this year the first National Wheelchair Marathon was sanctioned in conjunction with the 81st Boston Marathon and Bobby Hall was timed in 2:40:40, nearly 18 minutes faster, and bettering his own time is what pleased Bobby Hall most.

"That's what it's all about," he was saying now. "Winning and going faster."

He was inside the Prudential Center now with the others who had finished the marathon. His hands were dirty from pushing his black bicycle-tire wheels. He had a small blister on the little finger of his right hand.

"It's nothin'," he said of the blister. "Nothin!"

He acknowledged that his arms were tired, but not that tired.

"I can still push," he said. "But not uphill."

He had led from the start, zooming down the yellow line in the middle of the two-lane blacktop road on the hill out of Hopkinton, then rolling through the suburban towns as the throngs of spectators became thicker and thicker. In the beginning, he peeled adhesive tape off his fingers and threw the pieces away. Every so often he took a swig from a small plastic bottle, lifting it out of a metal holder near his right leg. Occasionally he splashed himself on the head. From the van a friend kidded him along.

"There's a right turn coming up, stick out your right leg . . . You should have a rear-view mirror clipped to your toe . . . Just wink at the pretty ones . . . I should've given you cards with your phone number on them."

With every wisecrack, Bobby Hall smiled. Stricken with polio when he was ten months old, he's now the program director for the New England Spinal Cord Injury Association and a member of the Greater Boston Track Club. Several runners know him. When Tom Fleming of Bloomfield, N.J., who finished sixth, passed Bobby Hall, he patted the wheelchair athlete on the head.

"He didn't say anything," Bobby Hall recalled. "But he patted me and turned around and looked at me. It was great, you know."

Down the hall appeared Curt Brinkman, a Brigham Young University senior who lost his legs at sixteen in an electrical accident. He had finished second among the wheelchair athletes in the 74-degree heat, followed by Dave Williamson of Bowie, Md.; Ken Archer of Akron, Ohio; Sharon Rahn, a twenty-year-old University of Illinois coed (the only woman among the wheelchair athletes); Larry Rowe of Union, Ill.; and Mike Keminaki of Tempe, Ariz.

"Did you," Bobby Hall asked, "come in the back way?"

"You didn't see me pass you?" Curt Brinkman said with a grin. "I went around some people and passed you."

Bobby Hall and Curt Brinkman each laughed. "But you pushed yourself the whole way in that heat?" a man was asking Bobby Hall now. "You really pushed yourself up all those hills?"

Bobby Hall smiled. "I didn't get a tow," he said.

(April 19, 1977)

Several months after that column appeared, an official of the New York Marathon took me aside. "Why did you have to write that column about Bobby Hall?" he asked. "We're getting all kinds of heat now because the wheelchair people want to be in our marathon too. I wish you hadn't written that column."

More than ever, I was glad I had written it.

But some little names are too busy to have a cause. Too busy enjoying life. Duke Stefano always had a smile and a handshake in his office as the assistant matchmaker of the Madison Square Garden boxing department. And he always had a rum and Coke anywhere else. Some folks consider drinking to be one of our most strenuous sports, especially on New Year's Eve, so Duke was my subject as 1972 turned into 1973:

Duke Stefano watched the bartender pour the rum over the ice cubes and then add the Coke to it.

"Always remember," Duke said. "There are drinkers and there are drunkards. There's a difference."

He lifted his glass in a toast to 1973 and smiled. 'Tis the season to be jolly, but with Duke, being jolly is always in season. He's a chesty little man with a big grin, the assistant matchmaker in the Madison Square Garden boxing department. To him, the best match he ever made was between rum and Coke more than forty years ago. Some drinkers are versatile. Others have no imagination. And then there is Anthony (Duke) Stefano, the world welterweight champion in his specialty.

"Only rum and Coke," he was saying now. "I tried scotch once, but it tasted like iodine. And rye gags me."

He first tasted rum more than forty years ago when he was an eighteen-year-old sailor stationed at the Panama Canal.

"We had this tough bosun's mate, an Irishman from Boston. We were assigned to a tugboat with the submarines," he recalled. "He liked me because he thought I was a tough kid. I was from Greenwich Village and I had boxed in the Golden Gloves, not good, but I walked like a champion. We went to this bar one night and the bartender said, 'What do you drink?' I'm supposed to be a tough guy, but I never had a drink before.

"I hear somebody else say, 'Rum,' and I say, 'I'll have rum.' The bartender says, 'With what?' and I don't know what to say, so the bartender says, 'I'll fix you up, son.' He puts a little drop of what he called gum in it, a white syrupy substance. I loved it. I really loved it. After that, every joint I went to down there, I had a rum and gum. I had to, because Coke wasn't down there yet. I went to the Coke later."

To the Duke, the rum is more important than the mixer.

"It can be Pepsi," he said. "Or even Tab, not as many calories. My favorite rum is Bacardi light, only eighty proof. Somebody gave me a bottle of one-hundred-fifty-one-proof rum, but I'd never drink that. It would take the varnish right off this bar."

He was in Harry M.'s, but soon he would be on his way to Toots Shor's and later to Jack Dempsey's.

"I like to bounce," he said. "And when I walk in, it's embarrassing, the bartenders have my rum and Coke on the bar before I get my coat off. They know me because I treat 'em pretty good. Like at Shor's, at Christmas when I go in, I put twenty-five dollars in an envelope and give it to one of the four bartenders. Now, who gives 'em twenty-five dollars? Plus I'm not a wealthy guy. Some guys maybe give 'em five dollars, but I thought beyond that. Anyway, that envelope with the twenty-five dollars, that's four drinks for nothing because each of the four bartenders buys me one right away.

"When the other four bartenders come back from dinner, they get the word about the twenty-five dollars, and now that's eight drinks. And then Toots would walk over and say, 'Do these creeps ever buy you a drink?' and

I'm up to twelve. And when I'm about to leave, I drop the customary deuce. 'You don't have to do that,' one of the bartenders says, but I tell him, 'One thing has nothing to do with the other' and that's good for another round. That's sixteen drinks for the twenty-five dollars. They're happy, I saved about four dollars and no wonder Toots went broke.''

He cultivates bartenders quickly, the old pros in Shor's or the college kids at the New Jersey shore.

"I walk into the Villa down there on Long Beach Island a couple summers ago, and the kid behind the bar is shorter than me. He says, 'Can I help you, sir?' and I say, 'What the hell do you think I'm here for?' But I'm kidding. I never get nasty, never. The first time I get nasty drinking, I'll quit. I made that promise to myself forty years ago. Anyway, I tell him I want a rum and Coke with a piece of lime in it, and he says, 'We call that a Cuba Libre.' I tell him, 'You're going to be with me all summer, don't say Cuba Libre again because I hate Castro and the hell with Cuba, and the next day, when I walk in, he says, 'Rum and Coke with a piece of lime and the hell with Cuba.' I say, 'Kid, you are in.' ''

At the Boxing Writers Association dinner at Grossinger's in 1969, his friends kept sending drinks to his table.

"Mike Pellegrino, he manages fighters, he sent over a bottle of rum, but what he didn't know was that nine other guys each had sent me over two drinks apiece. I had eighteen rum and Cokes in front of me. The whole joint was walking around, looking at the eighteen drinks on the table in front of me. I finished 'em all, then I took the bottle upstairs.''

He smiled and motioned to the bartender, who quickly refilled his glass.

"That's the only time I ever knew how many I had, because everybody was counting 'em for me. I never count. I can go two days and nights, but I always use my head. Like if I have a big weekend, like I will this weekend, I won't touch another one until Thursday or Friday.''

(December 30, 1972)

And sometimes a little name is a little person, as Jack Gregory's baby was in 1973.

As the N.F.L. season progressed that year, I read every so often that the New York Giants' defensive end had been excused from an early-week practice so that he might return to Jackson, Miss., where his infant son was ill. The emphasis was always on Jack and how soon he would return to the team. I was more interested in Jack's baby:

•　　•　　•

Two weeks ago, as the New York Giants and the St. Louis Cardinals waited during a time-out, Donnie Anderson turned to Jack Gregory. "How's your baby?" the Cardinals' running back said.

"He's coming along," the Giants' defensive end said.

Jack Gregory's baby is the National Football League's infant of the year, tougher in his tiny way than any of its players. When the Giants return to the Yale Bowl today, many of the Dallas Cowboys will ask Gregory about him, as they did three weeks ago, as Donnie Anderson did two weeks ago, as Gene Upshaw of the Oakland Raiders did last week. At the age of three months, Earl Jackson Gregory 3d, known as E. J., has "almost died five times," according to his father. About twenty physicians and ten nurses have kept the blond-haired, brown-eyed infant alive. He has had about twenty-five blood transfusions. Slowly he's progressing. With a miniature Giant jersey and a football near his isolette, he remains in Mississippi Baptist Hospital in Jackson, Miss., where he arrived August 5, two months and two weeks premature. At birth he weighed three pounds thirteen ounces. Within an hour, he was having trouble breathing. His lungs had collapsed.

"His hands and his face had developed fully," his father says. "But his lungs hadn't. The doctors thought he might die right then."

Jack Gregory, who owns a 700-acre soybean farm not far from Jackson, rushed from the Giants' training camp in West Long Branch, N. J., to be with his wife, Gwen, in the crisis of their first child. Several days later, the six-foot-five-inch, 250-pound pass rusher rejoined the Giants for their exhibition game against the New England Patriots.

"When we won, the players gave me the game ball for E. J.," his father says. "That's the ball he has in the hospital."

Soon another crisis developed. E. J.'s right lung, which has collapsed twenty-eight times, was hemorrhaging. In the hospital, one of the doctors took the infant's father aside.

"I think we're going to lose him," the doctor said.

"I'm a positive thinker," the big defensive end replied. "He's going to make it. I always look for the best to happen, not the worst."

"I realize that," the doctor said, "but . . ."

"May I see my son?" Jack Gregory requested.

When the doctor agreed, Jack and his wife walked over to where the infant was. Jack held his son's little hand.

"You've come this far," Jack told him, "you can't give up now."

When he turned away, Jack Gregory was crying. Somehow the baby rallied. Nurses watched him constantly. Transfusions kept his heart pumping. Tubes and needles kept his lungs pumping. Not long ago a tracheotomy eased his breathing. Gradually his weight has increased to five pounds four ounces.

"Hopefully, he's on his way," says Dr. Daniel Draughn, the thirty-six-year-old pediatrician who has supervised the baby's care. "He's got the genes to be as big as his daddy someday."

"E. J. has been a challenge," says Gloria Moody, the head nurse in the hospital's intensive-care maternity unit. "But now he's a growing premature baby. He's almost on his own."

He's on a bottle now. He no longer requires oxygen. He is fascinated by a red toy with bells, a present from Barbara Young, the wife of Willie Young, one of the Giants' offensive tackles. He is surrounded by cards, letters, flowers and presents from other Giants and other N.F.L. players. And when he hears his father's voice, he's transfixed.

"E. J. and Jack have had a bond from the very beginning," Gwen Gregory says. "E. J. knows when Jack's with him."

"I've gone home after games as often as I can," Jack says. "But it's starting to add up. It's really getting expensive."

The cost of the doctors and the hospital care is more expensive. Gregory estimates that his bills now total more than $20,000, with more to come.

"But," he mentions, "the N.F.L. Players Association pays eighty percent of them, up to fifty thousand dollars. I hope they don't go over that."

Through it all, Jack Gregory has tried to maintain his concentration on football as the Giants struggle in a six-game losing streak. It's not easy. He contends that "when it's time to play football, that's all I think about." But his son's illness surely has intruded on his concentration, as it would on almost anyone's concentration in any job. He hasn't been as effective as he was last season when he earned All-Pro recognition. Alex Webster, the Giants' coach, concedes that "Jack hasn't played up to his potential" this season, but the coach talks of it with more understanding than annoyance. As the baby continues to improve, perhaps Jack Gregory's performance will, too.

"In three or four weeks," Jack Gregory says, "E. J. might come home."

(November 11, 1973)

E. J. celebrated his fifth birthday in 1978; he's still in and out of a hospital occasionally but mostly he's home. And mostly, he's more important in his way than any of those big names.

10 · Olympics

I had never covered the Olympics until the 1976 Summer Games at Montreal, but I never felt I was missing much. Somehow the Olympics had never appealed to me. The events were fun to watch on TV but they were too political, too hypocritical. All those Soviet athletes were pros, not amateurs. Any of our Olympians who had benefited from athletic grants-in-aid at college were pros too, as far as I was concerned. The massacre of the Israeli athletes at Munich in 1972 turned me off even more.

And when I arrived in Montreal before the Olympics were to begin, the situation was as messy as ever—the Republic of China team was in the midst of a political dispute that threatened its participation. It wanted to be identified as the Republic of China— not as Taiwan, as Canada, the host nation, demanded.

My first morning there, I visited the Olympic Village, where each nation had its headquarters in a labyrinth of basement offices—the United States and the Soviet Union in large offices, the smaller nations in smaller offices. The door to the Republic of China office was closed, but I knocked and opened the door. Only one man was there. I introduced myself and he stood up to shake hands.

"My name," he said, "is C.K. Yang."

I knew that name, which is Yang Chuan-kwang in its proper Chinese form. He had almost won the Olympic decathlon in 1960 at Rome as a UCLA student from Formosa, as the Republic of China was then known. He settled in California and became a United States citizen, which enabled him to cross the Canadian border before the members of his team were turned back. We talked for a while, then he told me about the empty rooms upstairs where his team was supposed to have been lodged. One of the first rules of the Olympic Village was that journalists were not to go above the lobby floor. But to me, those empty rooms symbolized the Republic of China's dispute and I thought I should see them.

"I'd like to see your room," I said.

"Come with me then," C. K. Yang said.

He smuggled me upstairs in the elevator and led me along a long corridor to his room:

MONTREAL—He arrived a week ago but he never completely unpacked. Some of his clothes remained in the gray suitcase that was spread open across one of the five white-blanketed bunks in the Olympic Village room that C. K. Yang was supposed to share with four Taiwanese athletes.

"I am here," he said, "all by myself."

But today the Republic of China delegation, too proud to call itself anything but that, withdrew from the XXI Olympics that open tomorrow. Soon the athletes will upstage the politicians and that's the way the Olympics should be. But the historical and dangerous precedent of these Olympics is that the politicians of Canada, not the International Olympic Committee, established the guest list. And so tonight, or perhaps tomorrow, C. K. Yang, the winner of the Olympic silver medal in a memorable decathlon duel with Rafer Johnson at Rome in 1960 and now the Olympic coach for the Republic of China, will be closing that gray suitcase that he never completely unpacked. The room will be empty. So will the five other rooms that had been reserved for the Republic of China's athletes.

"The thing I'm really annoyed about," C. K. Yang was saying now, "is that Prime Minister Trudeau admitted this was a political move."

C. K. Yang is a big, husky man with shoulders almost as wide as a high-jump bar. He's a little heavier around the middle now, but not much. His hair has remained shiny black. And behind his black-rimmed glasses, his dark eyes flashed.

"Trudeau forgets that the Olympics is not politics, it's athletes," he said. "Trudeau is a coward. It seemed like somebody was putting a gun or a knife at his back. It was strictly a request by Red China."

C. K. Yang has been described as the spiritual father of the Olympic program in Taiwan, but he's a United States citizen. He and Rafer Johnson were teammates at the University of California, at Los Angeles, and he lives in the Los Angeles area now with his wife and two sons. He spent much of last year coaching Taiwanese athletes. He's also in the import-export business. But even as a United States citizen, he was hassled by Canadian customs officials when he arrived here last week.

"They asked me why I represent Taiwan," he recalled, "and I told them it was none of their business."

But when C. K. Yang was a candidate for a gold medal at Rome, the Republic of China compromised its pride.

"We had to go under the name of Taiwan or Formosa there," he remembered. "But the reason we accepted it was they knew I was going to win the decathlon or finish second. It would be a big sacrifice not to compete. We gambled. We got what we wanted when I finished second, so they were happy."

But with their Olympic athletes barred from Canada, nobody in the Republic of China is happy now.

"The athletes were in Los Angeles, Chicago, Detroit and Boston," C. K. Yang was saying, "and they were running out of money. I tried to call them in Los Angeles, but they had moved out of their hotel. I was giving them some training schedules over the phone, but I could tell they had no heart in it anymore."

During the political negotiations, the Taiwanese rejected the idea of marching under the Olympic flag.

"That would have been humiliating," C. K. Yang said. "We might have accepted marching under the Olympic flag if other nations had joined us. That way it would have been a great embarrassment for Canada." His eyes twinkled now. "I was even thinking of getting little Taiwanese flags made up and giving them to the members of the United States team and having them wave them during the parade. That would have been something. But the United States should not have pulled out for us. I approve of them trying to support us but not their pulling out. I was an athlete. I know. That would not have been fair to the United States athletes. Our problem is not your problem."

Victor Yuen, the secretary of the Republic of China delegation, nodded.

"If the United States had agreed to march in under the Olympic flag, I think we would have accepted the Olympic flag, too," Victor Yuen said. "That way we would have had some support. But not by ourselves. That would have been more or less an insult. We would have lost face."

During the dispute, ninety-five pieces of luggage belonging to Taiwanese athletes had been impounded at Dorval Airport here.

"It was so cold for us here," Victor Yuen said. "No feeling of Olympic atmosphere. Nobody seemed to want us here."

"The athletes from the other nations were with us, they understood," C. K. Yang was saying now. "But the other day, somebody walked into our office and said, 'I thought you had already left.' I told him, 'We have a right to be in this office, but you don't. Get out.' "

On the wall of the Republic of China office were the instructions for tomorrow's opening ceremony parade.

"I didn't carry our flag in Rome, it's too tiring," C. K. Yang said. "But I was going to carry it here."

(July 17, 1976)

The next morning, the day of the opening ceremony, C. K. Yang was gone. Teams from several black African nations also departed in a boycott aimed at South Africa's apartheid policy. Once again, politics had intruded on the pageantry of the opening ceremony. More than seven thousand athletes would march behind their nations' flags into the huge new Olympic Stadium, in step to the music of their anthems. Queen Elizabeth and Prince Philip were in the royal box to review the teams, led by the team from Greece, the original Olympic nation. As soon as I saw the Greek team, I thought of what C. K. Yang had said: "Trudeau forgets that the Olympics is not politics, it's athletes."

The hell with the politicians and the hypocrites, I told myself, enjoy the athletes. But first I found myself enjoying the role of impostor:

MONTREAL—The royal courier had delivered a royal envelope that had a royal mistake. It was addressed to "Mr. Walker Smith, The New York Times" but Red Smith's real name is Walter, not Walker—close, but one letter away from royal accuracy. Inside, the gold-edged invitation with an embossed gold crown announced an added Olympic event. "The Master of the Household," the invitation declared, "is commanded by her Majesty to invite Mr. Walker Smith to a Reception to be given by The Queen and The Duke of Edinburgh on board H.M. Yacht 'Britannia' at Montreal on Sunday, 18th July, 1976, at 5.00 P.M." In sports, Walker Smith is remembered as the baptismal name of the boxer known as Sugar Ray Robinson, a five-time middleweight champion but never a Pulitzer Prize winner. Walter Smith was not offended, merely curious as to whether the invitation included Phyllis Smith, his Olympic roommate. He telephoned a royal number for the protocol coordinator of the royal visit and inquired about her royal eligibility.

"No," a precise voice said, "only the press."

With two weeks of Olympic competition remaining, Walter Smith did not dare risk Phyllis Smith withdrawing for social reasons. Thoughtfully, he handed his invitation to someone willing to serve as an impostor. The impostor also had a clear conscience because his spouse would not arrive for several days. The impostor was equipped with the invitation, a presentation card and a blue parking sticker with a map showing where the *Britannia* was docked in the Bickerdike Basin of the St. Lawrence River.

"I'm surprised it's there," the cab driver said in his French accent. "But if they print up a piece of paper, we'd better go by the paper."

The yacht was there. But to describe the *Britannia* as a yacht is like describing Montreal as a village. It's an ocean liner, not a yacht. And a royal ocean liner. Nautical flags fluttered across its entire length. Its hull gleamed in navy-blue enamel with a wide gold vertical stripe. At the security checkpoint, the impostor wondered if he might be asked his name. But waving the invitation and the presentation card was enough to qualify for the electronic surveillance.

"All clear," the man in the brown uniform said.

As the impostor approached the yacht, a British sailor with a rifle stiffened to attention, his eyes riveted straight ahead as if Raquel Welch were in the distance. On the red-carpeted gangplank, the impostor was saluted by three British naval officers in dress white uniforms. With smiles from other officers, one with a red sash across his chest, the impostor was directed to the aft deck, where about two hundred newsmen, mostly Canadians, were gathering quietly under beige canvas.

"Look at the hawser," a guest said, glancing at the coiled rope on the deck. "It's painted purple. Royal purple."

Soon a gentleman in a blue suit spoke to the group in French, then in English, which was obviously his true language.

"This is a social occasion," he intoned. "No reporting, no tape recorders, no cameras, no notes. Thank you."

This was royal protocol which the British and Canadian newsmen accepted. But the impostor thought to himself, He didn't say no memory. And later, a British voice would say, "The London *Times* man, fearless of being imprisoned in the Tower, assures you, as a former colonist, that you may go ahead and describe the royal occasion." Except for Duke Snider, who wore the Dodgers royal blue with distinction, and King Clancy, the vice president of anecdotes for the Toronto Maple Leafs hockey team, the impostor had not traveled in the royal whirl. And moments later, the royal occasion began as the file of guests mounted the stairway to a deck tented in red-and-white canvas.

"Have your presentation cards ready," a voice kept saying.

Under the red-and-white canvas, a royal announcer would take the presentation card and read the name to the Queen and the Duke standing nearby. For the impostor, the moment of truth had arrived. He handed his presentation card to the royal announcer.

"Walker Smith," the royal announcer said.

In a green dress, the Queen extended a royal hand with a royal smile.

"How do you do," the Queen said gently.

"How do you do," the impostor replied.

Alongside was the Duke in a gray suit with a narrow blue tie and a striped shirt.

"Where are you from?" the Duke asked.

"The New York Times," the impostor said truthfully.

"Good," the Duke said, smiling brightly.

Instantly, a tall naval officer in a white uniform moved toward the impostor. Discovered at last, the impostor feared.

"You must have a drink," he ordered.

"Well, yes," the impostor stammered.

Instantly, a waiter appeared, holding a gleaming silver tray with a dozen glasses on it—scotch and water, scotch and soda, gin and tonic, vodka and tonic. Other officers, tall and handsome in their dress whites as if delivered by Central Casting, quickly mingled with small groups of guests.

"This is the veranda deck," one of them said. "We never come back here unless we're invited."

By now the Queen, who had opened the Olympics, and the Duke were circulating among the guests.

"Did you see your daughter [Princess Anne, a British equestrienne] in the opening parade?" a man asked.

"Perhaps. She had her [wide-brimmed] hat turned down over her face," the Queen replied, "but I couldn't pick her out. But my husband did."

The Duke will officiate later this week at the equestrian competition at nearby Bronton, Quebec.

"I must be there but I have so many to help me," the Duke said. "If you have a dog, why bark?"

After about an hour, the Queen and the Duke quietly excused themselves.

The royal occasion, the added Olympic event, had ended. Undetected, the impostor departed with another glance at the royal purple rope.

"The purple hides the dirt," an officer had explained.

(July 20, 1976)

That same day Nadia Comaneci arrived as a world personality. Six months earlier I was doing a piece for *Sport* magazine on Olga Korbut when gymnastics people kept telling me, "Olga won't do much at Montreal, she's had it. The little kid from Rumania is the best in the world now." Indeed she was:

MONTREAL—On the uneven bars, she whirls as easily as a sparrow fluttering from limb to limb on a tree. On the balance beam, she clings to it as surely as a squirrel would. On the vault, she lands as softly as a sea gull on a beach. In her floor exercises, she is part go-go dancer, part ballerina, part cheerleader. And today Nadia Comaneci, her dark pigtails tied with red and white yarn, won her first Olympic gold medal as the all-round champion in women's gymnastics. But at fourteen years old, she is not a woman. An athlete, yes; an artist, yes. But with her eighty-pound rubber body, she's hardly much more than a child. That, of course, is the essence of her charm. And she was carefully choreographed to project that child image in these Olympics by her Rumanian coaches. When she toured the United States a few months ago, she didn't smile.

"I never smile," she often said then.

She's so good, it is often said, "you get a chill watching her." Her coaches knew that a smile would warm that chill. Now she smiles. They also knew that more lively music for her floor exercises would increase her appeal. Her pianist resisted the change, but the coaches and the officials insisted.

"But did Nadia want the new music?" a man wondered.

"Over there it's not up to the kid," he was reminded.

Over there the Rumanians knew that Nadia Co-ma-NEECH was technically superior to any of the Soviet gymnasts. They also knew that Olga Korbut had used her charm to upstage her teammate, Ludmilla Turischeva, the brooding beauty who won the all-round gold medal at Munich four years ago. Gymnastics has been one of the purest forms of sport for one hundred and fifty years, but now, ever since television recorded Olga Korbut's tears and triumphs at Munich, gymnastics also is show biz, especially Olympic women's gymnastics. If there were prize money, the women would deserve more than the men. And so the Rumanians reminded Nadia to smile and wave. Not boastfully. Softly and naturally was enough, both for her and for the television people.

"We're trying," an important ABC television man said earlier in the week, "to make Nadia into what Olga was four years ago."

Olga's manner had been perfect for show biz—a smile, a wave, pigtails, a wiggle. And at Munich she won two gold medals and one silver medal. But so had Karen Janz of East Germany, but not many people remember her. No television impact. For the last four years, Olga Korbut was what gymnastics was all about to many people. But she realized that gymnastics wasn't what the world is all about. Despite her pixie appearance, Olga is twenty-one now, a woman who wears heavy Russian perfume and platform boots and is talking about becoming an actress.

"In Hollywood?" she once was asked.

"Oh, no," she replied, "in Moscow."

But at fourteen, as a Barbie doll with bangs, Nadia Comaneci was perfect as Olga Korbut's television successor. She also was perfect as a gymnast. Five times (all three on the uneven bars, twice on the beam) she has been awarded a perfect 10 score. It registers as "1.00" on the electronic scoreboard because 9.99 is the board's limit. The perfect 10 score was considered unattainable in the Olympics until Nadia attained it once Sunday, twice Monday and twice today. Not that she considered it unattainable.

"I've done it," she said, "twenty times now."

On a scale of 1 to 10, she has made the scoring scale outmoded. On a scale of 1 to 10, she really deserves an 11 for what she has accomplished in relation to the scores of other gymnasts. Because of the restrictions of the scoring scale, many gymnastic observers thought that her dominance over the other competitors was not as wide as it should have been. Her aptitude for gymnastics was discovered in kindergarten. It was confirmed in a recent aptitude test that some of the European nations give their gymnasts.

"The numbers from one to one hundred are mixed up on a piece of paper," says Art Maddox, the pianist for the United States Olympic women's gymnasts. "You get four minutes to go from one number to another. It might sound easy, but it's not. I'm told that Nadia had the highest score anybody ever got—seventy-two, as I remember."

Aptitude is one thing. Performance is another. And today, in winning the all-round gold medal, Nadia performed virtually impeccably at the Forum, the Montreal Canadiens' hockey shrine.

Outside, ticket scalpers were getting as much as $200 for a $16 ticket. Inside, the flags of the competing nations hung from the ceiling as Nadia was accorded an ovation usually reserved here for Guy Lafleur, the hockey idol. But the scene of the competition was much different from what appears on television. Understandably, the TV cameras zoom in on the competitors. But they seldom show the dazzle of the overall view—the march into the arena, to lively music composed specifically for the Olympics by Michel Conte of Canada—the little runners in white T-shirts and skirts, the recorders in white dresses, the judges and officials in yellow blazers and gray skirts, and finally the competitors in four groups of nine—swinging along as if they were the Seven Dwarfs on the way to the mine. Gymnastics is a four-ring circus—one group soaring off the vault, one spinning on the uneven bars, one somersaulting on the four-inch beam, one dancing on the floor, with each nation's pianist nearby.

"Nadia has great feeling in her body," says Art Maddox. "She is in complete control every moment."

In today's competition, Nadia Comaneci opened with a respectable 9.85 on the vault, added her third consecutive 10 on the uneven bars, another perfect 10 on the beam and concluded with a 9.9 in her floor exercises. By that time, all the other competitors were watching her except the Soviet athletes, who never seem to look at her as she performs. That assured Nadia Comaneci's coronation as the queen of the Olympics, the successor to Ludmilla Turischeva in skill and to Olga Korbut in show biz. Sometime in the fall the Rumanian doll will tour the United States, as Olga did after her Munich triumph. Before one of Olga's tours, an American promoter was assured that Olga would be accompanied by several other Soviet gymnasts.

"Never mind them," the promoter said, "just bring the little kid."

But now Nadia Comaneci of Rumania is the little kid.

(July 22, 1976)

For all its various sports, the Olympics is primarily a track meet. And even in the years when I didn't pay too much attention to the Olympics, the 10-event decathlon fascinated me. Long before the Olympics were on television, I remembered a 1948 wirephoto of Bob Mathias, then only seventeen years old, huddling in a blanket in the London rain between his events. I was nineteen then and here was a kid two years younger winning the Olympic decathlon. Maybe that's what hooked me on the decathalon—that and the versatility that it demands. But for me, the decathlon in Montreal demanded something else—a spotter. As the competition dragged toward the early evening with Bruce Jenner trying for the gold medal, I took out my typewriter and rolled the paper in. Next to me Frank Deford turned. "What are you doing?" he asked.

"I have to write an early column," I explained, "to get me through the first edition."

"How do you do that?" he said.

His respectful tone surprised me. Frank Deford is *Sports Illustrated*'s decathlon champion. But on a weekly magazine, he's not confronted with newspaper deadlines.

"I can do it," I said, "because whenever Jenner is about to do something, you're going to nudge me."

He laughed and I began to write. Every so often Frank would nudge me and say "Now," and I would look up to see Jenner approaching the pole-vault runway or measuring his steps for the javelin throw. After the final event, the 1,500-meter run, I phoned the office with a sentence that mentioned his gold medal. After he appeared in the interview room, I wrote a new column for the later editions:

MONTREAL—In his idle moments between the decathlon events, Bruce Jenner covered his red "USA" track shirt with a gray T-shirt that implored, "FEET, don't fail me now."

They didn't. Neither did his arms and his legs and his torso and his heart and, most of all, his concentration. In accumulating a world-record total of 8,618 points for the Olympic gold medal today, Bruce Jenner didn't fail himself. He was supposed to win the 10-event competition, and he did. He's now the ninth American to win the Olympic decathlon in the grand tradition of Bill Toomey, Rafer Johnson, Milt Campbell, Bob Mathias (twice), Glenn Morris, Jim Bausch, Harold Osborn and Jim Thorpe, although Jim was later disqualified for the sin of having played minor league baseball. But he's the first decathlete, as they call themselves now, to train with world-class athletes in his events rather than with other decathletes. That's why Bruce Jenner suddenly is a name known throughout the world today after all his years of obscurity. That's the way it is with the Olympic decathlon champion. Until he wins it, virtually nobody knows him. But after he wins it, his names lives on like the Olympic flame.

"If you train with a decathlon man," says Bruce Jenner of San Jose, Calif., "you can't visualize that you can do much better. But if you throw the discus with Mac Wilkins or throw the shot with Al Feuerbach, then they're twenty feet ahead of me. You learn much more that way."

But somewhere along the way, Bruce Jenner learned more than how to run, jump and throw. For an Olympic decathlon champion, the most difficult challenge is the eleventh event—his future. But after his 4:12.61 time in the 1,500-meter run assured his victory, Bruce Jenner behaved as Nathan Hale might have if he had only one decathlon to give for his country. After crossing the finish line, he suddenly had a small American flag thrust at him and he waved it with his left hand. On the other side of the brick-red track, he threw the flag into the crowd, as if it were a miniature javelin.

"I don't know where that guy came from," he was saying about an hour later. "The guy just gave me the flag."

Bruce Jenner suddenly is the only American star here. Nadia Comaneci was everybody's child but she's a Rumanian and that was last week. Some observers suspect that the ABC television network, in its dedication to the star syndrome, supplied the flag bearer. But whatever, Bruce Jenner was in a genuine ecstasy.

"It's over," he told his wife. "We did it."

Chrystie Jenner, a United Airlines stewardess, is the primary breadwinner. Bruce sells some insurance in San Jose, Calif., but not much. Mostly he trained for the Olympic decathlon.

"She has just as much invested as I do," he said later. "She works at a job she didn't really like so that I had time to train."

But now, after the gold medal was hung over his Prince Valiant haircut, he kissed it and waved to the thousands who had waited in the Olympic Stadium and clapped impatiently for the victory ceremony. His discus mentor, Mac Wilkins, had called the Olympics "just another track meet," but Bruce Jenner disagreed.

"If you get down to basics, yes, it is just another track meet, I've competed against all the other guys before," he said. "But, boy, when you look up in the stands and see sixty-eight thousand people, you know it's not just another track meet—we had one hundred and twenty-five at the national Amateur Athletic Union decathlon. And when you see the Olympic rings up there, you know it's not just another track meet."

Mac Wilkins had also called his discus gold medal "an achievement for myself" but Bruce Jenner showed better manners.

"I did all the work," Bruce Jenner said, "but I grew up in a country that allowed me to do what I wanted to do."

As for the future, Bruce Jenner will be very careful. He remembers how "Mark Spitz jumped on the Bob Hope Show and just died and there went the credibility of the seven gold medals." And after his gold-medal ceremony today, Bruce Jenner talked about credibility again.

"I feel I've built up a lot of credibility as an athlete and I don't want to do anything to tarnish that," he said.

Bruce Jenner will be known now as "the world's greatest athlete," almost as if it were part of his name. The decathlon scoring system awards points against a table of performance for each event, not against the other competitors. In his two-day grind, he ran the 100 meters in 10.94 seconds, did the long jump in 23 feet 8 1/4 inches, put the shot 50-4 3/4, high-jumped 6-8 and ran 400 meters in 47.52 yesterday. Then he opened today's events by running the 110-meter hurdles in 14.84 and followed by throwing the discus 164-2, pole vaulting 15-9, throwing the javelin 224-10 and finishing with a 4:12.61 in the 1,500-meter run. Then he jogged a victory lap while the other competitors gasped for breath.

"I won, don't forget," he said. "And don't let the secret out, but I'm not that tired."

Bruce Jenner might not be the world's greatest athlete.

"But the decathlon," he said, "is the only measurable test of running, jumping and throwing. Football players run, jump and throw but they don't have a measurable test."

Bill Toomey, the Olympic decathlon champion at Mexico City, talked yesterday about other athletes.

"There are probably thirty guys in the National Basketball Association who would be good decathletes," Bill Toomey said. "Basketball requires a lot of elements that are in the decathlon—stamina, jumping, agility. Some football players, too. O. J. Simpson would be a good decathlon man. He has all the materials."

But only Bruce Jenner has the gold medal.

"This was the last meet of my life," he said. "Now that I've won it, there's nothing left for me. The decathlon is nothing between the Olympics, and I've enjoyed the climb to the top."

And tonight Bruce Jenner enjoyed his last climb—the two steps to the top of the Olympic gold-medal platform.

(July 31, 1976)

At dinner later, Frank Deford sneaked up and nudged me again. "Now," he said, laughing.

Every laugh in Montreal was treasured, because there weren't that many. Too much was going on. Somebody mentioned to me later that covering the Olympics "must be fun" and I replied, "Not really. Spring-training baseball in Arizona, that's fun; the Olympics aren't fun." But they are a wonderful adventure. When they ended, I had a better understanding of what they meant, at least what they meant to me:

• • •

MONTREAL—Waving a small American flag, Bruce Jenner seemed about to leap over the Olympic Stadium in a single bound after winning the decathlon. On his victory lap after completing a double in the 10,000-meter run and 5,000-meter run, Lasse Viren was convoyed by countrymen with two fluttering Finnish flags. That's what the Olympics are all about. But on that same brick-red track, the tall Haitian jogged as slowly as a jogger in your neighborhood. Except that he was competing in the Olympic 10,000-meter run. Lasse Viren had lapped him eight times but the tall Haitian kept jogging around and around the track that was empty except for him. Eventually, the bell ringer in a yellow blazer signaled his final lap. That's when the cheers for him began. The cheers followed him across the finish line, about 15 minutes after Lasse Viren's time. Then the tall Haitian raised his arms in appreciation. That, too, is what the Olympics are all about. And that really is all anybody should expect from the Olympics now and in the future.

Don't expect the Olympics to be any better or any worse than the people who govern them and the people who participate in them. By their nature, the Olympics require a cast of thousands. None is likely to be submitted for canonization.

Because the Olympics involve sports, the idealists believe they should be exempt from the sins of mankind. When they aren't, the idealists call for their burial. Too political, they roar. Their solution is to adhere to the Olympic ideal—let individuals compete, not nations. What the idealists don't understand is that when the flag isn't there, the money isn't there.

As long as politics exists, politics will exist in the Olympics, as the African nations proved in their boycott and as Canada proved in demanding that the Republic of China accept identification as Taiwan or nothing.

But sometimes even the ostriches of the Olympics pretend that politics doesn't exist. Perhaps the most private party in Montreal was a gathering of the Israeli Olympic team at a downtown restaurant. Ankie Spitzer, the widow of an Israeli fencer killed in the Munich massacre, disclosed that she had asked Lord Killanin, the president of the International Olympic Committee, and Roger Rousseau, the commissioner of these Games, for a moment of silence in the opening Olympic ceremony. But her request was denied. Too political.

"And then Rousseau told me," Mrs. Spitzer said, "that I was being emotional."

Being emotional is also what the Olympics are all about. But not when it involves a memory the Olympic ostriches would prefer to forget.

Perhaps someday the Olympic ostriches will take their heads out of the sand and realize that the Olympics should be open to all athletes—professionals as well as amateurs. Until then, the Olympic ostriches will be supporting hypocrisy, not amateurism. The athletes in the Soviet Union and East Germany are not amateurs. They are subsidized by their governments. Many of the American athletes are not true amateurs, either. The track-and-field stars have received under-the-table "expense" payments from meet promoters. The swimmers and the basketball players have received college grants-in-aid as athletes. That makes them as subsidized as the Iron Curtain athletes.

With the emergence of the East Germans in track and swimming, some Americans are wondering how a nation of about seventeen million people can win so many gold medals. Some even are calling for a better organized Olympic movement that might produce more American gold-medal winners. But the East Germans' success is best explained in a message in their Olympic brochure from Manfred Ewald, the president of the East Germany National Olympic Committee.

"The Youth Law adopted in 1974 obliges all state organs to assist the children's and youth spartakiads," the message reads in part. "It is part of everyday Olympic life in our republic that at the same time when the world's best athletes compete for Olympic laurels at Montreal, district spartakiads are held in many places in the G.D.R. [German Democratic Republic] during which thousands of young boys and girls compete with the same elan as our Olympic team."

If that's what it takes, the East Germans can have it. Perhaps the Little League and other sports are overemphasized in America, but mostly, America lets kids be kids. That's what the Olympics should do —let competitors be competitors. But some nations won't let them. Perhaps the most chilling moment of the Olympics occurred in a TV screening room where Bud Greenspan's *The Olympic Symphony,* shown tonight on Canadian television, was previewed by perhaps three dozen guests. There were no words, only music by Beethoven, Handel and other composers. It seemed to be the perfect solution to the Olympics— eliminate the words and enjoy the competitors and the history. But when it ended, a Soviet Union television executive in a gray suit objected. Here to scout the Summer Games for 1980 when they will be in Moscow, he had been offended by a few 1936 scenes of Adolf Hitler in his Nazi uniform.

"You showed Hitler," he said. "This is shocking to us."

"It wasn't done to glorify the period," Bud Greenspan explained. "It was done to identify the period. To eliminate it creatively would have been as bad for us as your objection."

"But such a film," the objector said, "can't go on Soviet TV."

The debate lasted for perhaps fifteen minutes, without anything being resolved. And that, unfortunately, is what the Olympics are all about.

(August 2, 1976)

Within a few months the Olympics also were all about money—the $85 million that NBC paid to the Soviets for the television rights to the 1980 Summer Games in Moscow and the $1 million finder's fee for Lothar Bock, the mystery man of the negotiations. I had been exploring the possibility of doing an amusing column on the TV networks' talks with the Soviet Olympic officials when I stumbled on these financial arrangements.

I suddenly had a page-one news story as well as a much more significant column:

More than three years before the opening ceremony, the Soviet Union and NBC have set the first record of the Moscow Olympics—the $85 million TV deal. And the Soviet Connection, a West German impresario named Lothar Bock, has collected a $1 million fee from NBC and been guaranteed undetermined additional income by that network for his influence in the TV negotiations. Once again the Olympics have been exposed for what they are —big business, not sport. Except for the athletes. Cheers and a gold medal are the most an athlete can expect. But without the athletes, the Olympics would not exist. Perhaps someday in the next century the idealists of the International Olympic Committee will realize that if nations and TV networks and influence peddlers deal in millions during the Olympics, the athletes also deserve to make a buck. Perhaps someday the idealists will become realists and open the Olympics to professional athletes.

It won't happen in Moscow, of course, because there are no professional athletes as such there. Only professional politicians.

Lothar Bock had worked with the Russians before on cultural TV productions. He's lively and friendly, thirty-eight years old with longish hair and a Continental flair. He lives in Munich, drinks vodka and smokes West German cigarettes. When he comes to New York, he stays at the Plaza and goes to P.J. Clarke's for steak tartare and bacon cheeseburgers. He's not usually around sports, but he delivered the Olympic TV contract to NBC four days after having been released from his CBS commitment when that network withdrew from the negotiations.

"We wonder about that," says one international TV executive. "We wonder if Lothar Bock had that planned all along."

Outsiders familiar with Soviet intrigue wonder if Lothar Bock was a double agent really working for the Russians in order to jack up the price.

"No," says another television network official. "We never had any reason to believe that Lothar was a double agent."

With his $1 million fee, Lothar Bock put such sports agents as Jerry Kapstein, Irwin Weiner and Bob Woolf to shame. Forget about representing athletes, gentlemen, start talking to people in Tehran, Iran, where the 1984 Olympics probably will be held. Deal with nations, not draft choices, as Lothar Bock dealt with the Soviet television ministers. His ability to deliver preceded him. Robert Wussler, now the president of the CBS television network but then its vice president in charge of sports, was in Moscow in 1975, when he was introduced to Lothar Bock.

"If you want the Olympic Games," the man making the introduction told Wussler, "here is the man."

And now Lothar Bock has emerged as the main character, the Soviet Connection, in a plot that Chekhov would have cherished—bugged hotel rooms, vodka parties, an "$80 million cocktail party" and even Soviet jokes.

No matter which Moscow hotel the American network executives stayed at, they believed their rooms were bugged. Every so often they would shout at the vents where they assumed the transmitters had been planted.

"Let me repeat that," one of them often yelled, "in case you missed it."

For important conversations they talked in the hotel corridors. Some executives even developed code words that they practiced using in their New York offices. The morning and afternoon negotiating sessions were followed by dinner meetings in Moscow restaurants.

"Those guys," one network executive recalls, "were willing to go out to dinner every night to eat well."

And to drink well. At lunch, one vodka toast was mandatory. At dinner, several vodka toasts were mannerly. At one dinner party for twenty-two people, thirty bottles of vodka were consumed and not all of the twenty-two people were drinking.

"I've had hangovers," one network executive recalls, "but the next morning I felt like I'd been kicked in the head."

The night before the negotiations began in early December, the Russians threw what became known as "the $80 million cocktail party"—that's where the three networks first discussed pooling their funds and resources. The pool plan was submitted to the Justice Department for antitrust approval, but when CBS withdrew, the plan was abandoned.

Suddenly, only NBC and ABC were in the hunt and then NBC hired Lothar Bock.

But now even the network executives at ABC and CBS laugh at the most memorable joke the Russians told on themselves. It seems that a comrade and his small son were traveling on a Moscow trolley when the boy had a question for his father.

"How wide," the boy asked, "is Red Square?"

"About six hundred meters," his father answered.

"And how long," the boy said, "is Gorky Street?"

"About six kilometers," his father replied.

"And how high is the Soviet government?"

"That's a silly question," his father said. "There is no answer as to how high the Soviet government is."

Across the trolley, an old man looked up.

"Yes," the old man said, "there is an answer for your son's question as to how high the Soviet government is. I know I am 1.8 meters high. From that I know that the Soviet government must be 1.6 meters high because"—he touched his throat—"I have had it up to here."

Before the 1980 Olympics are over, NBC probably will have had the Soviet government up to here, but Lothar Bock will have had the last laugh.

(February 6, 1977)

Several weeks later I met Lothar Bock in the NBC offices. We chatted for more than an hour. He spoke easily and calmly until I mentioned the suspicion of some people that he had been working for the Soviets as a double agent in the Olympic negotiations.

"Not one dollar," he said, his voice rising. "No way, never. It's out of the question."

Whatever, that's the Olympics now—finances, politics and hypocrites. But thankfully, it's athletes too.

11 · Basketball

I remembered when Joe Namath was belittled by N.F.L. people because he was in the "other league," so I didn't pay much attention when Julius Erving provoked the same skeptical reaction by the N.B.A. establishment. At the time Doctor J also was in "the other league," the A.B.A., but he was doing more things with a basketball than anybody I'd ever seen. And doing them in midair. Doctor J did at altitude what Bob Cousy had done at sea level. To me, that's the ultimate compliment because until Doctor J arrived, Bob Cousy of the Boston Celtics was the flashiest basketball player I'd ever seen.

And yet, when Cooz was at Holy Cross, some people didn't think he'd make it in the N.B.A. because he was too fancy. I know. I was there with him. For posterity's information I believe I was the first sportswriter to spell his nickname C-o-o-z, the way it was pronounced. That spelling appeared in the *Holy Cross Tomahawk,* the college paper.

But for all his behind-the-back dribbling with a basketball, my favorite memory of Bob Cousy involved beer cans. His junior year, Holy Cross defeated Kansas in a big game at the Boston Garden soon after Christmas vacation began. I had stayed for the game and I returned to the empty snow-covered campus in Worcester, Mass., for a party.

In those years, beer was strictly forbidden for students on that

Jesuit campus. I mean strictly. Under threat of expulsion.

But with the campus empty and with an unbeaten basketball team, we assumed that the rules did not apply. Several cases of beer materialized in Beaven Hall, a dormitory where several players lived. Cooz was relaxing in an upper bunk when somebody tossed him an empty beer can and pointed to the window at the far end of the room. The window was open from the top. About eight inches, maybe twelve inches.

"Shoot it, Cooz," somebody said.

Cooz shot it, the beer can sailing end over end through the opening and down into the snow below.

"Shoot this one," another said.

That can also disappeared into the darkness. Cooz tossed out dozens of empty cans, each sailing cleanly through the open window at the other end of the room and into the snow below. If you think Bob Cousy could shoot a basketball, you should have seen him shoot those empty beer cans. But years later, when I wrote about the empty beer cans in a *Saturday Evening Post* piece that coincided with his retirement from the Celtics, he was disturbed.

"That couldn't have happened," he said. "We weren't allowed to have beer on campus."

I assured him it had happened. I still don't think he believes me. But at the beginning of his Celtics' career, not many N.B.A. people believed in his potential. Red Auerbach selected 6–11 center Charley Share of Bowling Green as the Celtics' first draft choice while putting down Cooz as "too fancy." Cooz eventually was drafted by Tri-Cities, a franchise that represented Moline, Ill., Rock Island, Ill., and Davenport, Ia., during the N.B.A.'s early years. When that franchise soon folded, Cooz's name went into a hat along with those of two experienced N.B.A. players, Max Zaslofsky and Andy Phillip.

Zaslofsky was chosen first, by the New York Knicks; Phillip was chosen next, by the Philadelphia Warriors; Bob Cousy joined the Celtics—by default, then helped them win six N.B.A. championships.

So when Doctor J was still being derided by N.B.A. people in 1976 because he was playing with a red-white-and-blue basketball, I knew I had heard that song before, about Bob Cousy because he was too fancy, and about Joe Namath because he was in the "other league." I hadn't suddenly jumped on Doctor J's bandwagon. I had written about Doctor J as early as the summer of 1972, when he was playing in a Harlem playground on weekends. I talked to him there in a small red-brick Park Department supply room with dusty cans and boxes. That was the locker room.

"No showers," he explained. "Usually the school next door is open and we change there. But it's closed today."

He was with the Virginia Squires then. He joined the New York Nets the next year but he still wasn't fully accepted two months before the 1976 treaty between the leagues:

He had stunned the Denver Nuggets with 31 points, including six in the final thirty seconds that provided the New York Nets with a 117–111 victory. He also had ten rebounds, four assists, two steals and four blocked shots —another merely spectacular game for Julius Erving, the merely spectacular Doctor J, the surgeon in sneakers. But the Nuggets appeared most stunned by the memory of two blocked shots in the closing minutes when the game was being decided. "He got there quicker than I thought," Chuck Williams said. "I didn't even see him," Bobby Jones said. "He came out of nowhere." That's not surprising. Doctor J performs in nowhere. He is the best basketball player in captivity, perhaps in history. But the Nets are competing for the American Basketball Association championship and, sadly, that's nowhere. Only 12,243 customers attended Thursday night's game. When the four-of-seven series resumes tonight at the Nassau Coliseum with the Nets leading, 2–1, a sellout might materialize, the way relatives gather at a deathbed.

Only six teams remain breathing in the A.B.A. as it seeks survival in a treaty with the National Basketball Association after nine seasons of struggle. The treaty negotiations involve economics—initiation fees, TV income, indemnities. Everything but basketball itself.

If the treaty involved basketball, the N.B.A. would be seeking it because the N.B.A. can't call itself the best basketball league until it includes the best basketball player. Without the merely spectacular Doctor J, the N.B.A. hasn't fulfilled its commitment to the public.

The N.B.A. without Doctor J is like boxing without Muhammad Ali, football without O. J. Simpson, baseball without Tom Seaver.

The shame is that some people, possibly many people, don't appreciate Doctor J's skills because A.B.A. games are not shown on national television. Out of sight, out of mind. It's as if Nureyev were dancing on a street corner, or Picasso were displaying his paintings in a park. But in three games against the Denver Nuggets, a team that is superior to most N.B.A.

teams, the merely spectacular Doctor J has scored 124 points in 123 minutes. He has averaged 41.3 points a game. Over his A.B.A. career, the six-foot-six-inch forward has averaged 30.8 points in 45 playoff games. The highest scoring averages in N.B.A. playoff history are 29.7 by Kareem Abdul-Jabbar in 57 games and 29.1 by Jerry West in 153 games.

The level of team competition might be tougher in the N.B.A., but that's not really the point. In the A.B.A. it's often tougher for Doctor J because he attracts double coverage. And his versatility enables him to do much of what Kareem Abdul-Jabbar could do under the boards and much of what Jerry West could do on the perimeter. His scoring average reflects only a portion of Doctor J's merely spectacular skills.

"Without him," says Joe Mullaney, who coached the Spirits of St. Louis this season and who once coached the Los Angeles Lakers, "the Nets would be a mediocre team."

With him, the Nets probably will win the A.B.A. championship for the second time in three seasons since he was obtained from the Virginia Squires, the latest A.B.A. team to go bankrupt. But the A.B.A. is not the proper stage for the merely spectacular Doctor J, the best basketball player. He belongs in prime time instead of obscurity. He belongs somewhere special instead of nowhere.

He still has time. He turned twenty-six years old about two months ago. He's not even at his peak as a player yet.

Doctor J professes not to resent the limited recognition he receives because he performs in the A.B.A.

"Not individually," he was saying now. "I have more feelings about the other A.B.A. players who aren't recognized for their talent: Ron Boone, Marvin Barnes, Bird Averitt—he doesn't even get recognition in our league —Jim Silas, Ron Buse, Billy Knight, George Gervin. But the players in the other league know these guys. The public doesn't, but the players in the other league do."

"What about a treaty with the N.B.A.?" he was asked.

"I'd receive it favorably," he said. "I think it would be good for all pro basketball."

"Would you like to go in with the Nets as a complete team?"

"Absolutely," he said, "and we would be a winning team."

"Are you satisfied that people know who you are?"

"I think most people know who I am," he said, "but they might not know what I look like."

"Do you feel," he was asked, "you could do in the other league the same things you do in this league?"

"Yup," he said quickly.

Julius Erving wasn't being smug or sarcastic. Julius Erving isn't like that.

He simply knows what he can do. And he knows that he can do more things better than any other basketball player. He doesn't talk about it, he just does it. Out in Denver he was shooting by himself after practice when a by-stander mentioned that David Thompson of the Nuggets was the only player who could do a full 360-degree turn in the air and slam-dunk a basketball. Without a word, the merely spectacular Doctor J hitched up his knee braces, retreated a few steps, soared into the air, spun 360 degrees, slam-dunked the ball and walked off the court.

Yup.

(April 8, 1976)

Following the treaty, Doctor J was sold to the Philadelphia 76ers in a $6 million deal—$3 million to the Nets, a $3 million contract for the Doctor—after a contract dispute with Roy Boe, then the Nets' principal owner. That was a mess. Doctor J was guilty of malpractice, Roy Boe was guilty of betraying his franchise. But on the court, Doctor J proved what everybody who had believed in him had expected—that he would be as spectacular in the N.B.A. as he had been in the A.B.A.

But because some of the 76ers have not related to basketball as a team game, the 76ers have had to struggle to win the N.B.A. championship.

More than any other game, basketball requires a *team* concept. One ball must be shared by five players, by five egos, really. That concept symbolized the Boston Celtics when they won eleven NBA championships in thirteen years. It also symbolized the Knicks, who won the 1970 and 1973 titles. None of the Knicks appreciated that concept more than their Rhodes Scholar who retired in 1977:

He never could jump high enough to dunk the ball. His hands never were big enough to palm the ball. But he has been the purest basketball player of all. Bill Bradley understood and appreciated the game for the game. And now it's almost all over. He's starting his last week of work for the New York Knicks today in a matinee in Madison Square Garden that's a cruel reminder of the glory years. Many of the Knicks' big playoff games at the Garden were in April and May on warm Sunday afternoons. Bill Bradley remembers those warm months.

"The warmer it was, the better it was," he says, "because it meant the deeper we were into the playoffs."

Twice the Knicks won the National Basketball Association championship. That's what Bill Bradley is most proud of.

"That," he says, "and the fact we played the game the way it's supposed to be played—together, as a team."

Ask him about his most memorable game and he'll say the fifth game of the 1970 playoff final with the Los Angeles Lakers. The Knicks rallied in the fourth quarter without Willis Reed, who had injured his thigh in the first half, for a 107–100 victory and a 3–2 lead in the series that they would win in the seventh game. Bill Bradley made several important baskets in the closing minutes of that game, but to him it's not memorable for anything that he did.

"It's a team memory," he says.

That's what the memory of Bill Bradley should be like—a collective memory, a montage of an arched left eyebrow, an angular smile, a gawky body that seemed about to tip forward, a mouth moving as he muttered to himself, his movement without the ball and then that quick one-hander, and his concentration. Especially that concentration.

"His philosophy," his Princeton coach, Bill van Breda Kolff, once said, "was so old-fashioned it was new—practice makes perfect."

And there are the small memories, such as that day in 1967 when the Knicks put their embarrassed rookie from Princeton and Oxford on display for photographers. After half an hour, the photographers put down their cameras. Bill Bradley stood up to leave.

"No, no," a photographer said. "I've got to shoot color now for a magazine cover."

"Me on the cover?" the rookie said. "That's not right. I haven't played a game yet."

"Don't worry," somebody joked, "the story will say, 'Why Bill Bradley Won't Make It.' "

"Oh, that's all right," Bill Bradley said, laughing. "This is the picture of a flop."

He never was a flop, he just needed a little time. But when Cazzie Russell broke his wrist early the next season, Bill Bradley was ready. And when Dave DeBusschere arrived in a trade to join Willis Reed, Walt Frazier, Dick Barnett and Bill Bradley, the Knicks had a team that thrilled the town. Some people believe that Bill Bradley provided the Knicks with intellectual credibility. If a Rhodes scholar was playing in the N.B.A., then the Madison Avenue people not only accepted it, they purchased season tickets and shouted "Dee-fense" like everybody else.

But the purity of Bill Bradley would not let him accept the Madison Avenue offers of TV commercials.

"I had three reasons," he says. "I was suspicious of the advertising industry that manufactures needs, then sells products to foster those needs. Second, some offers were coming to me as a 'white hope' and that offended me. Third, basketball was an important part of my life, I wanted to keep it pure. I cared about basketball, but hair sprays and deodorants and popcorn poppers were not basketball."

When the Knicks hierarchy asked him early this season if he would be interested in coaching, he reacted the same way.

"I don't know if that talk was exploratory or serious, but I responded negatively and that was the end of it," he says. "For me, the joy and the reason to be in basketball was to be a player. Being a coach or general manager was one or two steps removed from that primary experience. The real joy is playing."

When the playing ends next Sunday, he'll devote himself to politics.

"I'll work hard for the Democratic Party in New Jersey," he says. "I hope to campaign for the Democratic candidate for governor and I want to work on issues. I'll expand my role on the board of directors for the Cancer Research Institute and for the March of Dimes."

None of that work is salaried, but thirty-three-year-old Bill Bradley has earned about $2.5 million from the Knicks in his ten seasons.

"Now that I have more time," he says, "I plan to make a little money from writing and speaking."

Bill Bradley once was described by Phil Jackson as a "basketball junkie," but his addiction is cured. He doesn't plan to shoot baskets in the playground near his Denville, N.J., home where he lives with his wife and their four-month-old daughter, Theresa Anne, but he does intend to see the Knicks play "a few games" in the Garden next season. At one of them the Knicks should retire his number "24" and hang it on a banner from the ceiling alongside Willis Reed's "19" as another reminder of the championship seasons when the Knicks played the game the way it's supposed to be played—together as a team.

(March 3, 1977)

In their glory years, the Knicks were easy to talk to, easy to write about. But in every sport, there are subjects that challenge a sportswriter. In basketball, Kareem Abdul-Jabbar was that subject. When he was Lew Alcindor, a U.C.L.A. sophomore, I covered a Jets-

Raiders game in Oakland on a Saturday afternoon, hopped a flight to Los Angeles and hurried into Pauley Pavilion with my luggage and typewriter as the national anthem was being played for U.C.-L.A.'s season opener against U.S.C., his varsity debut. He scored 56 points that night and I described him as "awesome," wondering if perhaps that word wasn't too strong.

But when Coach John Wooden came out of the U.C.L.A. locker room to talk to the sportswriters, his first words were "Lew was awesome."

And as Kareem Abdul-Jabbar, he has continued to be awesome on the court. Off it, he was somewhat awesome too. He seldom smiled. He seldom appeared relaxed. At least not when talking to sportswriters. But there had to be a side of him that smiled, that enjoyed life. I was determined to discover that side but I knew I couldn't do it in a locker-room interview. I arranged to meet him in the Milwaukee Bucks' hotel on a trip to New York shortly before the 1974 playoffs. I brought along a rare picture of him smiling:

His image is one of glowering concentration. He leads the National Basketball Association in stares. But in the photo, Kareem Abdul-Jabbar was doing something he is rarely seen doing. He was smiling. He was sitting on the Milwaukee Bucks' bench and actually smiling. When he was shown the photo, he smiled again.

"This was at the end of a game when the subs were doing their thing," he said. "It probably involved one of our guards, Russell Lee, maybe a stuff shot. Russell is a very excitable young man."

He smiled as he continued to look at the photo. He was sitting in his room Friday night at the City Squire motor inn, where the Bucks awaited their game with the New York Knicks last night. Soon his face was serious again, as it always seems to be when he is performing as the N.B.A.'s most dominant player.

"That," he explained, "is mainly because I'm trying to do my job, and when I think about that I get very serious."

In repose, as he was now, he smiled easily and often. But when he spoke intently, his expression remained intent.

"I'm basically serious, but I laugh at a lot of things. People are funny," he said. "I'm not schizophrenic. It's just that most people relate to me either as a basketball player or as a seven-foot object, not as a person. That's what I have to deal with."

His extreme height as a youngster influenced his intent expression.

"I always was taller than other kids, but I was younger, too. You kind of withdraw in that situation. The things you don't know about, you let go by. After a while it came to be my natural demeanor. Like my freshman year at Power," he said, referring to his New York high school. "I was fourteen most of that year, but I was on the varsity with guys seventeen and eighteen, guys getting ready to go to college, guys with all the experiences of adolescence. You end up doing a whole lot of homework on what life's all about, figuring out certain things were cool and certain things weren't too cool. By the time I was a senior that age gap no longer existed, but because of my height the gap was between me and the people around me."

The gap will always be there, no matter where he is.

"In the off season I've traveled around the world," he said. "Outside this country, nobody knows I'm a basketball player, but they regard me as a giant. Like in Thailand, the people there are very short, and, wow, they didn't say too much, but they stared. One time in Pakistan I had three hundred people following me. That can unnerve you. I had to get in a cab. And in Istanbul, two little boys followed me. I doubled back and caught them, just to play a joke on them."

He glanced at his watch and phoned his wife in Milwaukee, but while he was speaking to her a room-service waiter wheeled in his dinner—broiled chicken, salad, pound cake and two glasses of orange juice. He signed the bill and handed a tip to the waiter.

"The tip's included," the waiter said. "Fifteen percent."

With a grin, he snatched the tip away from the waiter.

"An honest man," he said when the waiter had left. "I didn't expect that to happen in New York."

He grew up here as Lew Alcindor, but he's not always comfortable here now.

"I'll always be a New Yorker," he said, "but I don't like New York like I used to. After living outside New York you realize that a lot of the things people say about New York are true."

Four years ago, when the Knicks eliminated the Bucks in a five-game playoff, the Garden fans sang, "Goodbye, Lewie."

"I wasn't surprised by it. Having grown up here, it seems like something they would do. But I can't be that worried about it either. That's one of the quirks of human nature. But it hasn't made me think about needing to have a big game here. I don't want to get psyched out that I feel I've got to do this or do that when I come to New York."

As a youngster in Upper Manhattan he followed the Brooklyn Dodgers, the football Giants and the Knicks.

"My year was 1955," he said, recalling the Dodgers' first World Series triumph. "I was in third grade and everybody in my school were Yankee fans. They had an endless winter of me. I was a diehard Giant fan in the seventh and eighth grades. I went to all their games and sat in the bleachers. I used to buy two cups of coffee and just hold them to keep my hands warm. I spent about a dollar on coffee. That's why my number is thirty-three, that was Mel Triplett's number.

"I still don't like the Baltimore Colts because they beat the Giants, and I didn't like Wisconsin then because it was so cold whenever the Giants played the Packers there. And the Knicks in those years, very sad. Charlie Tyra, Donnis Butcher, Cleveland Buckner. In the summer I liked to swim at Rockaway, where my father was a lifeguard. I like horseback riding and tennis now. I like being alive on the planet earth, but even with Watergate I'm not into politics much. Politics is more or less the art of deception. You're dealing with illusions. The more that comes out about Watergate, the more confused you get."

Suddenly, he looked away from his dinner. He was staring at the night table where the white telephone was off the hook.

"I left my wife on the phone," he said, rushing to pick it up. "She hung up on me. Oh, wow, I got to call her back."

(March 10, 1974)

I wonder if Milwaukee people appreciated how fortunate they were to have had both Kareem Abdul-Jabbar, the N.B.A.'s most dominant player, and Al McGuire, college basketball's most colorful coach. But the world turns. Kareem forced a trade to the Los Angeles Lakers, and Al announced that the 1976–77 season would be his last long before his Marquette team got to the N.C.A.A. final:

ATLANTA—"Sports," said Al McGuire once upon a time, "is a coffee break." His coffee break is about over. He will retire as Marquette's basketball coach after the National College Athletic Association championship game Monday night. He is forty-eight years old, which means he is retiring on his schedule. "Can you imagine being in your fifties," he once said, "and still worrying if some cheerleader is pregnant?" Or even worrying about winning a basketball game. "Winning is only important," he has said, "in war and surgery." Long after Al McGuire's success as a coach is forgotten, his philosophy and his phrases will be remembered and repeated. Some of his words deserve to be chiseled on stone tablets or at least carved into the boardwalk at Rockaway Beach, where he grew up—

On aggressiveness: "If you haven't broken your nose in basketball, you haven't really played. You've just tokened it."

On his coaching habits: "I've never blown a whistle, looked at a film, worked at a blackboard or organized a practice in my life."

On his coaching style: "Every coach coaches the way he played. I couldn't shoot, so I coach defense."

On handling players: "My era is over. Dictator coaches are finished. I was good for the 'Burn, Baby, Burn' atmosphere. It's time now for coaches who sit in dens."

On his team's style: "The team should be an extension of a coach's personality. My team is arrogant and obnoxious."

On fundamentals: "I'm not sure I have the basketball knowledge of a good high school coach. I don't know if I coach. I think I'm like the master of ceremonies. I create a party on the court and keep it going. I have people with me who do a lot of coaching, but I never know what leg to tell a kid to put out first to make a lay-up."

On his team's philosophy: "We run a black defense and a white offense. Nobody could be a star under our system."

On strategy: "It's a Simple Simon game. Most of the time it's like a kindergarten. When you have the ball, you are king. But when I have it, I am king. When you dribble, you are king. But when you stop, I am king."

When his black players once threatened to stop playing during a nationally televised game to honor the memory of Dr. Martin Luther King: "You don't have to stop playing, I'll call a time-out."

On the value of pre-game meals: "Give me kids who'll win on a pizza and a Coke."

When some Marquette rooters questioned his players screaming at him: "It's healthy. I also notice that the screaming always comes when we're fifteen, twenty points ahead. When it's tied, they're all listening very carefully to what I have to say."

On his type of player: "I can't recruit a kid who has a front lawn. Give me a tenement and a sidewalk."

When he was trying to recruit Ernie Grunfeld, now an all-American at Tennessee: "Look, Ernie, if you want to wear a blazer, go to Tennessee; if you want to play basketball, come to Marquette."

When leaving on a vacation: "I'm going to Tibet, maybe I can recruit the Abominable Snowman."

On recruiting: "I got to get the best because that's the only way I can be good. If I want shrimp cocktail, I got to get shrimp, I can't get octopus."

On his New York accent: "Back in New York, I sound like just another bartender, but in Milwaukee, it's music, like a Southern accent."

On how to determine if a player has hung onto the rim after a dunk, a technical foul: "Electrify the rim. If a guy's hand touched it, you leave the juice on until he turns blue."

On coaching's social value: "Help one kid at a time. He'll maybe go back and help a few more. In a generation, you'll have something."

On teaching history at Belmont Abbey when he coached there: "All you do is stay six pages ahead of the class. When somebody asked me a question I couldn't answer, I said, 'It'll take too much time to explain, see me after class.' We had two doors in each classroom. When the period ended, I ran out whichever door the kid wasn't near."

On barroom brawlers: "If a guy takes off his wrist watch before he fights, he means business."

On racial philosophy: "The only two things blacks have dominated are basketball and poverty."

On education: "I think everyone should go to college and get a degree, then spend six months as a bartender and six months as a cab driver. Then they'd really be educated."

On priorities: "You have to know what's important. Don't come to me with a haircut problem. Come to me with a hit-and-run problem. Go after a parrot with a slingshot, not a cannon."

When a busboy dropped a tray of dishes: "The most expensive thing in the world is cheap help."

On his critics: "They call me eccentric. They used to call me nuts. I haven't changed. The only difference between being eccentric and being nuts is the number of security boxes you own."

As the vice chairman of Medalist Inc., a sports equipment firm, Al McGuire owns several security boxes. He's retiring as a coach in order to devote his time to that business. Without him, college basketball won't be quite the same.

"But you got to remember it's a game," Al McGuire once said. "If we lose, a new star will appear in the East."

But a new coach like Al McGuire will not appear anywhere. His legacy is that there will not be another like him.

(March 27, 1977)

Marquette won that N.C.A.A. title in a joyous, sentimental triumph that seemed to exemplify everything that is good about college basketball. In contrast, when Kentucky won the N.C.A.A. title in 1978 its championship seemed to exemplify everything that is bad about college basketball. At least to me:

ST. LOUIS—Out on the court his Kentucky players were cutting down the nets as mementos of the National Collegiate basketball championship. But the Wildcats' coach, Joe B. Hall, in his navy-blue three-piece suit, had walked back into the stands to embrace his family and shake hands with some rooters with blue-and-white buttons. "He's the greatest," one of the Kentucky rooters was saying now as the coach returned to the court for the presentation ceremonies. "He's the greatest coach there is." But a stranger asked the rooter what he would have thought of Joe B. Hall if Kentucky had lost to Duke last night. "I," the rooter replied, "would have cut his throat." Or perhaps Joe B. Hall would have cut his own throat. Sadly, that's the aura that Kentucky basketball projects. Before the championship game, Joe B. Hall had talked of how this had been a "season without celebration" because of the burden of being No. 1 in the wire-service polls and of being expected to win the title. But now that Kentucky indeed was No. 1, the jubilation of both the coach and his players appeared to be forced. They seemed to be celebrating having avoided defeat rather than having achieved a championship. Duke, its players hugging each other in genuine warmth derived from Coach Bill Foster, seemed to be enjoying finishing second more than Kentucky enjoyed finishing first.

College sports is supposed to be fun, supposed to be part of the learning experience. But about all that the Kentucky players appeared to be learning was how to survive in a torture chamber.

Don't put all the blame on Joe B. Hall for this atmosphere. The late Adolph Rupp created this atmosphere for Kentucky basketball and the Wildcat rooters have perpetuated it. Joe B. Hall succeeded Adolph Rupp six years ago, but he has never replaced him and probably never will, surely not as long as Kentucky's home court in Lexington is known as the Rupp Arena, a memorial to the baron of the blue grass who created the burden of success that Joe B. Hall must live with now.

"It takes you six to eight years to get over playing for Adolph Rupp," one of his players of two decades ago, Vernon Hatton, has said. "But once you get over it, you get to like him."

Adolph Rupp's teams won four national championships, in 1948, 1949, 1951 and 1958, and now Joe B. Hall has provided Kentucky with a fifth title, but its first with black players. One of the black players, Jack Givens, scored 41 points in the 94–88 victory over Duke, recalling a story, perhaps apocryphal, that is still told about Adolph Rupp from the years when Kentucky shunned black players. Every so often a scout would file reports on high school players in his area, along with newspaper clippings of box scores. But he never filed a report on a certain star.

"What about him?" Adolph Rupp is said to have asked the scout. "Tell me about him?"

"You can't use him, Coach," the scout replied. "He's the wrong color for your team."

"Wouldn't you think," Adolph Rupp growled, "they'd put an asterisk next to them."

But black or white, the Kentucky players have the haunted look of people who will need six to eight years to get over playing for Joe B. Hall, a sometime cattle rancher and tobacco farmer who is whispered to have raised $750,000 for a basketball dorm that was named for him until recently, when his name was removed because of university policy. Joe B. Hall was enraged.

"That's fooling with a man's name," he complained. "Your name is the most important thing you have."

Joe B. Hall sometimes seems to resent his role as Adolph Rupp's successor. At a news conference Sunday, the coach and five of his players—Rick Robey, Mike Phillips, Kyle Macy, Truman Claytor and Jay Shidler—sat behind a table on a platform as if they were on trial. And in a sense, they were, indicted by their own success and by their reputation as a "physical" team.

"So much is expected of us," Joe B. Hall said. "Our fans start out the first day in practice saying, 'We know you're going to win the N.C.A.A.'"

During the questioning, Rick Robey described Duke as "physical," a word that Joe B. Hall does not like to hear. The coach interrupted, saying with a rare smile, "Don't use that word. Say they play hard." Rick Robey, who smiles quicker than any of his teammates, laughed, and so did Joe B. Hall, briefly. But the four other players never cracked a smile. Perhaps they were afraid to smile. During a game, nobody on the Kentucky bench seems to smile, especially Joe B. Hall.

"In the two games here," said someone who sat close to the Kentucky bench, "there never seemed to be any joy until they finally won. Some of the coach's language was brutal in chewing out a player after a mistake. He wasn't supportive of his players. He hardly ever had eye contact with them as they came out of the game. Nobody seemed to be having any fun."

But the Kentucky fans had fun long into the night. And somewhere one of them was chuckling, presumably the one who threatened the life of Gene

Banks, the Duke freshman forward, in a telephone call to the Checkerdome before the game. If college basketball is so important in Kentucky that somebody would threaten a college kid's life in order to distract him in a championship game, it's to be wondered if somebody would've threatened Joe B. Hall's life, even as a prank, if Kentucky had lost the championship game.

And if that's what winning the college basketball championship is all about, Kentucky can have it.

(March 29, 1978)

The morning that column appeared in the Louisville *Courier-Journal,* my phone rang. Harold Claassen, the *Times* deputy sports editor, told me that a man in Kentucky had called to discuss the column with me. I phoned the man in Kentucky and he told me how he thought I had been unfair to the Kentucky basketball program and to its fans. Then he paused.

"I don't know what else to say," he said with a short laugh. "I didn't expect you to call back."

We had a brief, pleasant debate. But the next day the letters began arriving from Kentucky; more than one hundred of them. Almost all the letter writers denounced me. But there was one lady who wrote, "You're right, these people down here are nuts." I'll always wonder how many other Kentucky people agreed with me.

Two months later, the N.B.A. playoffs boiled down to one game in another significant plot:

If a sports event is not show biz now, it does not mean much. That is the gospel according to the TV ratings. How many homes? How big a share of the viewing audience? How much did the commercial minutes sell for? That's all that's important. On that premise, the National Basketball Association championship series has not been important. "No superstars, no Doctor J, no David Thompson, no Bill Walton," says a TV man. "And no ratings." That's because the public is imbued with the superstar syndrome. And that's a shame. But as the Washington Bullets and the Seattle SuperSonics await tomorrow night's decisive seventh game, they have provided a refresher course in the most fundamental aspect of basketball—that it is a team game, perhaps the most intricate and subtle team game. One ball must be shared constantly by five egos. And that's why the Bullets and the SuperSonics are still playing long after the "superstars" stopped slam-dunking. That's why the championship series between the Bullets and the SuperSonics has been one of the most important in N.B.A. history.

"All the store-bought teams are home," says Dick Motta, the Bullets' coach. "This is basketball for the purist."

"If we function as a team, nobody can beat us," says Lenny Wilkens, the Sonics' coach. "This is a team game."

It's also a coach's game. Dick Motta is now the oldest N.B.A. coach in point of service—ten years, including his first eight with the Chicago Bulls. As a phys. ed. graduate of Utah State, he has been a coach—a teacher, really —for a quarter of a century. Whenever a rival N.B.A. team hires an ex-player with no coaching experience, he smiles.

"I hope," he says, "they keep hiring them."

Lenny Wilkens once was an ex-player hired as a coach. As a smart N.B.A. guard, he knew the game. But it took him five seasons with the Sonics and the Portland Trail Blazers to learn how to coach. When he replaced Bob Hopkins as the Sonics' coach last November 30, he knew what he had to do—change the entire starting lineup.

"I knew that we couldn't win with that lineup," says Lenny Wilkens, who had been the Sonics' player personnel director. "I'd seen them too many times before."

The Sonics' starters had been Mike Green at center, Bruce Seals and Paul Silas at forward, Slick Watts and Fred (Downtown) Brown at guard. Lenny Wilkens put Marvin Webster at center, Jack Sikma and John Johnson at forward, Dennis Johnson and Gus Williams at guard. Green and Watts soon were traded, but the coach has used Silas, who had played on two championship Boston Celtic teams, as a powerful rebounder and Brown as a "sixth man" sharpshooter.

"Our success," Lenny Wilkens says, "has confirmed my belief that you can still put together a team of players who work, enjoy each other's good plays and respect each other's games."

That's how the Trail Blazers won the N.B.A. title a year ago in the championship series with the Philadelphia 76ers, who could not even get by the Bullets in the Eastern Conference final this year. With the ups and downs of other N.B.A. teams, only the Bullets have qualified for the playoffs in each of the last ten seasons. But when Dick Motta succeeded K. C. Jones as coach, the Bullets had problems. Truck Robinson did not want to play with Elvin Hayes, Nick Weatherspoon was asking to be traded, Dave Bing was not a true playmaker, Kevin Grevey was a small forward who was unable to cover Julius Erving, among others. But one by one, Dick Motta solved the problems.

"Bob Ferry [the Bullets' general manager] understood that Truck and Elvin did not play well together," Dick Motta says. "We decided to keep the big, great forward over the kid. We traded Truck to Atlanta for the playmaker we needed, Tom Henderson. And in the swap of draft choices, we were able to get Greg Ballard."

Weatherspoon also was traded and Bing eventually was let go. And before the recent season began, the Bullets signed Bob Dandridge, formerly of the Milwaukee Bucks, as a free agent. Dandridge is the only expensive free agent on the Bullets; Gus Williams is the only expensive free agent on the Sonics.

"We knew Bob Dandridge could cover Doctor J for us," Dick Motta says. "You structure your team to the best talent in your division."

With Dandridge at forward, Grevey was available to be converted to guard when Phil Chenier's back ailments occurred. But the Bullets had another problem before the season began. Wes Unseld, who is built more like the Capitol than the Washington Monument, was considering retirement.

"Lots of people wanted Wes to retire so that Mitch Kupchak could play more," Dick Motta says. "As good as Mitch is, I wanted Wes too. He's stable. He sets screens, he's the best outlet passer in the league. I was used to a center like that in Chicago, like Tom Boerwinkle, and I wanted Wes."

And when Phil Chenier stopped playing in January, the Bullets signed Charles Johnson, who had been cut by the Golden State Warriors.

"We were down to seven players and we had to dress eight according to the league rules," Dick Motta recalls. "We thought about Herm Gilliam and Ken Charles; we even hesitated in signing C. J. because he was the same height as Larry Wright, but we liked his experience. He fit in right away."

When the Bullets surprised both the San Antonio Spurs and the 76ers in the playoffs, one ball was enough.

"There are only enough shots for four guys, usually only three," Dick Motta says. "You need an Unseld, a Silas, a Bill Russell, a guy who doesn't need the ball to be effective. Or to be happy. You need that balance. The Knicks used to have it. They could all score but they loved to pass so that provided the balance. But they all didn't have to score every game."

Now the Bullets and the Sonics have come down to one game for the championship.

"It's almost like a death march," Dick Motta says of the long campaign. "At the start of the season, everybody has to walk two thousand miles. The twelve strongest survive. Shoot the rest. Then the twelve go until they drop, one by one."

Dick Motta should not give TV any ideas. Imagine the ratings a "death march" would get.

(May 6, 1978)

The Bullets won the title, but both teams won the respect of everyone who understands basketball.

12 · Golf

Golf is my game. Not that I play it well. But nobody enjoys it more. Even playing badly is better than not playing at all.

I usually shoot anywhere from 86 to 96, depending on how often I'm playing and how difficult the course is. My handicap never changes. It's 18, which I consider fair because I was eighteen when I started playing. My first round was at Dyker Beach, a municipal course in Brooklyn near where the Verrazano Bridge is now. I've forgotten what I shot that day but I've never forgotten Dyker Beach, which always promoted itself as the world's most crowded golf course.

Weekend golfers waited as long as six hours to tee off. Sign up, go back to bed, have breakfast, read the papers, drive to the course again, practice putting and tee off. And then wait on every shot in a six-hour round.

Many of the fairways at Dyker Beach were parallel with only a few small trees in between. Drives from other tees often sliced or hooked into the wrong fairway, like shells on an artillery range. Some of the golfers didn't even know enough to yell "Fore." I'll never know why the pro shop didn't stock helmets.

Perhaps that's why I appreciate difficult courses now. Their fairways usually are separated by trees. It makes the course tougher. But it's safer.

No matter what I shoot, I always enjoy a difficult course. I had

112 once at Pebble Beach the day after Jack Nicklaus won the 1972 U.S. Open there. The rough was still ankle-high in most places, knee-high in some. I couldn't hit a wedge ten yards out of it, but I didn't care. The most important thing was that the kid from Dyker Beach was playing Pebble Beach.

In my travels and in the spirit of research, I collect courses. At last count, I'm approaching two hundred.

I've played some of the world's best—Pebble Beach, Augusta National, Winged Foot, Merion, Pine Valley, the Olympic Club, Southern Hills, Shinnecock Hills, Riviera, Baltusrol, the Old Course at St. Andrews and the two Muirfields, the original near Edinburgh, Scotland, and Muirfield Village outside Columbus, Ohio. The best part of my game is my bag tags.

"Hey," I once heard a teenage caddie whisper to another after noticing some of my bag tags, "who is this guy?"

He soon found out that this guy is a hacker. Of all those famous courses, the only one I've broken 90 at was St. Andrews, the Scottish shrine of golf. If you're a golfer, you'll understand why that was one of the nicest days of my life. That sense of golf's romance is about all that some of us have in common with the good golfers. In the first round of the 1978 Bing Crosby tournament, Tom Watson shot a six-under-par 66 at Cypress Point, the beautiful course that Frank (Sandy) Tatum, now the U.S. Golf Association president, has described as the "Sistine Chapel" of golf.

"To shoot a round like that," Tom Watson said later, "I know it sounds corny, but it's a big event in my life."

I know it sounds corny, but just playing a famous course is a big event in my life. Just walking it sometimes. The first time I walked Pebble Beach at the 1972 U.S. Open, it was sunny and warm and the surf was crashing along the rocks on the beach and the birds were chirping in the fir trees. When golfers are lining up their putts in the silence of a big tournament, I always listen for the birds. That communion with the course itself is what separates golf from, say, tennis. I've never heard a tennis player identify a match with a court. Except for the variations in surface, a tennis court is a tennis court is a tennis court. In contrast, every golf course is different. When a golfer shoots 68 or 78, or 88 or 98, at Pebble Beach, it means something.

Put a famous golfer on a famous course in a famous tournament and it really means something. I wasn't covering golf when Arnold Palmer was Arnold Palmer, but when he returned to Cherry Hills in Denver for the 1978 U.S. Open, he still was special:

DENVER—In the distance, the snow atop the Rocky Mountains melted into the brown foothills. And as Arnold Palmer stood on the first tee at the Cherry Hills Country Club today, his hair, surrounded by a white visor, seemed to melt the same way, the grayish white blending into the soft brown above that leathery face and neck. Arnold Palmer is forty-eight years old now. He hasn't won a tournament on the P.G.A. tour since 1973 and he isn't likely to win the U.S. Open this week. But that's not important. What is important is that Arnold Palmer remains Arnold Palmer, win or lose. Not many people in sports retain that magic. And this is where that magic started, where Arnold Palmer the golfer turned into Arnold Palmer the legend, where he made his most memorable "charge," where "Arnie's Army" was inspired, if not formed, when he won the 1960 U.S. Open with a 65 in the final round. His "charge" began when he drove the green of what then was the 346-yard, par-4 first hole. When he arrived on the first tee today, somebody yelled, "Drive the green again, Arnie," and he smiled. With a new tee set back in a chute of trees, the hole is 399 yards now and nobody drives it.

The others in his threesome, Rod Funseth and Lou Graham, hit first, then John Laupheimer, the deputy executive director of the United States Golf Association, announced, "Arnold Palmer, Ligonier, Pa." Applause and whistles erupted from behind the yellow gallery ropes.

With that familiar lunging swing, Arnold Palmer, wearing a maroon shirt and gray slacks with black golf shoes, smashed a long straight drive about 260 yards into the middle of the fairway. "Whooooo," yelled the spectators. When he lofted a wedge shot toward the undulating green, a whoop went up when the ball landed near the cup, but it bounced and rolled about 15 feet beyond. And then his birdie putt stopped about a foot short.

"Short," somebody whispered. "He never used to be short. He always gave himself a chance."

Arnold Palmer got his par there, as he did for the first five holes. When he bogeyed the sixth and the eighth holes, his Army had a few deserters. But the loyalists remained, waiting for another magic tournament, another magic round, another magic shot like the 1960 drive that is commemorated by a plaque set in red brick near the old first tee that the members still use.

"The new tees at the first and the eleventh holes," Arnold Palmer had said in the men's locker room. "Those are the only real changes in the course since 1960."

But the men's locker room hasn't changed that much. That's where the drama developed that year. In those years the Open format demanded a 36-hole finish on Saturday, a round in the morning and another round in the afternoon. Arnold Palmer shot 72 that morning to fall seven strokes behind Mike Souchak, the leader. Thirteen other players were ahead of him and eight others were tied with him at 215.

"I remember I had only about twenty minutes, and I ordered a quick hamburger in the locker room," Arnold Palmer recalled. "And that's when Bob Drum came in."

Now something of a legend himself among golf raconteurs, Bob Drum then was the Pittsburgh *Press* golf writer who accompanied the Latrobe, Pa., golfer almost everywhere. Arnold Palmer asked Drum what he thought a 65 would do in the final round and Drum scoffed.

"No good," Drum growled. "You're out of it."

"The hell I am. A sixty-five will give me two hundred and eighty," Arnold Palmer said, "and a two hundred and eighty will win the Open."

"Forget it," Drum barked. "You're out of it."

Annoyed and angry, Arnold Palmer didn't forget it. Instead, he drove the first green for a birdie. Then he had birdies on the second, third, fourth and seventh holes.

Even with a bogey on the eighth, his 30 for the front nine tied the Open record. With a 35 on the back nine, his 65 for 280 won by two strokes over a chubby blond amateur named Jack Nicklaus; the Palmer "charge" had been copyrighted.

"Telephone call," a man was saying now to Palmer in the locker room today. "That phone over there."

When the phone conversation ended, Arnold Palmer laughed. "I just got my lesson before I started my round," he said. "That was an old golf-pro friend of mine." Then he walked out of the locker room toward the practice tee, but he was instantly surrounded by two dozen autograph seekers—men, women and children.

"Let's zing 'em today, Arnie," a man said.

"Can we make way, please," a marshal said.

But patiently, Arnold Palmer signed all the autographs, always looking up at the women and the girls and flashing that famous smile. Then he walked out onto the practice tee, where his caddie, who is also his new son-in-law, Doug Reintgen, waited in white coveralls. Doug Reintgen, with one more year to go at Duke Medical School, was married to Peggy Palmer last Saturday and he's spending his honeymoon caddying for his father-in-law, who now was hitting short iron shots.

"I always warm up with my driver first," a middle-aged male onlooker said. "I guess I been doing it wrong."

"His shirt is always out in the back," a middle-aged woman said when Arnold Palmer was hitting a 3-wood. "Always."

His warm-up complete, Arnold Palmer signed a few more autographs, then strode through the crowd and putted on the small practice green near the plaque and the old first tee. Soon he was striding toward the new tee when a gray-haired man approached him.

"If you sign this," the man said, "I'll guarantee you'll drive the green today."

Arnold Palmer laughed and signed his name. But he did not drive the first green. He did not shoot 65 either; he shot 76, which is five over par. And he had only one birdie. But he's still Arnold Palmer, and that's enough.

(June 16, 1978)

But, for all Arnold Palmer's popularity, Jack Nicklaus has been the supreme golfer of our time. Perhaps his best year was 1972, when he won both the Masters and the U.S. Open (at Pebble Beach); suddenly he had an opportunity to complete an unprecedented pro grand slam if he could also win the British Open and the P.G.A. championship. At the British Open at Muirfield that year, I was standing among a gallery of golf-knowledgeable Scots who were following Jack in a practice round. Next to me was a middle-aged man and his young son. As they watched Jack's iron shot bore through the breeze and land about 12 feet from the pin on the fifteenth green, the father turned to the boy. "Aye, lad," the father said, "there's a mon to watch."

When the tournament began, Lee Trevino was the mon to watch. After three rounds, he was the leader at 207, with Tony Jacklin of England one shot back and Jack six shots behind. Jack often had hit a 3-wood or a 1-iron off the tee to assure being in the fairway rather than in the high grass or heavy gorse. But in the final round he was blasting tee shots with his driver and then spinning wedge shots at the cup in the boldest round of golf I've ever seen:

MUIRFIELD, Scotland—Striding off the seventh tee today, Jack Nicklaus turned to a friend in his gallery. "Ask Barbara to stop at nine and get me a cold lemonade," he said, referring to his wife. "Tell her no lime juice. It's dry enough out here without any lime juice."

The dryness was from the electricity. In the final round of the British Open golf tournament, Jack Nicklaus was showing what makes him tick. At the start he had been six shots behind Lee Trevino, the leader, but he had to win to keep his chances alive for the grand slam. As he gulped the lemonade on the tenth tee, he had a 4-under-par 32 on the front nine to tie Trevino for the lead. And the electricity kept flowing. When he dropped a six-foot putt for a birdie on the tenth, he led by a stroke.

Another birdie occurred at the eleventh with a five-foot putt. He was 6 under par now, going for a 65, which would be a course record for the Muirfield links.

After four more pars, he came to the tee of the par-3, 188-yard sixteenth hole tied with Trevino, who had a birdie on the eleventh to produce one of many roars that rumbled across the moors. Nicklaus chose a 4-iron, but his tee shot into the cooling wind rolled halfway down the bank into low rough on the left side of the green.

"Another few feet in the air," he would say later, "and it would have stayed on the green, about twenty-five feet from the cup."

But it hadn't. And his pitch shot was also too far to the left, about five feet. As he stood over his putt, the sound of bagpipes in the distance intruded on the silence. The putt slid by the cup. It would be the only bogey in a 66 on his scorecard, but it would be remembered as the hole where his bid for the grand slam was lost.

But a playoff with Trevino almost did occur. After a par at each of the last two holes, Nicklaus came off the eighteenth green with a sad smile and a shrug. He glanced at the scoreboard, which showed Trevino and Tony Jacklin ahead of him by a stroke. Then he walked into the brown wooden shed where the Royal and Ancient Golf Club officials registered each contestant's score.

"Trevino's blown!" somebody shouted.

Out on the seventeenth hole, Trevino was in the rough on his fourth shot, creating a probable bogey 6, maybe a double-bogey 7.

"He just holed his chip!" somebody yelled.

Outside the scorer's shed, Nicklaus's caddie, Jimmy Dickinson, flung down his yellow vest in disgust.

"He holed a chip shot for a five!" he yelled to Nicklaus.

"What?" Nicklaus said, his voice shrill in the shock.

Moments later Jacklin took three putts for a bogey 6. Now, if Trevino had a bogey 5 on the 447-yard eighteenth hole, Nicklaus would qualify for an eighteenth-hole playoff tomorrow. When he emerged from the scorer's shed, he went into the R. and A. office to watch Trevino's final hole on television. His arms were folded, his legs in chocolate-brown slacks crossed.

"Hit a long drive, didn't he?" Nicklaus said.

On the screen, with his flat swing, Trevino quickly floated an 8-iron shot close to the pin, assuring his par.

"At long last," the voice of Henry Longhurst said on television, "we have seen the shot that has won the Open."

In the trailer Nicklaus scratched his blond head and departed without a word. Quickly he was escorted toward the press tent, where his wife, in a red-leather pants suit, waited for him.

"Hi, there," she said softly. "Beautiful round."

Without a word he kissed her and held her for a moment, while others congratulated him on his dramatic attempt. Then he listened to the roar that greeted Trevino's winning par.

"I was there and let it get away," he said. "I felt a sixty-five would do it. I had a sixty-five and let it get away."

He let the grand slam get away, too. But in his disappointment Nicklaus also showed what makes him tick. Asked about the odds on his producing a grand slam another year, he laughed. "They're pretty high now," he said. Then, seriously, he added: "I shot two hundred and seventy-nine, and nineteen times out of twenty that'll probably win. But it didn't. That's what you're fighting, that somebody'll beat you. For sixteen rounds, to put it together, that's difficult. I'm disappointed because I felt I could put it together, but I didn't. I got beat. That's why everybody enters and plays. You don't want to give it to one guy."

He stood up and said, "Lee Trevino is some good player. If I had to lose, I'm glad it was to him."

(July 16, 1972)

But before Jack Nicklaus talked about what it had been like to shoot the 66 that wasn't enough, he showed his quality as a human being. He had come into the press tent and he was sitting behind a table up on a platform, not saying a word. And none of the sports-writers knew what to say to him. Among us was Norman Mair, of the Edinburgh *Guardian,* who had planned to travel to the P.G.A. championship at Oakland Hills, outside Detroit, to cover Jack's bid to complete the grand slam. But now that was unnecessary. After a long silence, Jack looked down at Norman and smiled. "Well, Norman," he said, "I guess I cost you a trip to Detroit."

In perhaps the most disappointing moment of Jack's golf career, he was considerate enough to think of how it affected somebody else. That's perhaps the most gracious thing I've ever heard an athlete say.

But just as Jack Nicklaus and Arnold Palmer have been the reigning kings of men's golf over the last two decades, Nancy Lopez arrived in 1978 as the queen of the women's tour:

During the U. S. Open at Denver, a prankster tacked a name card on the press-tent scoreboard that read, "Lopez, Nancy." Next to it were the numbers "3-4-3-3," which would put her three under par for Cherry Hills' first four holes. The namecard and numbers soon were removed as too frivolous for the world's most prestigious golf tournament. But the message was clear. Nancy Lopez had transcended the women's tour. And when she won at Rochester last Sunday for her fifth consecutive victory, the word buzzed through Cherry Hills as quickly as Andy North's clutch putts on the back nine. Nancy Lopez suddenly is the biggest name in golf, bigger than Jack Nicklaus, bigger than Arnold Palmer. And if she wins a few more tournaments this year, she might be the biggest name in sports.

"The only thing wrong with Nancy," says one of golf's corporate types, "is that she doesn't know how to say no yet. But then Arnold couldn't say no either."

In that case, Nancy Lopez should never learn how to say no to autograph seekers or interviewers or photographers or anyone in "Nancy's Navy," as her gallery is known, in an "Arnie's Army" takeoff. It's her nature to be friendly, cooperative and obliging. To be nice. If her natural manner changes, her natural golf swing might change too. And then there wouldn't be anybody to say no to. Her natural manner is on display again this weekend in Hershey, Pa., where a sixth consecutive victory would lift her earnings on the Ladies Professional Golf Association tour this year to $137,698, although she is eight shots off the lead entering today's final round.

But the money does not make Nancy Lopez special. Her natural manner does.

In the tournament press tent the other day, Nancy Lopez started to say, "I'm going to play my—" then she quickly turned and whispered to Jeff Adams, the L.P.G.A. public relations coordinator, "—butt. Is it all right to say 'butt'?" Jeff Adams assured her it was.

"—play my butt off," Nancy Lopez continued with a smile.

When she arrived at the Greater Cincinnati Airport for the recent

L.P.G.A. championship, she was met by Tom Callahan, a Cincinnati *Enquirer* sports columnist who would take her to the Kings Island course. In the car, Tom Callahan confessed that he was not a tournament driver, that he had arranged to meet her in order to interview her during the trip.

"But how," Nancy Lopez asked, "can you take notes while you drive?"

"That's all right," Callahan said. "I'll remember what you say."

"No," she said. "Let's stop for an iced tea so you get it right."

When she won the L.P.G.A. title, she strolled into a Sunday-night party for the tournament volunteers who would have been delighted with a quick appearance. But she, her father, her boyfriend, her sister and her brother-in-law stayed for several hours. Eventually a small truck arrived with dinner for everybody.

"Somebody," says a man who was there, "had ordered Mexican food for one hundred people to be delivered."

During the Rochester tournament, one of her drives skulled a local dentist, Dr. Jerry Masolella, in her gallery. As he lay dazed, she held his hand and wept. The next morning she phoned him. And in her acceptance speech at the presentation ceremony, she pointed him out to the other spectators and blew him a kiss. All that is as natural for her as hitting a golf ball.

Moments later, on her way to the press tent last week on Father's Day, she stopped suddenly. "I've got to call my father," she explained. "I've got to call my father first on Father's Day."

Domingo Lopez, once a 4-handicap golfer who runs an auto-body repair shop in Roswell, N.M., nurtured Nancy's natural swing by telling her, "Hit the ball in the hole." Now that natural swing and natural manner have transformed her into a natural idol for thousands of young girls who suddenly will start playing golf just as thousands of young boys did when Arnold Palmer arrived as an idol two decades ago.

Equally important, Mark McCormack, who guided Arnold Palmer's career, has decreed that Nancy Lopez concentrate on golf, that she not be distracted by the business deals that appear almost hourly.

"We want to let her play," says Peter Johnson of Mark McCormack's firm. "She wants to get as much prize money as she can this year so that nobody will break her record for a long time. And there's no reason to rush into any deals now anyway. The offers keep getting bigger and bigger. Something that looked super a few weeks ago is peanuts now."

And in the back of Nancy Lopez's mind is the men's record of eleven consecutive tournament victories, set by Byron Nelson in 1955.

"Am I going after Mr. Nelson's record?" she said the other day with a grin. "Well, if I get to ten, I'll certainly go after the eleventh."

(June 25, 1978)

Nancy Lopez didn't win that Hershey tournament. But her streak had established her as a winner. Forevermore she will have the privilege of being able to lose without being accused of having "choked" on the final holes. That word has always annoyed me. If a golfer hits a bad shot, it doesn't necessarily mean that the pressure of the situation produced the bad shot. Sometimes a golfer just hits a bad shot.

More than any other golfer in recent years, Tom Watson had to endure that "choke" reputation. Unfairly, I thought, especially when he was leading the 1976 Masters after the second round:

AUGUSTA—On the eighteenth hole today, Tom Watson hooked a 5-iron to the left of the green, chipped up short and two-putted for a bogey 5. "Tom Watson," a man in the gallery muttered, "even finds a way to blow a thirty-six-hole lead." Two years ago Tom Watson won the British Open, and early this year he won both the Crosby and the San Diego Open in successive weeks. But three weeks ago he was leading the Tournament Players Championship by two shots with nine holes remaining, shot 77 and lost by four. Two weeks ago he was leading the Heritage Classic by four shots with eighteen holes remaining, shot 74 and lost by one. And when Tom Watson dropped into a share of the Masters lead with Rod Funseth at 139 today after a 3-under-par 69, golf people were wondering how Tom Watson would blow the Masters over the last two days.

It's not fair. As a touring pro, Tom Watson has earned $663,495, and he's only twenty-seven years old. Golf people should be emphasizing what he has accomplished instead of what he has failed to accomplish.

But that's the way golf people think. That's the nature of the game. They wonder how they're going to miss a putt instead of how they're going to make it. And that's the atmosphere that Tom Watson must cope with over the last 36 holes at the Augusta National Golf Club this Easter weekend.

Tom Watson would appear to be ideally suited to cope with that atmosphere. He was graduated from Stanford, where he majored in psychology.

But perhaps Tom Watson is too smart. Many of the young golfers on the tour never studied anything in college except the greens. When they play golf, they don't think, they react. With his reddish brown hair and his freckled face, Tom Watson resembles Huck Finn with a sand wedge and a diploma. But perhaps he thinks too much. Perhaps he worries about his swing too much, especially about how his swing will hold up under pressure. After all, a swing holds up only as well as the golfer holds up.

"Having a swing that will hold up," Tom Watson was saying now after his round. "When you don't believe in your golf swing, you don't hold up."

But when Tom Watson talked about his swing, he wasn't concerned with the flaws that bother most duffers. He was mostly concerned with what he called "tempo." He thought he had been playing too fast today, walking too fast, even waggling the club too fast. He had been hitting the ball with the bottom of the club face instead of the middle of the club face. That's a fine distinction that only a touring pro can appreciate. Not that he was complaining.

"I'm very pleased shooting sixty-nine today," he explained, "the way I played."

But then the word "choke" entered the conversation, the word that Tom Watson always seems to be asked about, the word that golf people always use so carelessly, as they did when Tom Watson blew his leads at both the T.P.C. and the Heritage tournaments.

"I didn't believe in my swing," he said. "I think that's different than choking."

"But how," the newsman persisted, "do you explain choking, how do you define it?"

"Everybody chokes," Tom Watson replied. "I choke, everybody chokes. But when I'm swinging well, I don't tend to choke as much as when I'm swinging badly. Very few players out here can play badly and win. I don't consider myself one of those players yet."

One of those very few is Jack Nicklaus, only three shots off the lead at 142 after a 2-under-par 70 in the second round.

"I'm a jumpy person," Tom Watson acknowledged. "Everything I do is fast—I walk fast, I waggle fast. I have to slow myself down. But when I won the Crosby, my tempo was very good. Much slower. I'm also a private person. I have to get away from golf every so often. That's one of the things that will let Nicklaus play for a long time. He can get away. But I can't. I've got obligations, I've got to establish myself. Another thing, I'm not as good with people and with crowds as some golfers are. I'm getting better, but I've got a long way to go. I don't talk that much. Leland [Duke] Gibson, the pro at Blue Hills Country Club in Kansas City, once told me, 'Let your clubs do your talking.' And that's what I try to do."

But it always comes back to his swing holding up under the pressure of the final round. Perhaps nothing in sports is more elusive than the golf swing.

"You feel different every day," Tom Watson said. "I had it off and on for six weeks in 1975 around when I won the British Open, but you never have it long."

The year before that, he was leading the U.S. Open at Winged Foot entering the final round but shot 79 as Hale Irwin won. The next week he finished with a 69 to win the Western Open. Most people forget that, but they remember how he blew the U.S. Open, and they'll remember if he blows the Masters this weekend.

"Does it irritate you," he was asked, "to be asked about choking?"

"No," said Tom Watson, "because I expect it. It's not true, but I know I'm going to be asked about it."

But then Tom Watson was asked whom he fears the most in the Masters over the final 36 holes. He smiled.

"Myself," he said.

(April 9, 1976)

Tom Watson went on to win that Masters in a theatrical duel with Jack Nicklaus over the final holes. Nobody accused Jack of choking when his 6-iron shot missed the eighteenth green moments after he heard the gallery roar for Tom's birdie at the seventeenth. Tom also won the British Open in another theatrical duel with Jack over the final holes. Ever since then nobody has accused Tom of "choking."

And let me say that in my moment of crisis as a golfer, I did not choke. The day after the first Memorial tournament at Muirfield Village in 1976 the committee members and sportswriters played the course. I was waiting to tee off with two committee members when Jack Nicklaus, the tournament host and architect of the course, strolled down from the clubhouse. The two committee members froze under his gaze. One chopped his drive into the rough to the left of the tee. The other shanked his drive into the woods on the right. Now it was my turn. I kept telling myself "Swing easy" and I did. I have hit better drives but not many. This one soared straight as an arrow, about 230 yards out. And as I watched it land in the middle of the fairway, I heard Jack Nicklaus say, "He not only can write, he can play."

Put it on my tombstone.

13 · Ali

He was Cassius Clay then. He was about to fight Doug Jones at the old Madison Square Garden in 1963 and he was staying at the Taft Hotel in midtown. I had never met him before. When he opened the door of his small suite, I was surprised that he was so tall, a big broad-shouldered six-four. But people don't think of him as tall. Then as now, he hardly ever mentions his size. He prefers to brag about his speed—his hand speed as well as foot speed. That day I settled into a soft chair and we had talked for half an hour when he suddenly was above me.

"Stand up," he ordered and I obeyed. "Put your hands up like a boxer. Now watch."

He was circling me now, flicking his left jab to within inches of my chin.

"Pop, pop, pop," he was saying. "Ain't never been a heavyweight fast as me."

He kept moving around and snapping his jab for maybe three minutes—just another round of shadowboxing. We sat down and talked awhile more, then I closed my notebook, thanked him for his time and got up to leave. At the door we shook hands. But as I walked down the hall, he kept talking.

"I am the greatest," I heard him saying as I got into the elevator. "I am the greatest . . . I am . . ."

He is Muhammad Ali now, of course, and he's won the world

heavyweight championship three times. But nothing else has really changed. He's still talking. He's still the most compelling and complex personality in sports. I treasure his genius as a boxer and as a showman. I laugh at his comic routines. I wince at his cruelty and admire his generosity. I yawn at his monotonous monologues. But there has never been a newsmaker like him in sports.

"And when I'm gone," he has said of his eventual retirement from boxing, "the game will go to the graveyard."

Not really. Boxing is bigger than he is. But he'll be missed. For nearly two decades, he has thrilled, entertained, confounded and conned the world as no other athlete ever has. I mean *the world,* because boxing is truly a world sport. And he's fought all over the world. I've followed him to Kinshasa and Manila and Kuala Lumpur, to Madison Square Garden and the Forum and the Superdome. When he won the title for the third time, I had covered thirty of his fights, including eighteen of his twenty-four title bouts.

I was still writing hockey in 1964 when he went against Sonny Liston, who had destroyed Floyd Patterson in two first-round knockouts. That night I sat in the darkness of the Teaneck (N.J.) Armory, watching a fuzzy closed-circuit TV screen. Liston stayed on his stool when the bell rang for the seventh round and Cassius Clay was the new heavyweight champion. The next day he announced his conversion to the Black Muslim sect. He first called himself Cassius X and then Muhammad Ali, although many people resisted using that name for several years. Some still resist.

Not long after Ali's reign began, I became the *Journal-American*'s boxing writer. Hugh Bradley had died and I succeeded him. One of my first assignments was to cover Ali's rematch with Liston, scheduled for the Boston Garden in November, 1964. But three nights before the fight, Ali needed emergency hernia surgery. He soon was up and around, often driving a big red-and-white bus with "World's Heavyweight Champion" inscribed on one side. The bus was his favorite toy then. To help promote the Floyd Patterson–George Chuvalo fight at Madison Square Garden that winter of 1965, he agreed to take about thirty writers and photographers in his bus to Chuvalo's training camp at Kutsher's, a Catskill mountain resort. The ride was routine until he turned into Kutsher's entrance. With snow covering the ditch alongside the narrow two-lane road, he moved the bus too far to the right. *Bump, bump, bump.* We were in the ditch, the bus tipped to the right. Up front, Ali slammed on the brakes. He turned slowly, his big eyes peeking back to see if anybody was hurt. Next to me, Bob Waters of *Newsday* yelled "Whiplash" and held his neck.

Bob also held back a laugh. Ali's feelings were all that were hurt. Apparently he was not the greatest bus driver. The bus had to be towed out of the ditch for the ride back to the city.

His hernia healed, Ali was soon training again for Sonny Liston, with the May rematch to be held in Lewiston, Me., this time. Two days before the fight, Liston looked old and slow in a long workout at the nearby Poland Spring House, where he was lodged. He was punched around by his sparring partner, Amos (Big Train) Lincoln, and when he skipped rope, he kept getting his feet tangled. Desperate to make Sonny look good at something for the spectators who had packed the gym, trainer Willie Reddish used an old routine—heaving a medicine ball into Sonny's midsection. His stomach muscles flexed, Sonny hardly grunted as the heavy leather ball thumped off him. Some onlookers gasped at his show of strength, but in a far corner, Angelo Dundee shook his head.

"Why," whispered Ali's trainer, "don't Willie throw that ball in Sonny's face. That's where my guy's going to hit him."

That's exactly where his guy did hit Sonny in the first round. At that moment, Ali's back was directly above me. From my ringside seat, I saw the muscles behind his right shoulder move but I didn't see the punch itself. Across the ring Joe Louis was sitting behind Jimmy Cannon when Sonny went down from Ali's looping right hand to the jaw.

"Wouldn't crush a grape," Joe mumbled.

On the canvas, Sonny appeared about to get up but rolled over as if in surrender. After some confusion over the count because Ali had not retreated immediately to a neutral corner, referee Jersey Joe Walcott finally stopped the fight. The chant of "Fix, fix, fix" filled little St. Dominic's Arena and cynics still believe Sonny took a dive. Maybe so, but when Jersey Joe waved his hands, Sonny was on his feet, mixing it up.

I've always thought that Sonny just got caught cold with that right hand. How hard a right hand, only he knew.

Another theory is that the Black Muslims had warned Sonny not to win. If so, Sonny took that secret to his grave. In those years the

Black Muslims were much more obvious around Ali than they have been in recent years. In black suits and black bow ties, about a dozen escorted him into the ring. Not that everybody around him was a Black Muslim; his longtime jester, Drew (Bundini) Brown, never subscribed to the Black Muslim beliefs, especially their ban on alcoholic beverages. But he did not want to incur disfavor. The week before Ali fought Zora Folley in 1967, about six months after the *Times* hired me, I was sitting with Angelo Dundee across from Bundini (pronounced Boodini) at one end of a long table in Gallagher's restaurant. At the other end near the wall were Ali and his manager, Herbert Muhammad, with about a dozen others between us. Angelo and I each ordered a drink before dinner. As the waiter departed, Bundini grabbed his arm.

"Bring me a double martini," Bundini whispered. "But in a water glass, not a cocktail glass."

The waiter nodded and started to walk away, but Bundini grabbed his arm again and whispered, "No olive. Remember, no olive."

As far as Ali, Herbert and the other Black Muslims knew that night, Bundini was drinking water.

That was the same week that Ali, after a workout in the basement of the old Garden, sat in his dressing room and implied that he would go to prison rather than obey his Army induction order.

"For my beliefs," he said.

Nearly five weeks later, on April 28, 1967, in a Houston induction center, an Army lieutenant called out, "Cassius Clay—Army" and waited for that inductee to take the symbolic "step forward" in compliance with the military draft.

Muhammad Ali did not take the step.

Within hours Ali was stripped of the title by both the World Boxing Association and the New York State Athletic Commission; his exile had begun. It would not end until three and a half years later, when a court order permitted him to fight Jerry Quarry in Atlanta on October 26, 1970—"The Return of the Champion," as the bout was billed, even though Joe Frazier was now the recognized champion. Dancing as if he had never been away, Ali was awarded a third-round knockout over Quarry, who was bleeding from a long deep cut over his left eye.

"I have the title now," Ali snorted the next day. "Joe Frazier would like to fight me to be recognized by the people. Joe is just another contender now that I have a license."

Soon after Ali registered a fifteenth-round knockout of Oscar Bonavena, the burly Argentine, a showdown with Joe Frazier was arranged for the Garden on March 8, 1971, with each gladiator collecting an unprecedented fee of $2.5 million. When the extravaganza was announced at Toots Shor's restaurant, Jerry Perenchio, one of the promoters, predicted a "total gross box office of twenty to thirty million." Hearing that, Ali jumped to his feet on the dais and glanced at Frazier.

"They got us cheap," he shouted. "Only five million out of twenty to thirty; we've been taken."

In retrospect, they were taken. But everybody who saw that bout got their money's worth:

Even now the danger is that people are beginning to believe what Muhammad Ali proclaims rather than what really happened.

"I really won," he likes to say. "Joe Frazier had to go to the hospital after the whupping I gave him. I'm the real champ."

He must be trying to convince himself for the rematch. But the night of The Fight, when the bell rang ending the fifteenth round, Ali knew he wasn't the real champ. Moments earlier, he had been knocked onto his back by a left hook. To his credit, he rose as quickly as a man could. But now, his pride pierced and his jaw swollen, he hung his head as he waited for the decision. When the verdict was announced, he turned to his cornermen and said, "Let's get out of here." He didn't protest. He didn't appear at the postfight interview area to complain. He departed for a hospital where X-rays would show that his jaw was not fractured. The next day, wincing with soreness, he sprawled wearily in a bed in his hotel room.

"When a man gets me going, that's a punch," he said. "And when a man drops me, that's a hell of a punch. I didn't give the fight to him. He earned it."

To remember it in that perspective is important. In years to come, The Fight will be cherished as the sports event of our time. Its arithmetic was compelling. Each gladiator received $2.5 million. The total gross, dominated by worldwide TV revenue, was announced at $20 million by Jack Kent Cooke, who guaranteed $4.5 million of the fighters' fees. The live gate at Madison Square Garden was $1,352,951, a record for an indoor bout. But even more compelling was the atmosphere.

Probably never again will such a pairing exist—two unbeaten heavyweights, each with a claim to the title, each a social symbol.

Ali, also known as Cassius Clay, was the champion recognized by many of the boxing public. He had been deposed in 1967 following his draft-refusal conviction, which would be reversed by the Supreme Court three months after the Garden bout. Frazier was the champion recognized by the boxing politicians and also by those who resented Ali's defiance of the establishment.

In the ring before The Fight began, Ali's defiance recurred. Whirling in his red velvet robe, he shouldered Frazier twice, sneering as his rival glared.

When the bell rang, Ali's defiance continued. Muscled against the ropes, Ali waved to his constituents and shook his head, mocking the power of Frazier's punches. Ali thought that Frazier would tire, then he would pounce on his weary opponent and fulfill his prediction of a sixth-round knockout. Ali misjudged Frazier's fury. Instead of growing weary, Frazier grew stronger with the joy of combat. In one round, he dropped his gloves and laughed. After another, he playfully cuffed Ali on the head, smiling through his puffed face. Ali frowned, his defiance deflated.

"Layin' on the ropes and playing pitty-pat was my guy's big mistake," acknowledged Angelo Dundee, Ali's trainer. "The other guy wasn't putting any hurt on him, but he was making motion and winning points."

On the official scorecards, Frazier was a decisive winner. Judge Bill Recht had it 11–4 in rounds; Judge Artie Aidala had it 9–6; Referee Arthur Mercante had it 8–6 with one even. But physically, Frazier was exhausted. He entered a Philadelphia hospital a few days later for what his physician described as "high blood pressure" and "athlete's kidney." Ali immediately shouted that Frazier's exhaustion proved that the verdict had been incorrect.

Actually, all it proved was that Frazier had needed a rest after The Fight, while Ali had rested during it.

In his own mind, perhaps Ali doubted that he would win. Several days before, he had bragged about how he had been awarded a championship belt, while Frazier never had.

"I'll bring the belt into the ring," Ali promised, "and when he whips me, I'll hand him the belt."

Notice that Ali said, ". . . when he whips me," not "if he whips me." The doubt was there. Now that Ali has lost, the doubt will remain for the rematch, if one develops.

But it might be better if the rematch never develops. That way, The Fight will remain unique, as it deserves to be.

(December 19, 1971)

• • •

Nearly four months later, on June 28, the loser of The Fight won his toughest fight. On a morning drive through the South Side of Chicago, he stopped for a glass of freshly squeezed orange juice. He was coming out of the store when the owner, a small black man, ran out after him.

"I just heard on the radio," the storekeeper yelled, "the Supreme Court said you're free, an eight-to-nothing vote."

The storekeeper hugged Ali, who let out a whoop at the reversal of his 1967 conviction for refusing Army induction. Then he returned to the store and bought orange juice for half a dozen other customers. On a tip that the Supreme Court ruling would come down that day, I had gone to Chicago to cover Ali's reaction. About an hour later he arrived back at the Travelodge, where he was staying while training for a July bout with Jimmy Ellis, but instead of bragging that he had been correct all along, he sat in the lobby and spoke softly, humbly.

"I'm not going to celebrate," he said. "I've already said a long prayer to Allah, that's my celebration."

"Now that you're free," one of the reporters there asked, "are you going to sue anybody for damages?"

"No," he said. "They only did what they thought was right at the time. I did what I thought was right. That was all. I can't condemn them for doing what they think was right."

And for the first of dozens of times, he talked about his wish to retire from boxing soon.

"I just want to sit one day," he said, "and be an ordinary citizen, go to the hardware store, cut the grass. Don't be in no more papers, don't talk to nobody, no more lectures. Just rest. But a man told me the other day, he said, 'You're marked.' He said, 'You'll never be free, young man, from here on out you'll be called for something.' "

Called for history, but not immediately.

After the Supreme Court ruling, Ali went on tour, winning easily against Jimmy Ellis and Buster Mathis in Houston, Jurgen Blin in Zurich, Mac Foster in Tokyo, George Chuvalo in Vancouver, Jerry Quarry again in Las Vegas, Al (Blue) Lewis in Dublin, Floyd Patterson at the Garden and Bob Foster in Stateline, Nev. Foster will be remembered as the first to cut Ali's smooth skin. The skinny light-heavyweight champion fired a left jab from the hip that snapped into Ali's left eye during the fifth round. Until he knocked out Foster in the eighth, Ali bled from a slit under the eyebrow. Not much. But he finally bled for his money.

"What's it like," he was asked later, "to be cut?"

"It's worth two hundred and fifty thousand dollars," he said, meaning his fee.

Despite his flip answer, the first thing Ali did in his dressing room was look in the mirror, peering at the cut on the face that he had often patted so vainly. He needed five stitches. His boxing physician, Dr. Ferdinand Pacheco of Miami, reached into his black bag for two Band-Aids.

"Two small ones," he explained.

"Not two, just *one,*" Ali said.

His pride had been cut too. And four months later, on March 31, 1973, his pride was wounded even more. While losing a twelve-round split decision to Ken Norton in San Diego, he suffered a broken jaw. It had to be wired shut. Mumbling through clenched teeth, Ali explained, "I just got caught with my mouth open." He had been virtually silenced, the worst possible blow to his pride. But six months later he pulled out a twelve-round split decision over Norton at the Forum in Los Angeles with a flashy final round.

"I knew if I closed the show," he said wearily in his dressing room, "I'd stand a better chance."

He was slumped on a leather couch, still wearing his long white satin robe. He had an ice bag on his right hand, which he kept flexing as Dr. Pacheco felt the bones.

"It ain't broke, is it?" Ali asked.

"It doesn't feel like it," the doctor said.

"It hurts in the wrist," Ali said.

"You jammed the bones of the hand into the wrist, that's all," the doctor said. "I don't think anything's broken."

"What's it hurt for then?" Ali demanded.

"It's a fighter's hand," the doctor said.

And what a fighter. Looking back now, I think Ali's victory over Norton that night was the most important of his career. If he had lost to Norton again, many people and many promoters would have doubted him. He might even have doubted himself. And if he had lost the final round that night, he would have lost a majority decision.

"Take it to him," Angelo Dundee told Ali before the final round. "You need this round to win."

Responding to the crisis, Ali somehow regained the speed that had deserted him after the sixth round. His punches weren't any stronger, but his legs were. For three minutes his legs did what he asked them to do. Those three minutes changed his life. Those three minutes not only prolonged his career, they provided it with an upswing—a twelve-round rematch with Joe Frazier at the Garden on January 28, 1974. But the year before, Frazier had been dethroned by George Foreman in a stunning second-round knockout. The rematch did not have the appeal of The Fight three years earlier. There were whispers that Ali's right hand was still sore. Ticket sales dawdled both at the Garden and at the closed-circuit TV locations. John F.X. Condon, the Garden boxing vice president, phoned Ali at his Deer Lake, Pa., training camp.

"You've got to come up here tomorrow," John said. "You've got to tell everybody your hand's all right."

"I can't do that, John, you know I can't do that," Ali said. "I got to train, John, goin' all the way up to New York and back takes me all day, John, that wears me out."

"But nobody's buying tickets."

"I'll be there," Ali agreed.

He rode up and vouched for the health of his right hand, although, as Dr. Pacheco acknowledged much later, it had to be injected with a painkiller the night of the fight. I thought Frazier won the rematch by landing the more punishing punches. But the officials awarded Ali a unanimous decision. Now he was really alive again as an attraction. Quietly, negotiations began for an Ali-Foreman title bout, although Foreman was about to defend the title against Ken Norton in Caracas, Venezuela. The day before I left for Caracas, I happened to be on the phone with Dan Shedrick, a TV producer on the outskirts of boxing.

"I just heard that Foreman is going to fight Ali in Africa, in Zaire," he told me. "Don King put it together."

Don King, a fast talker who had led a fast life as a numbers baron in Cleveland before doing time for manslaughter, was the new black promoter. His straight high hair looked as if he had plugged a finger in a fuse box. I found him in Caracas and mentioned that I wanted to see him—alone. He confirmed the site as Zaire, once the Belgian Congo, and told me that each fighter had been guaranteed a record $5 million. He also filled me in on the intrigue of the negotiations. It made a good Sunday column, a worldwide scoop—thanks to a fortuitous telephone conversation. And when Foreman destroyed Norton in a second-round knockout, the Zaire bout was announced for September 24, 1974, in a soccer stadium in Kinshasa, the Zaire capital once known as Leopoldville.

"The Rumble in the Jungle," Ali labeled it.

My world travels with Ali began. Video Techniques, the promotional firm, arranged a group rate for newsmen that included round-trip airfare, lodging and meals. About fifty of us gathered at the Holiday Inn near JFK International Airport on Sunday evening, September 15, but we had been given no details other than an assurance that "everything is all set." We didn't realize until we got there that to save money, we were to take Icelandic Airlines to Luxembourg, where an Air Zaire jet would be waiting. But first we stopped in Iceland.

"Ah," said Jim Murray of the Los Angeles *Times* as we landed there in a bleak, rainy dawn. "Palm Springs."

"I think," said Jack Griffin of the Chicago *Sun-Times,* "we were closer to Zaire in New York than we are now."

After we landed at Luxembourg, we boarded a chartered bus for nearby Trier, West Germany, where we were to spend the night and recover from the jet lag. Groggy from the all-night flight, I decided to take a nap before dinner. I didn't wake up until eleven o'clock. Too late for dinner. Still woozy and not that hungry, I went back to sleep. The next morning I was waiting for the elevator to the lobby when Tom Cushman of the Philadelphia *Daily News* joined me.

"What are you going to do?" he said.

"I'm going down to have breakfast," I said.

"No," he said, "are going home or going on?"

"Why would I go home?"

"Because of the cut."

"What cut?" I wondered.

"Foreman's cut," he said. "Didn't you know that Foreman got cut over the right eye in training yesterday?"

"I've been sleeping," I said.

But now I was wide awake. I knew the *Times* was covered because our African correspondent, Tom Johnson, was on the scene in Kinshasa, but the big question now was how long the fight would be postponed. Downstairs, publicity man Murray Goodman was saying that the fight might be put off for only a week. In that case I would be better off going to Zaire rather than returning home. But the Air Zaire flight was leaving that afternoon. I couldn't wait too long to decide. At the Luxembourg airport, I hurried to the overseas telephone booth and called the *Times* sports department. Lena Williams, now a cityside reporter but then a sports clerk, was the only one there at that time of the morning.

"Is there any word," I asked her, "on the new date for the fight?"

She went to check the wire-service machines. Moments later she was back on the phone.

"It's coming over now," she said. "The new date is October thirty there."

Outside the booth, a dozen other sportswriters had lined up to call their offices for travel instructions. But when I told them the new date, most didn't bother. With the fight now six weeks away, only a few went on to Zaire; the rest of us returned home. Shortly after the 1974 World Series ended, we left for Zaire again, this time on Air France to Paris and then on Air Zaire to Kinshasa. There, scruffy greenish brown plains resembled Texas more than my image of darkest Africa.

From the airport, a new Mercedes bus took us to N'sele, a cluster of stucco villas that Mobutu Sese Seko, the Zaire president, had constructed to house visiting diplomats.

Ali also was staying there, in a big villa on the wide Congo River, but Foreman had left a nearby villa for the Intercontinental Hotel in Kinshasa, about twenty miles away on a highway that ended a few yards past the N'sele turnoff. My little apartment had a bedroom with a portable air conditioner, a bathroom with scalding hot water and a sitting room with a small refrigerator stocked with beer—big brown bottles of Simba beer with a lion-head label. The beer was good, the food wasn't. Meals were served buffet style in a small dining hall. Monkey meat was the local delicacy, and Angelo Dundee, who had been in N'sele for weeks, told me how he had found a monkey's head on his plate.

"I haven't had any since," he said.

With that warning, I never had any, period. I wish I also could have avoided the martial music that blared out of big speakers on the N'sele streets. The music seemed inescapable, seeping into my consciousness while I watched Ali and Foreman train each day in a big hall with slow-moving ceiling fans, or while I wrote my column in the lecture room that had been converted into a press room. Rather than risk censorship or confusion by the Telex operators there, I phoned the *Times* recording room in New York each day and dictated my column. Because of the fight, the telephone service was better than usual that week. "No prob-lem," the Zaire operator would say in what became the motto of the trip. "No prob-lem." It took only twenty minutes to get an overseas call through. No prob-lem.

With the six-hour time difference, the fight was scheduled to start at four o'clock Wednesday morning, October 30, so it could be shown live at the closed-circuit TV locations in the Eastern time zone at ten o'clock Tuesday evening, October 29.

In order to accommodate Saturday-afternoon home TV in the United States, the weigh-in also was held at a weird hour, eleven o'clock Saturday night in the Stade du 20 Mai, a soccer stadium rebuilt for the fight. More than ten thousand Zaireans attended the weigh-in, many shouting, "Ali, *bomaye,*" meaning "Ali, kill him." But to me and to many others, Ali was the man in danger. When I witnessed the weigh-in, I became convinced. In his red satin trunks, Foreman stood on the scale in the ring and raised both his arms, flexing his biceps and glowering at the cameras. He appeared invincible, too big and too powerful for Ali, who at thirty-two would be unable to stay away from the big punch that had produced twenty-four consecutive knockouts.

But the night (actually the morning) of the fight, two small scenes made me think I might be wrong.

After testing my ringside telephone hookup to the *Times* office, I wandered down to the fighters' dressing rooms in the stadium catacombs. I wanted to make sure the two had arrived without incident. Foreman was already there, and when I approached Ali's room, I saw him walking toward me down the wide hall. Swaggering, really. His arms hanging loosely, his face unsmiling, he had on a black shirt, black slacks and his dark brown work shoes. In the hallway gloom, he appeared huge, as big as Foreman had looked at the weigh-in. Perhaps it was the imminence of the fight, but Ali has never appeared *that* big to me before or since.

The other small scene occurred in the first round. Across the ring Ali was backing away, moving smoothly to his left against the ropes, and Foreman stumbled awkwardly after him. Ali already was in command:

N'SELE, Zaire—Beyond his stucco villa, the Congo River flowed swiftly. On the lawn, several dozen Africans, men in slacks and bright shirts and women in long dresses, had come for a glimpse of the famous man, now that he was the world heavyweight champion again. They stood there quietly, thinking that Muhammad Ali probably was asleep. Five hours earlier he had dethroned George Foreman with an eighth-round knockout. But suddenly he appeared. He carried a carved mahogany cane with inlaid ivory. He wore a pale blue short-sleeved shirt, black pants and scuffed work shoes. When he saw Budd Schulberg, he shook hands with the author of *The Harder They Fall* and hugged him.

"We can make a pretty good movie now," Ali said.

"The fight turned out pretty good," Schulberg agreed.

The plot couldn't be better. In perhaps the most dramatic scenario in boxing history, Ali had regained the heavyweight title at the age of thirty-two by outpunching a twenty-five-year-old puncher who had recorded twenty-four consecutive knockouts in a previously unbeaten career. And he had accomplished it here before nearly sixty thousand Zaireans of what was once known as the Belgian Congo in a spectacle that began at four o'clock in the morning. Flags floated in the ring during the American and Zairean anthems. But strangely Ali did not float like the butterfly he warned he would be. Instead, he stung like the bee he once was. He accepted Foreman punches that had demolished Joe Frazier, Joe (King) Roman and Ken Norton in a total of only 11 minutes 35 seconds. Then he retaliated with punches that wearied Foreman and finally spun him onto the blue canvas. Muhammad Ali has been looked upon as a buffoon. He has been defiled and defrocked of his title for defying the military draft because of his Black Muslim beliefs. He has been castigated for his cruelty. But he has proved he is a gladiator. He just might be "the greatest," as he has always proclaimed.

"I got off the first punches," Ali said. "He never took a lot of punches before. I took his heart the first round."

Ali's right eye was bloodshot but he had no marks on the brown face that is recognized throughout the world.

"I was talking to George in there," Ali said. "I was saying, 'I'm taking your best shots, George, hit hard, show me something,' but he couldn't. After round six, he was tired. I told him, 'You are just an amateur, show me something, hit me hard.' But the man is not that good. The surprise is that I did not dance. For weeks I kept hollering, 'Be ready to dance,' but I didn't dance. That was the surprise. That was the trick."

Once again the styles of fighters influenced an outcome that was surprising to many.

"George knocked out Joe Frazier and Ken Norton but I didn't, and yet I knocked him out," Ali said. "Ten years ago I stopped Sonny Liston to win the title after he knocked out Floyd Patterson twice, but I never knocked out Patterson and I fought him twice. I could've danced. I was saving that in case I got in trouble."

Behind him, the Africans began to shout, "Ali, *bomaye,*" the chant that had become his war cry here. He turned and waved.

"George was the champion, but all these people were yelling 'Ali, *bomaye*' for me," Ali continued. "I learned a special prayer of Allah. What you saw was the power of Allah in helping me win. That must have been Allah in there because I can't punch. My hands were so sore for Frazier and Norton, I needed Novocain. But they were good this time. I'm not known for being a hitter. Can you picture me making George Foreman helpless?

"His punch is strong if he hits you. He still hits hard. But his punches ain't no good after five rounds. You've got to dance on Frazier, got to dance on Norton, but dancin' ain't no good with George because he'll push you around. Dancing doesn't work with him because he fights from a distance. He's not like Frazier, who fights in close. That's why I switched to the ropes."

"Whose idea was it not to dance?" he was asked.

"Me," he replied quickly. "I don't have no trainers. They just work with me. I had to beat George at his own game. Once he's there in front of me, I knew I could pop him. He hits hard but he's coming from here. Let me tell you something. He would accept me as his teacher from now on. I told you I was the greatest. The first round, I let him blast his butt off. In the second, I was praying he keeps throwing. I knew I could whomp him. Wasn't that a beautiful heavyweight championship?" He chuckled. "I told him, 'You the champ, George, and I'm beatin' you up.' Don't ever match no bull against a master boxer. The bull is stronger but the matador is smarter."

Patterson was the only other heavyweight champion to hold the title twice.

"I'm greater than Patterson was. He fought a white fella, that Ingemar Johansson, and won it back the next year. I fought a strong good, black scientific boxer [Liston], who beat Patterson twice, whipped him at twenty-two, and ten years later I fought another black fighter. Black fighters are better than white fighters. That's really getting that title back. Wise people listened to me but a few fools bet on him."

"Was this your greatest fight?" someone asked.

"The greatest fight I ever had was the first fight with Joe Frazier, had to go fifteen, off three and a half years, jaw swollen. That was the greatest. And the second fight with Norton was my most satisfying. Frazier's a better fighter than this man. George kept looking over to Dick Sadler for instructions. He's a mechanical man. He didn't want to take no whippin'. That man probably could have got up. Do I look like a fellow who's got a few more years left? George look like he be through before me. This was like the *Titanic* sinking."

Ali smiled slyly. "Been a great day," he said. "President Ford called."

"Did he?" someone bit.

"No," said Ali, laughing.

As he turned and strolled toward his villa, he pretended to punch a few of the Zaireans. Everybody laughed.

"Did it mean more to you," he was asked, "to win back the title here in Africa, the home of your ancestors?"

"It's a good feeling but it don't mean nothin'," Muhammad Ali said. "I'd rather have done it in Madison Square Garden or Yankee Stadium because that's where the bulk of the nonbelievers are. The nonbelievers, the real fight crowd."

(November 31, 1974)

Ali was on top again. And on tour again. He went to Cleveland and stopped Chuck Wepner, the Bayonne Bleeder, who would inspire Sylvester Stallone to do *Rocky,* the Oscar-winning film; he went to Las Vegas and stopped Ron Lyle; then he was off to the steamy tropical metropolis of Kuala Lumpur, Malaysia, to oppose Joe Bugner of England on July 1, 1975—his third title defense in exactly one hundred days. Only six American sportswriters made the long trip—six hours across the Atlantic to London, nine hours across Europe and the Middle East to Kuwait for a fuel stop, nine more hours across the Arabian Sea and the Bay of Bengal to Kuala Lumpur's beautiful modern airport. Soon we checked into the Merlin Hotel, spotless and pleasant.

"Here they come," Ali shouted the next day when we approached the ring in the indoor arena where he was training. "All these writers see the world because of me."

The next day we saw him retire—for the first time. He called a news conference high in the Kuala Lumpur Hilton overlooking old British colonial homes and a racetrack shaded by palm trees and tropical foliage in the fashionable area of the city. In the distance were a rain forest and lush green mountains. With that backdrop, he solemnly announced that the Bugner bout would be his last.

"Horses get old, cars get old, the pyramids of Egypt are crumbling," he said. "I want to retire while I'm still on top. As of now, this is the last time you will see Muhammad Ali in a fight."

As of now. The formality over, Ali invited everybody up to his suite to view a video cassette of Bugner's loss to Joe Frazier in a twelve-round decision in London two years earlier. Ali ostensibly was scouting Bugner, but when a close-up of Frazier appeared, he snapped, "Ain't he ugly." He was slouched down on a couch and he spit the words out. "When I fight him, I'll kill him, I'll whip his ass. Joe Frazier's too dumb to whip me." His retirement, such as it was, had lasted half an hour.

In my news story that day, I reported his retirement and his comeback in the same paragraph.

As a boxer, Ali needed Joe Frazier again. As a showman, he needed a stage again, as he will need one forever. But with Ali, a stage can be almost anywhere:

KUALA LUMPUR, Malaysia—Possibly not since C. Aubrey Smith took his gin and tonic and departed with the British in 1957 has there been anything in Malaysia quite so official, also quite so incongruous and quite so amusing. On a dais with pale yellow and red tropical flowers today in the orchid-shaded softness of the Chempaka Room above the lobby of, yes, the Holiday Inn here, Muhammad Ali and Joe Bugner sat on opposite sides of Tan Sri Abdul Aziz Yeop, the president of the Malaysian Boxing Federation, and in front of a huge green-and-white "Holiday Inn" banner that destroyed the whole effect. Here they were amid some of the few peaceful palm trees in Southeast Asia, but that banner made it look as if the gladiators had upstaged a convention of cement salesmen in a Holiday Inn off the Ohio Turnpike somewhere. They had gathered for the reading of the rules and the selection of the gloves for next week's world heavyweight title fight. Behind the gladiators were the American and English flags. Some peace treaties between nations have been signed with less ceremony. But in Malaysia the rites of boxing are taken very seriously. At least they were until Muhammad Ali got bored with the formality.

"We are presenting the fighters," the Malaysian boxing commissioner said, "each with a boxing glove of Selangor pewter."

With a face the shade of coffee ice cream and an accent formed in London schools, the commissioner sounded like Alec Guinness made up to play a mod Malay chieftain. Ali accepted his twelve-pound pewter glove, cast from Malaysian tin, and holding it with both hands, pretended to punch Bugner with it. Even the challenger laughed. Then the commissioner began to drone the rules, one by one, as Ali yawned.

". . . the fighters will not use the ropes," the commissioner said.

With that, Ali awoke. In his red-flowered Malaysian batik shirt, he leaned back and stared up at the commissioner.

"I can't use the ropes?" Ali asked. "I can't use the rope-a-dope?"

"You can use the ropes," the commissioner explained. "But not take advantage of the ropes."

"I won't hang him," Ali said.

The champion was really awake now. When the rules had been read, Ali's trainer, Angelo Dundee, and Bugner's manager, Andy Smith, signed their acceptance. Then a dozen pairs of red boxing gloves, manufactured in Japan, were placed on a table below the dais.

"Red gloves!" Ali said. "Now we can't see the blood. The gloves should be white."

Ali leaned over the dais, then peeked back at the commissioner sitting alongside him.

"Are these gloves," the champion asked quietly, "large enough to put a horseshoe inside?"

"All we know," the commissioner replied stiffly, "is that they are eight ounces."

The champion walked down to the table to find the gloves that fit best. He put several left-handed gloves on, testing them by jabbing at Dundee's upraised left palm. Some spectators gasped at his speed.

"I'm puttin' fear in his heart," Ali said, glancing at the twenty-five year-old challenger. "He's tryin' to be cool, tryin' to make me think and the world think that he's not psyched out. But he's scared to death."

He found the proper left-handed glove, then he quickly approved a right-handed glove.

"I'm so fast," Ali said, sneering, "I hit you before the cameras detect it."

Now it was Bugner's turn. He mostly tested right-handed gloves as Ali stared.

"I'm glad to have a boxer who can talk," Ali said. "You're handsome and intelligent. But after the fight you'll be ugly and illiterate."

Bugner was enjoying the byplay rather than resenting it, as some Ali foes have. He even playfully grabbed Ali on returning to the dais.

"We're a photographer's dream," Ali said, laughing.

Now, with the gloves chosen, two of the commissioner's aides put them in separate boxes. Each box was wrapped with white tape. The tape was sealed with melted wax.

"Where they gonna put the gloves?" Ali asked.

"They will put them in the prison," the commissioner said, referring to Pudu Prison here. "In the prison for security."

"They didn't kill nobody—yet," Ali said. "Might have to go to jail after."

Ali suddenly realized that this Malaysian precaution was unique, if not unprecedented.

"The gloves are goin' to jail," he said, his voice rising. "I been in boxing twenty years and I ain't never seen gloves put in a jail. The poor gloves. The gloves need a lawyer. I never seen anything like this. They're puttin' the gloves in jail. Where in the jail, in a cell?"

"In a safe in the prison," one of the aides said.

"They're puttin' the gloves in jail," Ali repeated.

Soon the commissioner asked the fighters to determine the color of their trunks. Ali, as the champion, selected white. "White looks better on me," Ali said, holding the white satin against his skin. "Black looks better on you, Joe, 'cause you're white. You can't see white against white. You don't want to get in the ring like you don't have trunks on. If you're white and the trunks are white, it might confuse the people."

Joe Bugner laughed, everybody laughed.

"You're too nice a guy, Joe," the champion said with a grimace. "I can't get mad at you."

Moments later the meeting was over. Some cement salesmen probably will use the room tomorrow.

(June 27, 1975)

* • •

And a cement salesman might have put up a better fight than Joe Bugner did. Ali won a fifteen-round decision so decisively he didn't even bother to wait for the voting to be announced. He hurried back to his dressing room to get away from the blazing tropical sun. In order to accommodate closed-circuit TV in the United States, this fight had started at ten o'clock in the morning. Six hours later Ali, his retirement officially renounced, appeared barefoot in a bathrobe in the Hilton and joined Joe Frazier in announcing Manila as the site of their third confrontation.

"The Thrilla," the champion yelled, "in Manila."

But first there was the Belinda incident. His second wife, Belinda Ali, arrived in Manila in the midst of a scandal involving Veronica Porche, a beauteous member of the champion's entourage. Whispered to be Ali's mistress but declared to be a secretary and babysitter, she had been on location in Zaire, Cleveland, Las Vegas and Kuala Lumpur; some people even claimed that the Black Muslims had permitted Ali to have a second wife. On a quiet afternoon in Kuala Lumpur, I had asked him about that.

"No, no," he said. "Two wives are against the law of the land. But ain't she beautiful."

At that time Veronica was part of Ali's private life—part of Belinda's too. The two women were often seen together in apparently friendly coexistence, although Belinda was believed to have scratched Ali's face in Zaire during a quarrel over Veronica's presence there. But when Ali arrived in Manila, only Veronica was with him. I hadn't written about Veronica before because, to me, public figures are entitled to a private life. If sportswriters were to cover athletes' private lives, there wouldn't be room for the box scores. But when an athlete commits a public indiscretion, he or she loses that immunity. Ali lost his in Manila when Veronica accompanied him to several public social functions, including a visit with Ferdinand Marcos, the president of the Philippines.

"I told him [Marcos] that he has a beautiful wife," Ali explained later, referring to Mrs. Imelda Marcos, "and he told me, 'You do too.' I just let it drop."

Others contended that Ali introduced Veronica as his wife on several other occasions as well, and the Manila newspapers began to identify her as his wife. The champion's private life had become public. And after a workout in the modern Folk Arts Theatre alongside Manila Bay, he was asked about it.

"I know celebrities don't have privacy," Ali answered. "But at least they should be able to sleep with who they want to. The only person I answer to is Belinda Ali and I don't worry about her."

Obviously not. When the mother of his four children arrived in Manila after a twenty-hour flight from Chicago, the champion did not bother to meet her at the airport or even to dispatch a chauffeured limo for her. She rode to the Manila Hilton in a car belonging to a friend who happened to be at the airport. She checked into a suite connected to her husband's. Soon she burst in on Ali, who was being interviewed by Dick Schaap for the NBC television network.

"We've got to talk," Belinda said.

She and Ali went into another room, where, Dick told me later, "things got loud." But at his workout later, Ali minimized his marital discord, saying, "She don't worry about publicity, she knows I love her and she's my wife." With his marital situation apparently calmed, I was thinking about doing a column on Ali's huge entourage. I wanted to talk to him privately about what each of the people actually did.

"Come up to my suite about four this afternoon," he said. "I'll be up from my nap by then."

But at four, he was still sleeping. Rather than go down to the lobby, I waited in a chair near the security desk there on the twenty-first floor. I was reading a Manila newspaper when I noticed a bellboy pushing a car with six suitcases on it out of a suite down the hall—Belinda's suite. Minutes later, statuesque in a long white suit and white turban with gold earrings, Belinda emerged. Ali's bodyguard, Pat Patterson, was with her. He hurried to press the elevator button. As she came down the hall I approached her with my notebook open.

"Why are you leaving?" I asked.

"I'm not wanted here," she snapped. "Muhammad Ali doesn't want me here. Nobody wants me here. I'm not going to force myself here. I don't like an impostor coming in and taking over my family after eight years and destroying my life."

"Belinda," Pat Patterson called softly across the hall, "the elevator's here."

"I don't like one woman," Belinda continued, moving toward the elevator, "wiping me and my whole family out—"

"Belinda," Pat called softly again.

"—because she wants to show off."

The elevator doors closed. I took the next elevator downstairs. But she was gone. She had stormed through the lobby to Ali's chauffeured limo, which took her to the airport. She left Manila only twelve hours after she had arrived. Upstairs, waiting to see Ali about something else, I had been in the right place at the right time when Belinda departed. The harder you work, I've learned, the luckier you get. I had seen flashes of Ali's cruelty before—torturing Floyd Patterson and Ernie Terrell in the ring, lashing others with vicious remarks—but his humiliation of Belinda, a "Muslim woman" whom he had always professed to honor, was his cruelest hour. Soon he divorced Belinda and married Veronica, but that day, with Belinda's quotes in my notebook, I went back upstairs to see if Ali would comment on his wife's departure.

"The champ," I was told, "ain't talkin'."

The next day he still wasn't talking, at least not about his wife's walkout. "I'm just talkin' about Joe Frazier," he said. "Got to fill the theaters up. I've got so many problems—can the champ do it?" Three days later, on October 1, 1975, the champ did it in the best fight I've ever seen:

MANILA, the Philippines—In the most brutal confrontation of their five-year rivalry, Muhammad Ali retained the world heavyweight boxing championship today when Joe Frazier's manager, Eddie Futch, surrendered from the corner moments before the bell was to ring for the fifteenth round.

Frazier, dominating the middle rounds with the fury of his youth, had been battered by the champion throughout the three rounds prior to Futch's merciful decision.

"I stopped it," Futch explained, "because Joe was starting to get hit with too many clean shots. He couldn't see out of his left eye. He couldn't see the right hands coming."

Ali was far ahead on the scoreboards of the three officials. Using the 5-point must scoring system, referee Carlos Padilla, Jr., had the champion ahead, 66–60. Judge Alfredo Quiazon had it 67–62 and Judge Larry Nadayag had it 66–62. On a rounds basis, Quiazon had Ali ahead 8–3, with three even. The others each had it 8–4–2.

Ali's victory was recorded as a knockout in the fourteenth round, since the bell had not rung for the final round.

"My guy sucked it up," said Ali's trainer, Angelo Dundee. "When he looked completely out of gas, he put on another gas tank. I thought we were in front. My guy was hitting him better shots."

Futch believed that Frazier was ahead, which only added to the humanity of his decision to surrender.

"Joe had two bad rounds in a row," Futch said. "Even with three minutes to go, he was going downhill. And that opened up the possibility in that situation that he could've been seriously hurt."

Wearing dark glasses to hide his puffed eyes, especially his right eye, Frazier agreed with Futch.

"I didn't want to be stopped, I wanted to go on," Frazier said, "but I'd never go against Eddie."

Frazier dismissed questions about retirement, saying, "I'm not thinking that way now." But the weary champion indicated that the "Thrilla in Manila" might have been his last fight.

"You may have seen the last of Ali," the champion said. "I want to get out of it. I'm tired and on top. What you saw tonight was next to death. He's the toughest man in the world."

Ali attempted to register the early knockout he had predicted while dominating the early rounds. But then, Frazier, in his relentless attack, smashed and slowed the thirty-three-year-old champion. They resembled two old bull moose who had to stand and slam each other because they couldn't get away from each other.

Through the middle rounds, Frazier took command. On the two score-cards of *The New York Times,* the thirty-one-year-old challenger won eight of the first eleven rounds. But then Ali searched for the knockout punch that would assure the retention of the title.

Moving on weary legs, Ali began to measure Frazier in the twelfth with a flurry of punches to Frazier's face, which resembled a squashed chocolate marshmallow. In the thirteenth, the champion quickly knocked out Frazier's mouthpiece with a long left hook, then landed a left-right combination.

Frazier was shaken now, wobbling on his stumpy legs, but his heart kept him going. Then Ali's straight right hand sent Frazier stumbling backward to the center of the ring, but somehow the former champion kept his feet. His mouthpiece gone, Frazier kept spitting blood as he resumed his assault moments before the bell.

In the fourteenth round Frazier hopped out quickly but Ali shook him with a hard right, then jolted him with several left-right combinations before the bell and Frazier stumbled to his corner.

Moments later Futch waved his surrender to the referee. On the stool in his corner, Frazier appeared exhausted. He didn't protest.

Unlike the first two fights, Ali-Frazier III maintained a level of boxing violence seldom seen. During their 1971 classic, Frazier earned a fifteen-round unanimous decision and undisputed possession of the title with a relentless assault as Ali often clowned. In their twelve-round nontitle bout early last year, Ali's holding tactics detracted from his unanimous decision.

But from the opening bell in the Philippine Coliseum, the estimated crowd of twenty-five thousand, including President Ferdinand Marcos and his wife, realized that Ali had not come to dance. Moving out, flat-footed, he shook Frazier with several right hands in the early rounds, but Frazier kept attacking.

At the bell, Ali came out, hands high in a semipeekaboo. He stood flat-footed instead of dancing, as if looking for the early knockout he had predicted. Frazier, in contrast, moved in aggressively, trying to unload his left hook, but the champion tied him up effectively in two clinches.

Ali landed a left-right combination, then jarred Frazier with a left hook that sent him against the ropes. Ali also landed a hard right hand before the bell.

In the second round, Ali remained flat-footed, using his pawing jab to keep Frazier at bay. When he cupped his left glove around Frazier's head, the referee warned the champion. Ali then landed a hard right to the head that shook Frazier, then landed two more as Frazier kept coming in.

Ali covered up against the ropes, then easily pushed Frazier away, displaying complete control of the tempo. But suddenly, Frazier landed a hard left hook to Ali's jaw before the bell.

Before the third round, Ali bowed and blew kisses to President Marcos and his wife. Ali then taunted Frazier with his pawing jab, using his six-inch advantage in reach to keep Frazier away. He landed a series of hard punches to the head, but Frazier burrowed through them to land a left.

Ali covered up against the ropes, and when Frazier stepped back, Ali waved his right glove at Frazier, as if inviting him to return. Ali was talking to Frazier now, then burst out of his cocoon with a flurry of lefts and rights in a toe-to-toe exchange that had the spectators in a frenzy.

But in the fourth round Ali's tempo slowed as Frazier's increased. By the fifth round, a chant of "Frazier, Frazier" filled the round arena. As the struggle continued, the crowd sounded as if it favored Frazier, one of the few times that Ali hasn't converted the live audience into cheering for him.

Ali, at 224 1/2 pounds at last Saturday's weigh-in, had been the 9-

to-5 betting favorite in the United States but he was a 6-to-5 choice here. Frazier had weighed 214 1/2 at the ceremonial weigh-in.

Ali's won-lost record is now 49-2 with 35 knockouts. He has lost only to Frazier in 1971 and to Ken Norton, who broke Ali's jaw in 1973 in a twelve-round decision that Ali later reversed. Frazier's record is now 32-3, losing to Ali twice and being dethroned as champion by George Foreman in 1973.

In the decades to come, Ali and Frazier will be remembered as two of boxing's classic rivals through forty-two rounds. As memorable as their first two fights were in Madison Square Garden, their masterpiece developed halfway around the world from where their rivalry began.

(October 1, 1975)

That fight also had begun about ten o'clock in the morning for closed-circuit TV, but by nightfall both gladiators were up and around. Red Smith went with Joe Frazier that night while I followed Ali:

MANILA, the Philippines—Eight hours after Muhammad Ali left the ring following his epic in brutality with Joe Frazier, the champion's face tonight resembled a mask that had been stretched to fit. His narrowed eyes appeared to be underlined in purple crayon. His forehead had small lumps on it. The bridge of his nose was scraped pink. When he walked, he moved stiffly, almost in a limp.

Muhammad Ali had never looked like this before. But in a howl of sirens and flashing red lights he had arrived at a reception for the two gladiators given by President Ferdinand E. Marcos and his wife, Imelda, at the Antique House, a Philippines restoration showplace with high ceilings, expensive oil paintings, red carpeting, dark wood, a mother-of-pearl chandelier and the scent of flowers.

At first, Ali seemed to be fulfilling a social obligation. In his beige suit, white shirt and brown figured tie, he was almost overdressed. He hardly smiled. He cupped his hands together as if he were holding a small bird. When he shook hands with the other guests, he winced. And when he sat on a sofa next to Mrs. Marcos, his body was hunched in soreness.

Unobtrusively, a maid handed him a guest book to sign. Slowly he wrote, "To Mrs. Marcos—Muhammad Ali—death is so near and time for friendly action is so limited. Love and peace always." Around him waiters were serving drinks and caviar. He took a Coke.

When the Frazier people arrived, Joe wasn't with them. "His eyes," his manager, Eddie Futch, explained, "are just about completely shut." But the loser's wife, Florence, walked over to congratulate Ali, and when they shook hands the champion extended his fingers and smiled. To most of the others he had only extended a softly folded fist.

Soon the Frazier group departed. Downstairs the buffet line was forming. Candles flickered on small tables set for two hundred and fifty guests. From the porch a six-piece combo was playing and Joy Salinas was singing "You've Got to Love Me for What I Am." Sitting with President and Mrs. Marcos and their daughter, Imee, a Princeton junior, Ali was toasted with champagne.

"To the champion," President Marcos said.

Ali picked up his water glass and sipped.

But now, slowly, he smiled. He looked around, as if enjoying himself for the first time in the elegance of the room.

"I'm livin', ain't I?" he said, laughing.

The combo accompanied the Temptations in a rendition of "Old Man River," as Hugh O'Brian, the actor, softly patted Ali on the shoulder.

"I like him," Ali said, brightening again. "Wyatt Earp."

The combo swung into "Tie a Yellow Ribbon Round the Old Oak Tree" and Mrs. Marcos got up to dance with Don King, the promoter. Moments later President Marcos also got up to dance.

"Let's give the First Lady some support," he said.

Soon the dance floor was filled with couples as Ali looked on from his chair.

"They don't do this at the White House," he said.

Ali was laughing often now. And soon he was talking about the fight, about how he had preserved the title when Eddie Futch surrendered from the corner with Frazier on the stool moments before the bell was to ring for the fifteenth round, ending one of the classic fights in boxing history, probably ending one of the classic rivalrles.

"This'll kill you," the champion said. "This is next to death. I'm a superhuman. So when I'm that tired, it's dangerous. I hope he's all right. My face is swollen, but it's all right. No cuts. It'll go down. But my right hip hurts. He hit me with his left hook there. That stops you from dancin', stops you from movin'."

After the fight, Ali had spoken of retirement, as he often has lately.

"I got a lot on my mind," he was saying now. "I got eight million saved."

Ali shook his head, remembering the left hooks that had landed there.

"He's great at his style," Ali said. "He's not scientifically great, but he's great at his style. He's great. But they all get up for me. Chuck Wepner, Ron Lyle, Joe Bugner, they all fought better than they ever fought when they fought me. They get ready for me. If they beat me, they know they got the world."

He moved to another table, laughing and joking with the Filipino guests. Soon he was ogling the pretty girls.

"I can pick 'em, can't I?" he said, grinning and hugging one of them. "I'm actin' cool again, watch me."

Perhaps two dozen of Ali's entourage were at the party. But Veronica Porche did not appear, just as she did not appear at the Philippine Coliseum for the fight. His wife, Belinda, was in Chicago, where she returned last week.

"Time to let the President rest now," Ali said after the music stopped. "He's been too nice to us."

The champion shook hands softly with the President, kissed Mrs. Marcos and Imee on the cheek and walked out onto the balcony overlooking the courtyard as his entourage assembled. Soon he was walking, not as stiffly as before, toward the chauffeured limousine that has been at his disposal here.

"What a showman," Mrs. Marcos was saying on the balcony. "What a showman."

On the street now, the limousine had been surrounded by Filipinos who had gathered waiting for a glimpse of the champion. As theatrical as ever, Muhammad Ali got out of the limousine, picked up small children and kissed them, hugged pretty girls and reached out to touch those who couldn't touch him. But soon he was back in the front seat.

The limousine zoomed away, in a howl of sirens and flashing red lights.

(October 2, 1975)

During that reception, I got Eddie Futch aside. I wanted to know what there was in his background that persuaded him to stop the fight even though he thought Joe Frazier was ahead entering the fifteenth round:

MANILA, the Philippines—During the fourteenth round, Eddie Futch was watching Joe Frazier from the steps below the corner, watching the sweat and the water spin off Joe Frazier's face every time Muhammad Ali hit him with a right hand, watching Joe Frazier squinting to see that right hand through his left eye that had narrowed into a slit. But in a crevice of his mind, Eddie Futch was watching Davey Moore and Jimmy Doyle and Talmadge Bussey and a young middleweight named Billy back in Detroit, where he first was around fighters. Somewhere else in Eddie Futch's subconscious, Bob Dylan was singing, "Who killed Davey Moore, why, what's the reason for?" Up in the ring now as Eddie Futch watched, Joe Frazier kept getting hit in the face with that right hand because he couldn't see it coming. And when Joe Frazier tottered back to his stool after the fourteenth round, Eddie Futch looked at that left eye and he knew what he had to do. But he knew that he had to talk to the fighter about it.

"What's with his right hand?" the manager asked.

"I can't see it," Joe Frazier mumbled. "I can see the left, but when I move away, I get hit with the right."

"I'm going to stop it," Eddie Futch said.

"Don't do that," Joe Frazier said, starting to get off the stool. "I can finish."

"No, this is the best thing to do."

And it was. But the butchers in boxing will never understand that. The butchers are sneering, "Only three more minutes, he deserved three more minutes after what he done," especially with the world heavyweight championship at stake, as it was in the Philippine Coliseum here Wednesday morning. And especially if you think your fighter is ahead, as Eddie Futch did. But the butchers in boxing will never understand Eddie Futch, just as he doesn't understand them.

"Only three more minutes," Eddie Futch was saying today, shaking his head. "I'm not a timekeeper. I'm a handler of fighters."

Eddie Futch, a sixty-four-year-old great-grandfather, has been handling them for about forty years, but until he began working with Joe Frazier and earlier with Ken Norton, he handled fighters in Detroit and Los Angeles in the smaller divisions.

"Only three more minutes," he said again. "But it only takes one punch. I could see he was getting hurt by that right hand."

Eddie Futch didn't handle Davey Moore but he saw Davey Moore die in a world featherweight title bout in Los Angeles in 1963.

"He was a strong, well-conditioned fighter, a great champion," Eddie Futch said, "but that didn't help him. And in Cleveland in 1947, when Jimmy Doyle died after Sugar Ray knocked him out, I remember seeing him coming out of the ring on a stretcher and he looked at me as if he recognized me."

But mostly, Eddie Futch remembers a lightweight named Talmadge Bussey and a young middleweight named Billy in Detroit because he handled them.

"I was supposed to take Talmadge to Caracas but the trip was canceled because of a revolution down there and he fought Luther Rawlings instead," he remembered. "It was a savage fight. He went down just before the bell ended the eighth round and they dragged him to his corner. His father and his brothers were in the corner. When the referee came over, he told them they ought to stop the fight between rounds. But their family pride wouldn't let them. When the bell rang, they pushed him out. As soon as the bell rang, the referee had the authority to stop it himself, but he didn't. Talmadge got hit again and he later died. Then they passed a rule disallowing family members in the corner. Too much emotion involved. But it was too late to save Talmadge."

Eddie Futch can't remember Billy's last name. The kid had only six pro fights.

"He was a great prospect, he looked like a smaller Ezzard Charles—his father and his uncle brought him to me. One night at the Arcadia Club he got hit a shot and he went down. The moment he went down, the doctor was in the ring. The doctor told me, 'This kid's in trouble, he's seriously hurt.' We got him into the dressing room and we called an ambulance. I can still hear the doctor telling me, 'We almost lost him in the ring.' In the hospital it took him three days to come out of it. While he was in there I asked his father and his uncle if he ever had any head injuries as a kid. They told me that when he was six years old, he hit his head on the sidewalk. I told them, 'And you brought him to me to make a boxer out of him.' He recovered but he never boxed again."

Another time Eddie Futch was watching his welterweight, Hedgemon Lewis, being battered by Indian Red Lopez in a title elimination.

"There were only thirty seconds to go in the last round and I was sure Hedge was ahead," Eddie Futch recalled, "But I had to stop it."

And so, when Eddie Futch was watching Joe Frazier getting hit in the fourteenth round with that right hand, watching Joe Frazier squinting through his left eye that had narrowed into a slit, Eddie Futch knew what he had to do and he didn't hesitate to do it.

"There isn't enough money in the world," Eddie Futch said, "to let him get hurt."

And there aren't enough people in boxing like Eddie Futch who understand that.

(October 3, 1975)

Eddie Futch didn't want Joe Frazier to fight anymore, but Joe had to try George Foreman again. This time Joe lasted into the fifth round before Eddie Futch jumped up on the ring apron and stopped it. Joe "put the gloves on the wall" that night, June 15, 1976, but I believe that at his peak Joe Frazier fought better than Muhammad Ali at his. Joe's peak was the night he floored Ali in their first fight. But with his smokin' style, he burned out quickly. Because of Ali's three-and-a-half-year exile, nobody knows exactly when his peak was —maybe it was when he was giving college lectures instead of boxing.

And just as Ali burned out Frazier, so, too, Frazier burned out Ali, who has never been the same since he was "next to death" in Manila.

I thought Ali lost to Jimmy Young early in 1976 at the Capital Centre; many thought he lost to Ken Norton later that year at Yankee Stadium, although I agreed with the three officials who gave him the fifteenth round, thereby enabling him to salvage a unanimous decision. The next year he struggled through fifteen rounds against both Alfredo Evangelista and Earnie Shavers in unanimous but unspectacular decisions. Then he was matched in 1978 against Leon Spinks, an Olympic gold medalist with only six victories and a draw as a pro. Ali didn't take Spinks seriously, didn't train properly, didn't even talk up the fight, taking an unnatural vow of silence instead.

But until the fight began, not even Leon Spinks realized how vulnerable Ali was to a shocking upset:

LAS VEGAS—Like the old bull who, thinking he is still what he once was, lets the young bull gore him until it's too late to retaliate, Muhammad Ali had lost the world championship to Leon Spinks tonight. But now as the ex-champion walked slowly from the ring through the crowded aisles of the Hilton Pavilion toward his small upstairs dressing room, people were shouting "Ali, Ali" and "You're still the greatest." Wearily, he raised his right hand a few inches to acknowledge the chant, but he didn't resemble "The Greatest." His face, that wonderful face which once was hardly ever marked in a fight, suddenly had seemed stretched and aged as he plodded out for the final round. And now, up close, there were purple bruises above and below his right eye and over the bridge of his nose. His forehead was swollen near his left eye. Blood from his cut lower lip spotted his white satin trunks and his white terry-cloth robe.

"Nobody but his family," somebody was shouting now at the door to his dressing room.

Ali's bodyguards ushered him inside, where his wife, Veronica, and several members of the Ali entourage waited. The door slammed.

"Keep away," an Ali bodyguard in a brown suit was shouting. "Clear this hallway. Clear this hallway, I say, clear this hallway."

Virtually nobody moved. Not at this moment, not when Muhammad Ali had been dethroned on a split decision over fifteen rounds. Moments later, his trainer, Angelo Dundee, appeared.

"I thought we had an edge," Dundee said. "The guy who voted a five-point difference should be thrown away."

In the confusion, Leon Spinks somehow had entered Ali's dressing room and spoken to his boyhood idol. But now the new champion was moving down the hall toward his dressing room with his trainer, George Benton.

"Jab, jab, jab, that was the plan," Benton said. "Hit him on the left shoulder all night with that jab."

Bob Arum, the Top Rank promoter, followed the new champion. Moments later he visited the ex-champion, for whom he has promoted fights for more than a decade. When he appeared in the hallway, Arum was asked what would happen now in the heavyweight division.

"Nobody is really thinking about that, if you can believe it," Arum said. "Ali is disappointed. But he's a man. The way he fought the fifteenth round, he's a man. And he just said that if he lost the title, he's glad he lost it to a nice guy but not to count him out."

Suddenly the door opened. Hundreds of newsmen were waiting for Ali at an interview area in another part of the hotel, but Ali, always aware of history, was ready to talk now. He sat slumped in a chair in a corner of the room with Veronica curled at his feet.

"Spinks proved all of you wrong," the ex-champion said almost in a whisper. "All you people didn't think he'd win."

One of his handlers, Luis Serria, was pressing towel-wrapped pieces of ice on the purple bruises around Ali's right eye, then he moved it to Ali's left forehead as the champion combed his hair.

"He surprised you," Ali said.

"Did he surprise you?" he was asked.

"No, he had the will to win and the stamina. He hit pretty hard."

"Will you continue to fight?"

"Yeah," he said quietly, "I'll win it for the third time. I'll be the first one to get it for the third time. I'll get in better shape. I'll get down to about two hundred and fifteen next time. I made a mistake in the early rounds. I was hoping he'd tire. He didn't tire."

"Was the decision correct?"

"I didn't know. I knew it was close. The judges were watching it. They called it."

"What did Spinks say to you?"

"We both were clownin' here."

"What would you do differently?"

"I'd fight the first rounds like I did the fifteenth, keep movin', don't go to the ropes, get in better shape. We'll have a rematch."

"Did Spinks promise you one?"

"No, but the public will want it. The only one who can make him a few million in one night is me."

"Do you feel bad about losing the title?"

"Nothin' to feel bad about. You lose and you win. The battle plan was wrong."

"Did you decide the battle plan?"

"Yeah, let him wear himself out early. What made it hard was trying to make up the points. But one judge had me ahead."

"What punches bruised you?"

"Caught a thumb once in the eye and a couple of glancin' rights."

"How did your lip get cut?"

"I got it cut in the gym," he said, referring to when he was training in Miami Beach, "and it reopened."

"You look very tired," someone said.

"I don't feel that bad," Ali replied.

Several minutes later, the ex-champion walked wearily to the interview room, where he repeated his plans for a comeback in a rematch with Spinks for the title, although the World Boxing Council edict calls for Spinks to defend the title against Ken Norton first.

"If he beats me again," Muhummad Ali said, "then I'll give it up."

(February 16, 1978)

The next night George Benton told me, "Leon might have won the title too soon." Indeed he had—as a person more than as a boxer. By the time he started training for the rematch, on September 15, 1978, in the New Orleans Superdome, the kid from the Igo-Pruett projects in St. Louis had been hounded by continuous conflicts with promoters, managers, attorneys and police. He was arrested five times for traffic violations, once for possession of a tiny amount of cocaine. He was photographed in handcuffs. Unsophisticated, almost primitive, Leon couldn't seem to understand why every arrest was in the headlines. But one of the first commandments of journalism is that names make news. And he was now "Leon Spinks, the world heavyweight champion," as if that were his full name.

"But why do the papers make me out to be different now?" he said in New Orleans before the fight. "I ain't no different. I don't want to be no different."

Leon Spinks didn't want to be different, whereas Muhammad Ali has to be different. Ali's timing was terrible. His punches often missed awkwardly, sometimes sadly. But he was determined to win. In contrast, Spinks appeared determined to lose. He went through the motions, as if hoping he could now return to obscurity, where he wouldn't be different from anyone else. Ali fought as if he had to win in order to be different—the first three-time champion. And he did.

More than anything else, Muhammad Ali wants "the world heavyweight champion" to be part of his name.

Ali keeps talking about retiring, but he'll always need the millions he'll be offered. And he'll always need the stage. In his shrill of victory in New Orleans, he was in his hotel room the next morning shouting, "I am the greatest—of all times . . . of all times . . . of all times." He was still shouting it after I left.

Standing at the elevator and hearing "I am the greatest—of all times," I had to laugh. That's where I came in.

About the Author

DAVE ANDERSON grew up in Brooklyn, and on graduating from Holy
Cross in 1951, went to work for the *Brooklyn Eagle,* and then for the New
York *Journal-American.* At present he is a sports columnist for *The New
York Times.* His long career has brought him many awards for his coverage
of various sports; three out of the last five years he has been chosen "Sports
Writer of the Year" in New York. The most recent of Mr. Anderson's
Random House books is *The Yankees,* written with Murray Chass, Robert
Creamer and Harold Rosenthal.